The Other Side of Time

The Other Side of Time

A Combat Surgeon in World War II

by

BRENDAN PHIBBS

LITTLE, BROWN AND COMPANY

BOSTON   TORONTO

FIRST EDITION

The author gratefully acknowledges permission to quote from the
following copyright material :

The excerpt on page 307 from ''Wernher Von Braun'': Copyright
© 1965 by Tom Lehrer. Used by permission.
The quatrain on page 338 : From *W. H. Auden: Collected Poems,*
edited by Edward Mendelson. Copyright © 1976 by Edward Mendelson, William Meredith and Monroe K. Spears, Executors of the
Estate of W. H. Auden.

Library of Congress Cataloging-in-Publication Data

Phibbs, Brendan.
  The other side of time.

  1. Phibbs, Brendan.   2. World War, 1939–1945 —
Medical care — United States.   3. World War, 1939–1945 —
Personal narratives, American.   4. World War, 1939–1945 —
Campaigns — France.   5. World War, 1939–1945 — Campaigns —
Germany.   6. United States.   Army — Surgeons — Biography.
7. Surgeons — United States — Biography.   I. Title.
D807.U6P48   1987   940.54'7573   87-2939
ISBN 0-316-70510-1

RRD VA

DESIGNED BY ROBERT G. LOWE

*Published simultaneously in Canada
by Little, Brown & Company (Canada) Limited*

PRINTED IN THE UNITED STATES OF AMERICA

Contents

Preface

EVERYTHING in this book happened as it's set down: the conversations, while not verbatim, are reproduced accurately enough for the needs of reason and history.

Ho ho, cries cynic, and of course you had a tape recorder in that tank column.

Of course I didn't: nobody did. There were no tape recorders in those days, certainly not of a size to carry around in a half-track.

What I had, and what I used, was some advice I'd picked up, at a long remove, from a couple of heroes. Two hundred years ago, Stendhal came down from the mountain with the first and second commandments for all writers: never describe a face you haven't seen, never write a line of dialogue you haven't heard. The obvious corollary states that the writer must record faces and speeches before they're forgotten.

Scott Fitzgerald's (sober) life was a sustained frenetic attempt to find words to catch the present before it plunged away into the past: he was a compulsive recorder of images and phrases, scribbling notes like "the yolks of their eyes" on backs of envelopes and shirtcuffs, catching gems and flakes for the mosaic of his books.

Bowing to the two masters, I've been an inscriber of daily events, confrontations, and illuminations throughout my adult life. All that's needed is a pencil and a small blank space. In battalion aid stations a few hundred yards behind the line, in armored columns when we medics were jammed between tanks and guns, I wrote in diaries, on the backs of requisitions and report forms, and even, as the best revenge, on the empty side of Nazi propaganda sheets.

Cynic backs away mumbling. But time? When was there time?

Too much time is one of the worst features of any war. There are intervals of terror, certainly, and strenuous hours, but the great part of any war consists of boredom with a halo of chronic fear and discomfort. What does anyone do in a gunpit or an aid station when there are no targets or casualties? Try sitting in a hole or a cave, without books or radio or television, for only six hours and the truth about wars will be inscribed in flaming tedium on the dirt walls. There was time to have written *Paradise Lost* or the Old Testament, and writing was an infinitely better use of thought than brooding about future mutilation.

I've juggled names and units, sometimes to provide continuity and sometimes to protect the feelings of survivors. Battalions, combat commands, and even divisions have been shuffled, but the essence of events is minutely correct. Conversations are easier to record than you might think: a few key phrases will define a whole exchange. Most of the dialogue here is a combination of precisely recorded fragments with approximations of surrounding words, but in the chapter called "An Easy Leap" the exchanges are almost verbatim: I wrote most of them that same night, when nobody slept. I've deliberately changed the name of the hero of that chapter because there are still Nazis around, fouling their national waters, ready to commit murder.

We have a Division Association and a monthly newsletter that keeps us all writing and talking and meeting, but in every issue the "In Memoriam" list grows longer and with it the knowledge that we'll soon be washed over the edge of history, remote as Gustavus Adolphus's prayerful gunners or the legions of Julian the Apostate. What we were and what we did, at our best, and what happened around us, is slipping out of knowledge. That's a pity. Please, young people, listen to us before we leave.

The Other Side of Time

1

Dialogue with a Box;
Antigone

THIS IS A COLLECTION of war stories, all true. They started
with some scribbling between loud noises when I rode across
France and Germany with an armored combat command, and for
thirty-five years they waited, locked in a box that was buckled
in a bag, a musette, a lazy swatch of canvas the U.S. Army fixed
with straps and flung over an officer's shoulder as a place to carry
junk.

I put the box in the bag when I came home from France in
1945 to that brave new world all we heroes had just made possible,
and for a generation, half a lifetime, it slumped in neglected
cupboards and shelves. I had a profession that stretched the hours,
I had a large and infinitely rewarding family, I had the prairies
and mountains of Wyoming for wandering and happy danger,
but in all that crowded time the musette would not be forgotten.
I saw it when I went poking for guns or fishing rods or climbing
ropes, and I learned what the Greeks meant when they spoke of
demons living in cold stone or in bronze.

I'm here, it said, waiting; one day you'll come for me. I always
answered inwardly that I knew, and that I would, but it wasn't
until I was alone in the world, my wife dead and my children
scattered, that the noises of life receded enough to let me hear

what the box had been muttering down there in the dark all those years.

One sunny winter day in Arizona I took the bag to a valley high in some mountains near the Mexican border. The place and the time sorted well: the valley was a niche, an eyrie really, cut far up into a giant mountain wall, a rare place with the miracle of a perpetual spring and a twinkling of light swaying across a floor of leaves under hundred-foot sycamores and pines. A thousand years before, the Hohokam, the Old Ones, had loved the place and they had signed the earth with chert flakes and with shards. Exquisitely civilized beings that they were, I was sure they had had the good sense to sit still, as I did that day, to let themselves drift into the gulf of silence that washed between towering green walls and ended someplace in sapphire, an immensity scored and defined by the rare screech of a jay and the soundless wheeling of hawks.

I knew I was going to need a long stretch of quiet and a universe of solitude, and maybe the thronging of some kindly ghosts, if I was to turn and face what had been padding along behind me, just out of thought, most of my life.

With a sycamore log for couch and desk, I built a fire against the gentle chill, and opened the box. Inventory:

Item: Three leather-covered notebooks, one stained with long-oxidized blood. Inside, names, events, geography, dates: my diaries.

Item: Assorted writings in almost every prose form known to the English language on the backs of official reports that were supposed to record casualties or ammunition shortages.

Item: A few pages of military jargon about battles, dead and wounded, and numbers of prisoners.

Item: Some topographic sheets of fearful localities along the German border.

Item: Some odd bits — a French First Army warning to its soldiers about venereal disease (great, thundering, lecherous prose), a German soldier's paybook, and last, at the bottom, a proclamation about the death sentence to be inflicted on some French citizens for crimes against the Third Reich, signed by a Nazi official.

For five hours I hardly moved except to go to the spring for water for coffee, and, another time, to the fire to warm tortillas and beef. By twilight, tilting pages to the firelight, I finished reading.

As I stretched in the early dark, I had a sense that something powerful had slipped its leash. The past was raging and present reality was remote: I was standing on some ghostly highway waving at images that flew past, winking and exploding, too swift for definition.

Nothing will come of nothing, said an ancient king, and after a lifetime as a scientist, I knew that nothing useful ever came out of unsorted incoherence: I sat on my log, threw branches to brighten the fire, and tried to fit words around battles and faces.

Name any object and you'll see it. Well, I knew that — any physician has to be a working psychologist — but what astonished me that night was how clear everything seemed. By simply saying Colmar, or Strasbourg, aloud, I could fill the night with images. There they were, the white, cold faces in tank-turrets, the cathedral Dom in mist, a red sky screaming with dive-bombers, heroes with carbines and armbands, traitors howling away their last minutes, everything bright as the day it was etched.

I was a shaman, the words were magic. I named friends and rivers and battalions, and the apparitions bloomed, brightly colored, straining to be invoked. In minutes the firelight held a whole horizon of burning towns, twenty drunken singers in a Rhenish castle, terminal screaming in Dachau, the shout of a brave man across snow, and the embarrassing weeping of a coward. My log was a rare temptation: a Roman poet once commented that there's nothing as fascinating as a battle observed from a safe distance, and here I was, secure on the other side of time, ready to be enthralled by what used to be terror. I could have watched far into the night, but I knew a trap when I saw one.

The villagers clap hands over their ears when they hear the honk of the tedious veteran.

I had to march into that uproar, not float away on it, and I listened while the inner voice gave precise direction.

Everyone's a vessel for some unique knowledge (I said), and

mine's there, in that box. I have to fit words to it, and not simply words about battles and battalions — who captured what and how many died — nor yet words to list ordered agony and official screaming. We have those in redundance.

What I have to find, I think, is the rare epiphany that happens in research, if you're lucky, when marks on recordings and the architecture of certain cells and the statistics of mortality abruptly reach a mutual resonance, and there's a chiming, like a found chord. There's light, there's truth, shining and virgin, yours to bring to the world, and the excitement runs close to mania. If God can feel pleasure, it must be like that.

In the anarchy that's flooding tonight there are nodes and harmonics, elements of human dimension and time and circumstance, already composed, waiting to sound, and it's my charge to find them.

Find them? That's arrogant.

From a Himalayan valley a voice advises me to stop catching crickets with the fingers of the will. Pray to silence, I hear, let certain doors blow open, hope for thunder. Say please.

Humility's potent: so is the absence of twitching. In minutes an April morning spreads its light and there we are in 1945, sitting on a half-track, passing a bottle of brandy around, talking about spring. Since many of us were western Americans, we had never seen spring before: where we came from the seasons consisted of winter — cold — followed after a few muddy days by summer — hot. Our division had started fighting in the freezing slop of November (trench foot); winter had been an endless space of terrifying cold (blue-glass frozen hands and feet, ice-white corpses), and none of us suspected when we left Lorraine in the gray, blowing, tag-end of winter that we were starting a march toward spring. There were hints: there were a few days of grateful gold between rain while we tore across the Saar, and there were occasional hours of brightness between fogs as we fought our way up through the dank and drip and fir-dark of the Odenwald, and then suddenly we broke out into the open, rolling country toward Würzburg, and a whole continent lay glowing with the soft light of Gulf Stream air, shimmering, new to our senses, intoxicating. We drove through landscapes out of the colored picture books of our childhood; through shining fields and forests, clock towers and streams, half-timbered villages and winding cobbled streets, days shining with emerald and sapphire and nights drenched with silver and, permeating everything, an air that created a subtle whispering against our skins, the gentlest of warmth, still far from summer, fragrant, infinitely caressing, a velvety, inexhaustible mistress. I saw men take off their helmets and put down weapons and run their hands over their faces as if they were looking for the source of that soft, stroking loveliness; I heard them make stammering comments that everything looked like a picture postcard, or that the country was too goddamn beautiful for them goddamn Krauts. They were legitimately dazed; the spring of northern Europe is an intensity of beauty that has inspired and defied the best labors of poets and troubadours; it's an intoxicant no American understands until he has breathed it and walked through it.

The day of which I write was the loveliest of a succession of lovely days, which made it all the harder to sit on the half-track and look at our friend's body slumped in the gutter. Winter and corpses had sorted well; a frozen, torn member was a reasonable sight against a background of snow and burned ruins, but in this time of pulsing warmth and light, death and mutilation were really obscene; they jarred on the life that sang all around; they evoked outrage.

Consider further that for a long time we had had to leave our dead lying around anyhow, in roads and ditches and fields, and we had hated it. More times than any of us cared to remember we had looked up at a circle of faces and said simply, "He's dead; leave him."

"There? On the ground?" It was a standard challenge, and our standard response was a mumble that Graves Registration would be along pretty soon; but this never satisfied the faces, which had grown in a culture that never allowed death to be visible for long. They expected us somehow to whisk the torn bodies off into decent invisibility like undertakers, but in our world a dead man simply had to lie there, naked to the snow or the rain, dying over again anytime anybody looked at him or came into the range of his staring eyes. Our dead had to be dumped like rubbish and ignored.

A corpse is like a newborn infant in its terrible need for protection; it cries out for care. We always performed some small ritual: we pulled a field jacket over torn viscera, we covered a face, sometimes by turning a man on his abdomen (covering people's faces seemed important), and we often stuck his weapon in the ground by the muzzle or the bayonet and put his helmet on it. Then we ran to catch the column or pick up the next casualty.

We learned to be selectively callous; German dead didn't count at all, and men from other units not as much, but our dead from our own battalions, our friends from our terribly close family of survivors, *their* deaths diminished us, and we left bits and parts of our being sprawled in the mud or snow from Lorraine across Germany.

Wally had been an infantryman; all of us in the medical section knew him well. He wasn't a malingerer or a goldbrick, simply a decent man who had had some severe illnesses and several injuries that he had borne with cheerfulness and in the course of which we had helped him. He had become a close personal friend of most of the men in the section. In the attack that dawn he had been riddled by burp-gun fire; now his body was slumped in the familiar old-clothes pattern against the wall across from us. The trouble was that the cobblestones, as in many European villages, ran up to the wall; there was no sidewalk, and Wally was really lying in the street. Traffic was starting to boil; medium tanks, scout cars, jeeps, and guns went roaring and squealing past, spattering his body splash after splash. Finally, to our horror, a battery of giant eight-inch guns shouldered its way up the street. We were sure the body was going to be squashed under the wheels, but the drivers of the prime movers couldn't hear our yells and kept on their mammoth way; they all missed him, just barely, but the last gun's wheel caught his leg and made the body twitch and turn half over.

Out of the dust of the passing guns came a squalling vision in white — a fat German woman, arms flung wide, mouth issuing a high, steady stream of low German. Like most civilians, she ran toward our red crosses, and since I looked comprehending she ended screaming at me. The goddamn Amis, it appeared, had broken the windows in her house when they shelled the town last night. ALL the windows! Who was going to pay for this atrocity? What did they think they were doing with their stupid guns? Couldn't they shoot straight and not break people's windows? (Shades of Nuremberg: Krupp protesting outraged innocence while he worked slaves to death; frozen-faced Wehrmacht generals barking "*Nicht schuldig*" in the dock with the complete conviction that their systematic slaughter of millions of innocent people had been absolutely proper. Was this really a culture without the capacity to feel guilt or shame?)

"What's the old bag want, Doc?" an aid man asked.

"She's pissed off because her windows got broken in the battle." I started to giggle, realizing that I was starting to feel drunk and light-headed, knowing perfectly well that the screeching tub before me had been yelling "Heil Hitler" and cursing the goddamn Jews only days before, knowing too the utter impossibility of conveying to this red-faced, red-armed, sputtering hulk the insane inappropriateness of her footling injury weighed against a background of a devastated world and God knew how many mountains of corpses and square miles of widows and orphans. She could wipe all this away and expect the avengers of murdered civilization to be cowed by her sense of backyard outrage. The gulf was uncrossable: it really seemed funny.

The aid man didn't think so; he pictured the balance of damage more simply and directly.

"Knock it off, lady, for chrissakes," he requested, and when she kept right on he put a finger under her nose, turned her toward Wally's body, and said, "Fuck your goddamn windows. *Wass von* him? Huh?"

"*Ach, dass!*" The beldam was in an ecstasy of frenzied hausfrauhood, the state I assume she employed to terrorize the unfortunates in her family. "*Dass — pfui!*" and she spat at Wally's body.

With a swift motion the aid man picked up a folded litter — a formidable double pole eight feet long. Seeing it coming, she turned to run; the litter caught her square across her heaving behind, her arms flew out like the wings of a frantic chicken, and her fury turned to squawks, remarkably like the noise a hen makes when you chase it across a barnyard. The aid man and the hag disappeared down the street, he making wide, erratic, drunken swipes with the litter, she screaming to all the Germanic gods and to the neighbors who, from the grins on the faces in the windows, were enjoying the spectacle enormously.

"I'll bet she's the community pain in the ass," someone speculated. "Look at them other Krauts."

Silently, during all this, Sergeant Feehan had been unfolding a litter, placing it in the street, and draping it with an old gray German army blanket.

"Who's wounded?" I asked.

"It's for Wally." Feehan was drunk, like the rest of us, but he was in that mixture of anger and drunkenness when a man speaks with ferocious, biting clarity. "We ain't gonna let Wally lie there in the street with them goddamn tanks runnin' over him and maybe squashin' him, and them goddamn Krauts pissin' on him. We're gonna put him somewhere, goddammit." He glared, looking for dissent. "We're just —" he paused, searching for the definitive phrase, "just damn well gonna put — him — somewhere." He thumped the half-track with his fist with each of the last three words, challenging argument.

We agreed. We understood. We lifted Wally onto the litter, put the German army blanket over and around him, and put his helmet in the middle of his body with the quick, almost eager motions of men who had been waiting to do this for a long time.

"Where should we take him?" someone asked, and every face turned to me as the source of authority.

The street ahead was jammed with vehicles and marching men; it looked blurry and busy, but there was nowhere else to go.

"Down there," I said. "We'll find someplace that way."

I took the front left corner, Feehan the right, two other men picked up the back, and we started off.

"Hey," someone called, "what about the litter exchange?"

For combat medics, the litter exchange was the stuff of life; when you put a casualty in an ambulance, you made sure you took an empty litter and an equal number of blankets from it. If you didn't, there wouldn't be any litters or blankets and our wounded would soon be lying on the ground. The litter exchange was never far from our minds; someone was always counting blankets. We hesitated. Then Feehan pronounced the ultimate offertory of our world.

"*Fuck* the goddamn litter exchange!" Heresy. Ultimate sacrifice. We bowed our heads and started down the street.

We hadn't gone a hundred yards before I noticed that something strange was happening in the street around us: we were becoming a kind of wave, with noise ahead of us and stillness behind. Charlie Company, Wally's old company, was ranged along the street in half-tracks and jeeps. Soldiers were eating looted food, passing around bottles of brandy and poking into packs, while some dedicated souls were fiddling with machine guns, but as we came along, the noise and motion seemed to stop simply because we passed. Men were jumping down from half-tracks, walking quietly up to us, asking who the dead man was, calling out his identity to the man ahead, and starting to walk behind us. Many took off their helmets. Voices were calling with a soft, shielded quality.

"Wally from the Second Platoon."

"Medics are gonna put him somewhere."

"You taking him somewhere, Doc? Good for you guys."

The voices came from both sides and just ahead; behind was an increasing mass of men walking along, dangling helmets, until after a couple of hundred feet I realized the whole company was filling the street in our wake: we were at the head of a real procession. There was an extraordinary projection of warmth and closeness from the men marching behind us, but I was also aware of a faint knocking of angst because I had an uneasy presentiment that this natural, kind, human procedure was going to be regarded as somehow improper or even subversive by those dedicated to organizations and chains of command. More to the point, I realized that we hadn't the faintest notion of where we were taking the dead man, and it became increasingly clear that the whole company expected us to do something formal, significant, and consoling.

Cemetery, I remember thinking through the brandy, there's a churchyard or a cemetery; there always is.

At the first cross street, my forebodings were justified: there was a jeep with division headquarters markings on the bumper. Two infantrymen were holding it back from crossing in front of our procession and an annoyed-looking major was standing up in it to see what the hell.

"How in the name of Christ did he get up here?" muttered Feehan, and, following his glance, I saw with a sudden dull, deflating recognition a division medical staff officer, obviously lost, away far forward from his usual safe rounds, and scared as hell. He was ducking every time our eight-inch guns let go with a ranging blast.

God, I thought, in the middle of this high and solemn occasion why did you let this pissant loose on us? I could see quires of paperwork (reply by endorsement hereon) about field grade medical officers carrying corpses around; I could hear sniggering back-fence gossip at division about Phibbs's thinking he was an undertaker. My gloomy, swift reverie was interrupted by Feehan's voice.

"Major! Major! You'd better sit down! Snipers! They're shootin' a little high. That's how they got this guy...."

The major not only sat; he squinched toward invisibility. The faces of the infantrymen crowded behind the litter were a mosaic of stunned surprise and slow, fiendish comprehension as Feehan passed the wink. Now that I reflect on it, it was amazing how quickly they grasped the situation; they reacted brilliantly. Clarkson, a University of Chicago BAR gunner, caught on first, and the others followed his lead. Here before them they had the despised, usually invulnerable enemy, the rear-echelon brass, reduced to a quivering hulk, radiating cowardice, helpless, at their mercy. The Abbey Theatre in its prime couldn't have improved on the farce they organized.

"Counterattack," one of them bellowed, "right down that street off of the hill, that's where they're gonna counterattack. We ought to set the machine guns up right here after Doc gets Wally buried."

The major was echoing from his huddle behind the jeep windshield in a chirpy little call.

"Snipers," he quivered. "Counterattack. This street here." The men kept a little ahead of his responses. They staged an argument about where the German tanks would come into town, pointing in every direction.

"Surrounded, that's what we are, by God," someone yelled in convincing tones. "We better get the fuck out of here. Listen to that barrage."

The barrage was our own guns firing registration, but the major couldn't distinguish between one loud noise and another; the jeep spun around and headed away; over the screech of tires floated a hodgepodge of swiftly dwindling excuses about — so help me — about an important meeting at division headquarters and keep up the good work, men...

"Christ, that was fun," somebody breathed. It had been fun, of course, rare, wonderful, soul-cleansing fun; we had staged our own mystery play in Wally's honor. It took everybody a minute to wind down to the solemnity of our mission.

"Come on," I said, picking up the litter, "we'll find a park or cemetery or something." Our procession, larger now, went on down the street. We hadn't gone more than another fifty feet when the sound of a jeep coming up from behind us caused everyone to move to one side. The jeep drew abreast; I groaned; it was a season for pissants. Here was a visiting colonel, all nerved up and twitchy, doing his West Point best to hide his flap. He jumped off and looked reverently at the litter.

"Doc," he asked, "is that Colonel Kelly?"

I shook my head.

"Who is he, then?" he asked, still waiting to be impressed. Obviously he expected at least a battalion commander.

"Name's Wally," I finally told him. "Friend of ours. PFC. Got killed this morning. We're gonna put him somewhere out of the way."

"PFC?" He stressed the letters incredulously. "You — all these — all this — for a —" He turned up the corners of his mouth in what I always used to think of as a silly pumpkin grin.

"Look, Doc," (the tone descended from the dizzying heights of the upper Hudson; it rang with shakoes and the thin gray line and square meals), "this is very touching, but if we go on holding funerals for every — every — I mean, we *are* fighting a battle."

The colonel swaggered across the street and turned, facing us, blocking the whole procession. He put his hands on his hips; he wagged his helmet in what he obviously hoped was a mixture of stern command and pitying condescension. There was a silence of a few seconds as the men behind us realized that the colonel was deliberately blocking the street.

"FUCKHEAD!" My ears rang; the roar went on from behind my head in fluent, ear-shattering New York Italian, bass register. "YOU COWARDLY FUCKHEAD SON OF A BITCH! YOU BURY YOUR GODDAMN COLONEL FRIENDS AND YOUR MAJOR FRIENDS, AND US, WE AIN'T GONNA BURY OUR FRIEND — HE'S GOTTA LIE LIKE GARBAGE! FUCK YOU!"

I knew who it was before I turned: it was Falcone, the machine-gunner. He was six feet three, he weighed about two hundred fifty pounds, and when he was scrubbed and shiny for a parade he looked like a truculent gorilla; now, yelling with drunken rage, unwashed, unshaven, he was enough to chill the bravest man, and no one had ever considered the colonel particularly brave. He lunged past me at the colonel; I barely caught him, hanging on to the back of his web belt, and we waltzed around the street while the colonel scrambled back to his jeep with much more haste than dignity.

The other soldiers looked stunned: this was a real official colo-

nel from a much higher headquarters, even if he was kind of a
dumb one who never did much. They were genuinely frightened
for Falcone and some of them tried to shush him. Falcone went
on roaring and the colonel, a little recovered, tried to toss in some
crisp, soldierly commands and reproofs.

FALCONE: "WALLY DONE MORE TO BEAT THEM
KRAUTS THAN TWO THOUSAND COWARDS LIKE
YOU SITTIN' ON YOUR ASSES IN HEADQUARTERS!"

COLONEL: "Have you arrested; insubordination; face of the
enemy; *I'm supposed* to be in headquarters."

FALCONE: "WE DO THE FIGHTIN' AND THE FREEZ-
IN'. LAST WINTER, WHERE WAS YOU, YOU STEAM-
HEATED PRICK, WHEN WE WAS IN HERRLIS-
HEIM?"

COLONEL: "I'm an officer. I'm a colonel. Of — of course we
have stoves in headquarters." (He started becoming defensive
to the specifics of Falcone's bellowed accusations and thereby
lost any chance he had of gaining ascendancy.)

FALCONE: "AND WE GONNA TAKE OUR FRIEND AND
PUT HIS BODY SOMEPLACE DECENT LIKE THE
PRIEST DOES WHEN YOU DIE A CHRISTIAN AND
YOU GO BACK AND FUCK YOUR MOTHER SOME
MORE, YOU PILE OF SHIT!"

COLONEL: "Have you arrested. By God, you're under arrest,
you hear? Right now. Consider yourself under arrest."

They both wound down together. The colonel's last words broke
into the silence. I think all of us, with our years of disciplined
conditioning, were impressed at the word *arrest;* we certainly
wondered what Falcone found so funny, for he suddenly sat on
the cobblestones roaring with laughter, rocking back and forth,
slapping his thighs, bellowing and hooting.

He held both hands out to the colonel and began in mock Italian
accent. "Arrest me, Colonel Bambino. You gonna send me to a
nice quiet stockade where they feed me good three meals a day
and no one shoots my ass off?" He stood up and walked over to
the jeep; he held out his hands as if to have them manacled. He

wheedled, Sicilian, exaggerated, "Please, Colonel Bambino, arrest me, arrest me real good now." He turned to the silent, stunned faces. "You horse's asses, he ain't gonna arrest us — for chrissakes, what can they do to us worse than they done? We're gonna die, you goddamn fools. What can they do any worse? Slap your wrists? You dead men: you gonna die in the dirt while this prick sticks pins in maps. Arrest you? Put you in the stockade? You ain't that lucky!"

I turned from Falcone to look at the drunken, stunned faces behind us; they were beginning very slowly to break into relieved grins. Their world was turning upside down; a shattering, releasing truth was dawning. The second enlightment in a few minutes was brightening those tired, drawn faces. Nobody could do anything worse to them than what had already been done; they really could tell the whole world to go screw itself. They grasped slowly and in fragments what had been the truth of their lives all along: they were the ultimate sacrifice of the whole war, the point platoon of an infantry company, and all that kept them there was their pride in their own manhood and their friendship for each other, while the world behind them drank the liquor they had liberated and slept in the beds they had fought for and made fortunes selling them stuff to fight with and screwed their girlfriends and stole their jobs.

(It's a merciful God that keeps the future dark. These men couldn't have survived the knowledge that all their sacrifice was going to mean exactly nothing when they went home — those who lived to go there. They were going to be poor while others would have grown rich. Fat, safe generals from plush-lined headquarters would make speeches at banquets and hand each other medals and call each other heroes, and at American Legion halls the parasites from the quartermaster battalions would wave flags and scream about patriotism and nobody in the world would know or care that they, the tiny ten percent, had pulled the whole war machine forward.)

The men turned to each other with relaxed, astonished, suddenly knowing grins. Only a third or so of their original number was still alive and unwounded, and that third, they well knew, was going to diminish swiftly in the days and nights ahead. The colonel, with his threats of MPs and stockades, was a bad joke. Into the tired, chronically frightened minds of that infantry platoon burst the shattering, releasing truth that sent the sans-culottes boiling through the streets of Paris and the men of 1917 through the October night toward the Winter Palace.

"They've done the worst anybody can do to me; I have absolutely nothing to lose." When a man utters those words, he is ready for anything; a terrifying freedom is born. Princes and principalities are well advised to run for cover.

The reaction in the platoon was like a small spark igniting, flickering, flaming; the men started calling, restrainedly at first, as if putting a toe timidly into the pool of sacrilege, and then louder:

"What do you say, Colonel? You really going to arrest us?"

"We ain't doin' nothin' wrong, you know, Colonel, we're just trying to bury one of our friends."

The calls rose quickly. Long-suppressed anger tightened the air. Suddenly they were hooting and yelling. I suppose it was the closest thing to an actual mutiny that took place in the whole western front.

"Hey, Colonel; baby." Twittering yells.

"Look out for them nasty privates. They all got VD."

"Tell 'em, Falcone, for chrissakes, tell 'em what it's like in the war."

"Yoo-hoo, Colonel."

The colonel looked really frightened; his face flooded red and white as he tried to summon soldierly sternness against what was becoming a pathetically obvious wave of panic. The men were inching closer across the square, angry, threatening, and I began to feel I ought to shut everybody up — I was, after all, a major — when the yelling cut off with a knife edge. I turned. Salvo Gagliardo, the company commander of B Company, was standing among the men. Their manner became quiet, shuffling, sheepish, defiant. I was relieved: Salvo's authority was amiable but absolute. He had moved up from some headquarters job when their first company commander had been killed back at Herrlisheim, and he had become a legendary soldier. His men would have followed Salvo's lanky figure and dark Spanish-aquiline face across minefields into the inferno. Falcone was looking up from where he had sat again on the cobblestones as a worshipper might look at the sudden eruption of a friendly warrior god, unafraid, simply waiting for instructions for the day.

The colonel saw refuge; he began a stream of West Pointese: Captain Gagliardo, by God, arrest these men; these men were guilty of, in the face of the enemy, insulting an officer, the man on the pavement attacked me, and so on.

Salvo's smile didn't change; his dark face seemed to absorb the colonel's half-hysterical gibber. When he heard no response, the colonel stopped shouting and they confronted each other across fifteen feet of space, the colonel red-faced from shouting, Salvo and his men, statues. As I looked at their worn uniforms and the sudden death they carried slung around them as their usual and comfortable set of tools, their deadly potency spoke with tongues louder than words, while the colonel's starchy uniform and ridiculous forty-five seemed sillier the longer they stared at him.

Salvo finally spoke. "The guys are sorry they yelled at you, Colonel. You shouldn't stop a funeral. It's real bad luck. You really shouldn't have stopped them. This is one of our guys." That was all he said. He turned to me and waited for me to get on with the ceremony; the colonel might as well not have existed. I suppose he turned his jeep or drove away or did something, but I can't remember; the fact was that he shriveled into a functional nothingness as we all turned our attention to the serious business at hand, picked up the litter, and began our walk down the street, all of us feeling much more intense now, somewhat less drunk, in a silence emphasized by the scraping of many feet and the tinkling of steel, filling the street for a long way behind us.

After another block came the final interruption, the one we couldn't turn away. As I talked to a German girl, trying to ask the way to the cemetery, a runner came from the command post with orders. The battalion was attacking toward the Tauber River to seize a bridge in columns of companies: C after A; deploying thus-and-so; maps; overlay; move out at once. . . .

We were surrounded briefly by a wall of handshakes and back-slaps and kindly commands to take care of Wally, and then the street emptied itself behind us; half-track motors roared over yells and the clash of thrown arms, and the column turned down the Street of the Medical Staff Officers' Flight, men waving at us from steel sides, over machine guns, around mortar barrels.

We sent back the rest of the medical detachment, telling them we'd be along in the jeep, and in a matter of moments, it seemed, we were wandering down the street in a suddenly shrunken procession — just four of us and Wally.

Shrunken, but not alone; with the disappearance of the infantry company the civilian world began to come to life. Faces peered from behind curtains; figures stood in doorways; children ventured into the street. Fragments of German floated to me.

"Sanitater."

"Sie tragen 'ne Kamarade."

"Guck mal. Die Sanitater tragen sogar keine Waffen."

I began to feel very lonely. We were, after all, in an enemy city and, as the Germans were observing, we didn't carry weapons. I kept remembering that it was the rule for snipers to hide out for hours or sometimes days: we were certainly prime defenseless targets. In another block the street was almost lined, and I was listening anxiously for the dwindling roar of the tank motors. An astonishing number of people poured out of doorways and passageways: in any newly captured German city there was always a gush of civic relief when people discovered they weren't really going to be raped or gutted by the Jewish American Bolsheviks. Curiosity replaced terror; fingers pointed, a wall of faces grew, like bricks rapidly heaped in place, eyes peering over shoulders.

Lemurs, I thought, ghouls, enemy, let us alone with our dead; also, stop making me uneasy. Our sense of remoteness and danger was so acute that it took some time before we all realized that the faces were harmless: they were the faces of women, old men, and children. As had every community, this one had been drained of any male remotely capable of carrying a gun; I realized, too, the profounder truth that the eyes that hemmed us in weren't seeing us at all. They were looking at the body with a strange and tragic intensity; hands went over mouths; lips were bitten. Why? I wondered. What was Wally to them?

The answer came with the shining of the obvious: they hadn't seen their own dead, but the number must have been legion. Probably everyone along that street had lost someone, had mourned bodies moldering in Africa or Russia or France. Now they were seeing for the first time what Friedl or Joachim would have looked like if he had come home. A world of abstract statistics was suddenly, tragically concrete in the load we were carrying along the street. We weren't in any danger: Wally was our mantle and our shield.

A church stood ahead, tall, cold, dark, flinty; the doors were heavy, made of dark wood curlecued with iron. Next to it was a churchyard with some gravestones, the kind of place we'd been looking for. We stopped. The churchyard was dominated by a heroic figure of a German soldier, World War I model; across the base of the statue the words "*In Treue Fest*" shouted in bronze.

Someone asked if we should leave Wally inside, but I felt a revulsion. The German churches, Protestant and Catholic, had played a contemptible role during the Nazi lunacy. At the best they had been supine, spineless, passively cooperative; at the worst they had actually helped to launch the irruptions. The hell with them, I thought, they're the enemies.

(And just where, asked a mocking voice in my head, in this alien enemy city are you going to find someplace or something that isn't? Where is innocence in Nazi Germany?)

"It's a Protestant church," I told the men. "Wally was Catholic."

I was speaking to an Irishman and two Italians, who of course regarded that statement as final. We walked on through an aisle of stone and brick walls surrounded by whispers, mutters, pointed fingers, windows alive with peering eyes.

At the next cross street a curious atmospheric change filled the air. It was a phenomenon I had seen once or twice during the war: the blast from the eight-inch guns and the dust from hundreds of tank treads had created a swirling cloud of mist and dust rolling across the street ahead, dense, like a Maine fog hugging the sea. It shimmered with golden motes in the sunlight; it offered a comforting tarn-cloak of invisibility against the prying, whispering, pointing civilian world. We walked into the swirl and were lost in a maze of glittering particles so dense we could hardly see each other. The men at the handles of the litter were silhouettes, black against gold; it was impressively quiet, or at least we felt quiet, shrouded as we were.

As we came out the other side — it seems too pat as I write this — we saw what we'd been looking for. It was the first house on the left side in the block ahead. The street had changed its character completely; this house sat back from the street with a garden in front and on either side. It was one story, with a colored rustic roof and low windows across the front; below the windows was a bed of long-stemmed flowers, red and blue, rippling in the light breeze. Around the garden was a small ornamental black iron fence about three feet high, with a gate fastened with a brass latch. The place was lovely, set apart, obviously loved: it shone. Without a word we turned to it; I unfastened the little brass latch and we carried Wally into the garden, across the grass and over to the flower bed. I don't know what kind of flowers they were but I can see that dense, nodding, twinkling surface as if it were yesterday. The important thing was that the flowers were beautiful and also that they were tall; they were tall enough to cover a man. As we lowered Wally's body into them, they bent over the old gray blanket; he disappeared in starry red and blue. Each of us performed some final act: we straightened the blanket, pulled the flowers to cover him, tucked his head out of sight, or put his helmet precisely in the middle of his body. As we did, a woman and two children peeked out of the low window — big, scared rabbit eyes on the children, easing fear and slow understanding emanating from the woman.

"*Amerikanischer Soldat,*" I told her. "*Unser Kamarad. Tod. Er bleibt hier; nicht ruhren.* Don't disturb him."

"*Nein, nein,*" she answered quickly, and from the way she bobbed her head and from the look on her face I knew she understood and even sympathized. We took off our helmets and stood around the flower bed a minute. I know the others felt the same grateful peace that I did as we watched the innocent flowers sprinkle the stiffening limbs with loveliness. I had an irrational feeling that we had beaten the system: before long the ghouls of the Graves Registration Units would come along with their mattress sacks, their stapling tools, and their stencils, and Wally's mortal parts would be dumped into the returning chain of the vast assembly line that had brought him here, but none of that would matter. Wally had escaped into the flowers.

God rest his soul, I thought, but I knew as I thought it that it was for our own souls I was praying. Nobody really appeases the spirits of the dead; we appease our own out of the necessity with ritual and with tokens of beauty to mitigate the terror of the irreversibility of time.

Nobody said anything; we put on our helmets and, as the little gate clanged behind us, we stepped back into our world. Walking down the street, we began talking about maps and casualties and rations. By the time we trotted the last few yards to the jeep, we were ready for a tearing ride after the infantry column, yelling like children just out of church. The engineers had gotten a bridge across the Tauber River, we heard; we were going to be marching and fighting all night.

Across an ocean and a lifetime, in the high dark of my Arizona mountain the night was still crowded. Something had been appeased, liberated by my comprehension of it, but other ghosts were still breathing close. In the rising wind I could hear the rattling of unpaid bills.

Mike, Pico, Chuck, I thought, all you torn warriors in Baker Company, you've been patient. It's been a long time. Let us now speak of rare heroes and frequent bastards and evisceration.

I put out the fire and slung my pack.

2

Don't Volunteer

WHEN THE ANNOUNCER INTERRUPTED Shostakovich's First Symphony to tell the world what happened at Pearl Harbor, I wasn't in a position to be much help. Halfway through the required twelve-month internship, I was no use to anyone — certainly not to the armed forces — until July 1, 1942. My role in the months between was maddening, suspended animation, the bee caught in amber, all the more intolerable because for two years I had been hopelessly in love with the Second World War. So were many of my generation; permit me to defend our sanity.

In those innocent decades a war was something picturesque that happened three thousand miles away. After a hard day in the world of reason, we loved to relax with rotogravures and newsreels showing men in odd clothing killing each other. Blame anthropology; we're genetically selected over millions of years to be Pleistocene pack hunters, and the wink of civilization hasn't given mutation a chance to work. Peace and the ordered society do not come easily; they're not our natural state. They demand enormous exertion, and they often leave us snappish and hysterical. Prenuclear wars were often welcomed, much as we might deny it, for reasons we couldn't admit; we dropped a lifetime of pretense and gave ourselves up to official, condoned, violence, often dramatic and sometimes beautiful, like a parched man gulping his first draft of cool water. Neuropathology, double-entry bookkeeping, torts and wills and wheels and gears, all these were froth, the work of days tripping the superficial meadows. To tickle our profound ganglia we needed pictures of exploding destroyers.

Oh, we made dissenting noises, back in the thirties. We prattled of peace, we straggled across campuses bearing signs deploring war, we wrote with loathing of Schneider-Creuzot, but these were bubbles. In our deep unreasoning pools, there were cavalry charges, and the French foreign legion, and Saxon longbowmen, and Jean Harlow swooning across the bed under a World War I fighter pilot.

Sex and violence! Freedom from the need to keep motivations chugging against the hard current! A long, soft, effortless, backward sprawl into juvenile fantasy! There were some agonal twitches by the rational mind, but down in the dark animal structures of the thalamus and midbrain, the resident monster sneered. Beastliness won, going away.

My generation went rushing off to glandular violence and left me forlorn, condemned to wander far from danger, sticking needles in buttocks and placating the resident furies of the operating room. My fellow Americans were being clubbed into humiliation by subhuman Japanese, our antique planes were blooming into matchsticks over invaded islands, and the Japanese navy was running amok through a wandering fragility called the U.S. Asiatic fleet. Safety was a disgrace. I had to do something, and what I did was to march down to Fifth Army headquarters on Michigan Avenue to announce that I'd like a commission. To my surprise they were delighted to see me.

A regular army colonel, medical corps, made parade-ground noises.

He looked at papers. He was glad to see me. Northwestern University? St. Luke's Hospital? Bully!

I'd be commissioned at once, first lieutenant medical corps, Army of the United States (Ground Forces). My orders would arrive soon after July 1, and why hadn't he seen more of my colleagues?

I explained that they were patriotic but patient, waiting until they'd finished their training.

The colonel boomed.

They were needed now! Took time to cut orders! Army had to plan who to send where! War, dammit!

I said yes and raised my right hand and pledged true faith and allegiance, and went back to my slumlike intern's quarters, officially a first lieutenant medical corps, Army of the United States (Ground Forces).

Ground forces? The colonel assured me that was as good a way to join the army as any, and I was burning so brightly I would have volunteered for the paratroops or the rangers, if I'd been asked. (If there were elvish chuckles from underneath the typewriters at Fifth Army headquarters, I was in no mood to hear them.)

Enthusiasm's a nasty virus, very catching. In a week, another intern made the same trip and for the rest of that terrible winter, while the Allied world teetered over catastrophe, the two of us pursued our healing rounds with a smugness that must have been infuriating. We had done our bit.

In April we learned about consequences. Our gifted chief of surgery was asked by the army air corps to organize a base hospital unit: it was to include the best men on the staff with a few lucky interns and residents as junior officers. When we heard that we were among those selected, and when we were told that the unit was going to Denver, Colorado, where we could train in our specialties while we served our country, we were so happy we felt guilty. What a delightful war!

Then the club fell. Foster Mac, the chief, stopped us in the hall one day to tell us about a little problem. Those commissions we had. Army ground forces. You'd think, said Mac, it would be easy to move a couple of files from one office to another, but he'd spent a middling fortune on long-distance phone calls and all he heard were well-modulated snickers. Army ground forces had us by the tender parts and their clutch was fond and final. What the hell, he wondered, had we gotten ourselves into?

In June, while our colleagues were packing to go to the post they already referred to as Shangri-La, we received our orders. Report August 1 to the Medical Field Service School, Carlisle Barracks, Pennsylvania.

The medical field service? What the hell, we asked, was that? Our friends speculated: pushups, leggins, the outdoor life? At least it sounded healthy.

✳ 3

The Decent Army

WE WERE LUCKY in 1942. We didn't have to shrink from pictures of screaming Vietnamese about to be raped and murdered by American soldiers at My Lai.

There were no dead students scattered across the grass at Kent State.

Where we stood in 1942 the air was charged, clean, dangerous, honest. We stood in direct line of descent from Nollichucky Jack's Tennessee mountaineers riding over the Smokies to Kings Mountain, or Dan Morgan's Virginia riflemen marching to Saratoga, and we could say so without self-consciousness or pretense. We could say so because the Second World War wasn't one of those polite confrontations when the losers sign some papers and everybody goes home.

In 1777, defeat had meant mercenary bayonets in the belly and tomahawks in the skull and whole families burning in their homes and farms; in 1942, defeat would be even worse. Terrified, helpless people all over Western Europe and half of Asia had learned that defeat was going to mean Gestapo torture chambers, and mass machine-gunning by SS troops, or possibly rape, castration, or decapitation by hysterical Japanese. From France to Malaya, the world was littered with broken bodies that bore witness to the kind of war we faced in 1942.

We could claim as ancestors those privates of the 24th Iowa standing before a table in a forest volunteering to reenlist for a third time in 1864, knowing that they could leave honorably right then for their farms, not under any compulsion to reenlist, and knowing further that reenlistment meant that they would probably die, but reenlisting anyway because they believed enough in the Union to die for it.

We could claim as great-great-great-grandfathers the men who faced the massed British fire at Lundy's Lane or who stood behind the cotton bales at New Orleans, knowing that their bravery and possibly their lives interposed between a nation of free men and an empire of glum enslavers.

In sober historic truth there have been times when the United States Army gleamed with high purpose, fit challenge for manhood and capacity for dedication, and that, you may or may not believe, is how we felt in 1941.

It's hard today to remember the glow that bathed our armed forces as the country hitched up its weapons for the Second World War. It was a springtime, a virginal encounter when a generation distracted and sometimes desperate could turn happy and relieved to the ancient, simple virtues. First, everybody felt pleased surprise to find out that we had any armed forces at all, because sometime during the twenties and thirties the United States Army had largely disappeared. While the rest of the world rumbled and flamed through a tortured decade, the United States Army was visible only in rare rotogravure pictures of men in campaign hats and leggins running around the Mexican border. They looked quaint, vaguely like cowboys. They certainly didn't seem any match for the well-drilled hordes that thumped and banged their way across the newsreel screens, flaunting the terrors of Germany, Russia, Italy, and Japan.

The people of America rejoiced when the armed forces marched back into their world, and they had reasons. First, and very clearly, unless the American armed forces were brave and efficient, Americans in places like Pittsburgh and San Diego were going to discover the facts of life in Manila and Kharkhov and Amsterdam and Grenoble.

Second, the armed forces ended the Great Depression. It was so simple nobody believed it. The spending was all that was needed. Thoughtful economists have pointed out that we would have accomplished the same end if we had built all those planes and tanks and mess kits and bayonets and dumped them in the Pacific Ocean. Why is the obvious always invisible?

The government, with a wisdom never displayed before or since, imposed effective controls on prices, wages, and rents, and thereby stated what the money was worth; despite unprecedented shortages of all material goods, there was no inflation because we, the people, didn't let it happen. Everybody who could work had a job, and the money everybody worked for retained its value because we, the government, the people, fixed its worth.

Out of the romantic past came the army we had forgotten, and on its olive-drab shoulders came riding a wild, happy, sustained prosperity. The army was such a sacred image in 1941 that all the Madison Avenue Pandars had to do to sell cigarettes or booze or nose-wipes was to show a soldier smoking or drinking or blowing his nose, and hey, presto! Instant identity with the totally good and the completely irreproachable.

I swam in that national radiance like all about me. I couldn't wait to chuck my intern's whites and swank about in my new uniform — the more so as it seemed the army was going to need a lot of help in getting itself sorted out.

This last was no joke: any thoughtful student of military history shuddered to read the accounts of our rearming.

Picture in *Life* magazine of maneuvers, new style: "In the attack the infantry will advance, standing erect, shooting from the hip, until fire superiority has been attained...." Last time this lunatic maneuver had been tried, whole rows of marines had sprawled in their blood in the fields below Belleau Wood. Nobody in the Second World War ever actually attacked anything like that, but the proposal shed frightening light on the quality of our military leadership.

Headline from maneuvers: "Military leaders discount the tank as a factor in modern warfare.'' This was the year before the Germans erupted across Poland. Other American military leaders were still emphasizing the essential role of the horse.

Headlines from the training camps were unnerving: ''Soldiers near mutiny; vow they didn't join Army to cut the general's lawn.'' ''Soldiers threaten to desert: We join the Army to learn how to fight a Blitzkrieg, and all we do is ten hours a day of close-order drill.''

The litany was long and worrisome, but not chilling. Everybody knew we had no choice; we had to raise an army and that army was going to have to fight and beat the Japanese Imperial Army and the Wehrmacht, the best-led, best-trained, most savagely unscrupulous soldiers in the history of warfare.

Unscrupulous; add terror. Here I must apologize to the world and to time and to certain Belgian ghosts. I apologize for amiable knots of young gigglers in the thirties, shaking their heads over the atrocity stories of the First World War. Women shot in the streets! Families burned in their homes! Innocent hostages dying on stakes before firing squads! We were embarrassed about our parents — they believed such drivel. British propaganda, patent and palpable!

It's one thing to be a dolt; it's another, and much worse, to be a lazy, opinionated dolt. With minimum effort we could have discovered those pathetic monuments in every Belgian town, inscribed with the names of men and women ''*fusillée par les Allemands*,'' guilty of no crime worse than ruffling the feelings of a local German commander, shot by the thousand facing clean, well-drilled German firing squads. Solid history, 1914. It was enlightened not to know about it.

Our giggles died in our throats in 1942. There were the pictures, not to be denied, of the goggled eyes and monstrous protruding tongues in the faces of the hanged, men, women, even adolescent children, hands tied behind backs, swinging in the wind over marching German columns.

And the Japanese; the clever, the clean, the quaint. More solid history: British wounded bayoneted on their litters, routine practice, Malaya, 1942. Pregnant women's bellies slit open to let them scream themselves to death. Nanking, 1938, Manila, Singapore, Hong Kong, 1941.

Australian soldiers crucified to trees, hung with placards saying ''They took a long time to die,'' Milne Bay, New Guinea, April 1942.

Maybe we should never use total black or clear white to symbolize the caperings of the human animal, but in 1942 we didn't have to concern ourselves with shades of gray or quibbles. We knew we were marching out against the closest approximation of total darkness the planet had known for centuries.

There was something else, a quality, a definition about us and what we were that we couldn't have known back then, a set of outlines that would be washed into recognition only by the flood of years and events.

We were a reenactment of American history, from Louisburg to Château-Thierry, a levee en masse around a skeleton of barely competent professional soldiers, when somehow, always, the carpenters and salesmen and tavernkeepers and foundry workers got themselves sorted into ranks, most of them to become adequate and some of them to become heroes. The very incompetence we saw gave us a possessive sense; if anything was going to be made of the army, we would have to do it. It was going to be our army, we were prepared to love it, and I suppose we would have felt even more strongly if we had known what we really were: the last American crusade, an army marching out with the cheers and blessings of a whole people, to save our country and the world from black, unrelieved villainy.

We were marching out to become the last people's army in the history of the United States of America.

4

Metamorphosis

CARLISLE BARRACKS, July 31, 1942. This is my wartime diary, first entry. It's long after taps and I'm sitting in a puddle of light at one end of a large dark barrack, scribbling. There are a thousand of us here, young physicians new-fledged out of internships, and we've certainly joined the army at an interesting time. It's not at all clear that we're going to win this war, and if we lose, there'll be no place in the world fit to live.

Shall I then presume? Certainly: when the Earth shudders, there's usually something worth recording. With that grandiloquent justification, I begin. *Meine Kriegserrinerungen,* me and Clausewitz.

8:00 P.M., July 31. In the humming tensions of this summer night we wander the barracks, exchanging names of schools and hospitals, trading in speculation. The army took us in kindly enough, but to what purpose?

The military knife sliced us out of youthful America with precision; in age, profession, and state of training we're stamped from the same die, with only geography and attitude for difference. I soon hear overtones of both.

On a nearby cot a figure is bowed, rocking, head in hands, in the attitude of someone passing a gallstone. Another lieutenant stands nearby, patting a shoulder, consoling.

Erect figure: "What the hell, we haven't got it all that bad. They made us first lieutenants right away and we get pretty good pay, a hell of a lot better than the nothing we got for being interns."

The face lifts from hands; it's one of those stuffed structures with subcutaneous protusions that force the eyes into slits. In purest accents of Chicago I hear outrage. (Diphthongs of Northern Illinois: in Chicago they'll tell you they *heeyave* a thing.)

"Lousy first lieutenant's pay's all right for you guys, you know what this fucking war is costing *me?* I heeyad a three-year surgical residency" — he pounds the bed with each word — "all signed up. Partnership with the richest guy on the staff at the end. Guy with two Cadillacs, house in the country . . ." He drops his head, shakes it, continues with effort. "Thirty thousand dollars. A year. Guaranteed. You want to know how much a war costs, ask *me*. Fucking draft board, prejudiced. Against our hospital. No deferments even when my mother called."

I commented that we had all been offered deferments at our place. Most of us had turned them down.

"Turned them down? You guys crazy? What hospital?" I told him.

"Oh shit, one of those university white-rat places."

And his?

He named a near–North Side butcher shop, notorious for appendectomies and salpingectomies, a place not approved for training in any specialty. Smart draft board.

By now the listening circle has widened. Speech opens.

"We're in a war, for chrissakes. We lose it, where's your thirty thousand?"

"What about the guys on Bataan, tonight? M.D.s like us killed, captured, maybe tortured?"

"Oh shit, they always get up these wars." (Presumably, we gathered, to exploit him.) "Somebody's making a fucking bundle. Out of us."

I have never seen greed naked and dancing like this: the most avaricious usually clutch some fig leaf of professional decency, but this creature's dangling his horrors before the world. I revert to the idiom I heard in childhood.

"Jaysus, man," I console, "I'm sorry for your troubles. It's destroyed you are surely."

The Gaelic syntax is lost on him, but the tone isn't. We are not friends.

A pleasant curved face from Pennsylvania sounds reason, morbling. (When a Pennsylvanian wants to name the stuff Michelangelo carved, he says "morble.")

"What does the ohrmy think we're good for? What do they think we know? What will they ask us to do? I feel, well, insecure."

"Insecure, shit — incompetent."

The brave vowels of New York are a trumpet.

"Incompetent is what we should feel. Our official rank ought to be first lieutenants, medical corps, Army of the United States, incompetent."

Consensus flickers around the cots.

"If the public had any idea how much a twelve-month intern didn't know ... !"

"The great void. Miles between facts."

"Two, three more years of training, we might be worth something to the world."

"Right now we're a menace to life and health."

We compare exposures on our rotating internships. Two to three months on surgery, one or two months of orthopedics, with luck. We've held retractors during operations, we've put in stitches. We watched while great surgeons performed feats years beyond our training. Major surgery? It would be criminal if we tried.

Nasal Iowa grinds out the hardest resonants in the English language to ask what the hell we'd do if we had a guy with a bullet that went in the back and came out the front. Like in through a costovertebral angle and out just above the symphysis pubis?

New York answers that he could put a great bandage where the bullet went in and where it came out. Then he'd pray.

We talk impossibilities. Chest wounds, pneumothorax, amputations.

"Anybody know how to do a major amputation?"

"Why not ask us if we can do brain surgery?"

Now the laughter is nervous.

Another Pennsylvania accent wanders to our circle with the hot dope. Unimpeachable source. He has it on the very best authority. The army has special residencies in trauma and surgery all organized for us. We'll go on what they call detached duty and get all this great training. Hospitals are screaming for help, the army's not fighting anywhere right now.

The night blooms with professional ease. We're soldiers in a sensible army. A fearful ton lifts off our shoulders. Any physician with a pinch of conscience lives with an occupational Fury, the always-present, always-intolerable thought of a life slipping through incompetent fingers. We exhale. We're free to turn to the war, to our new livelihood, to the evening news and the map pinned to the barracks wall.

Heavy black crayon marks on the cellophane map cover show the edges of the fighting; as we listen, we hear that they're moving at a rate that may soon be terminal.

Somebody puts a finger on a Nazi arrow curving down through the Caucasus Mountains to Maikop.

Another finger points to a very efficient German arrow poised a few miles east of Suez.

Strategists move fingers together; nails touch somewhere between Turkey and the eastern Mediterranean littoral.

"They meet there, they'll cut off the Suez Canal."

"Good-bye Near East."

"Good-bye oil."

"Good-bye the British Empire."

"Probably good-bye the war."

"Jesus, the British and the Russians get knocked out of the war, the Germans have two continents and all the iron and slaves in the world. They can take their time and build a navy and an air force so big nobody can keep up with them. We'll be alone, waiting.''

''That is pure damned silly propaganda. What the pinkos want you to believe. Like the WPA running a war. Fucking New Deal.''

We turn to a face drawn tight with the need to convince us. A blond Ivy League haircut swims above social jowls lifted from a prognathous horse. Boston mounted a prep school to get those terminal consonants.

Words come pouring through a stutter.

''M-M-MacArthur. F-fighting the Japs. Yellow Japs. Real American, only one around. Roosevelt-Russian-socialist-communist-Churchill.'' Nouns gasp for lack of verbs; there's a pause for exhalation of pure hate.

The machine begins its next discharge about Martin Dies, the Un-American Activities Committee, and the laughable-sinister New Deal commies.

Here's a Roosevelt-hater, bubbling and boiling : will our grandchildren believe such creatures existed ? He should be stuffed and arranged in a lifelike pose in a glass cage. I know the type : I've lived with it. My father and his successful friends used to go all purple-irrational at the mention of the President's name. He threatened their purses, their true testicles, the only goal and good of their lives.

Now the two-legged pathology facing me is descending through a vocabulary of excretion, obscenity, and scatology with a giggling air of release from stricture : he's learned that in the best locker rooms and bars one can mouth any foulness and be roundly clapped for it, as long as Roosevelt's the victim.

For the moneyed, disapproval of Hitler is forced, primly stated, but hatred of Roosevelt is a fury from the deeps of their propertied hearts : they hate him enough to commit treason for it. Is something like this happening in France ?

The Hater starts a joke about Eleanor and the black WACs; everybody turns away, embarrassed. We seek refuge in the fireflies and cut-grass smells outside, until taps sounds and conversation dwindles through the dark.

Now I'm sleepy.

August 1. Army life begins. We gather papers, notebooks, class schedules, and stroll out the front door, assuming we'll walk to the class building, a few hundred yards away. This, we quickly learn, is the army. We line up by alphabetic platoons and march off behind a brass band.

Voices in front mutter that we're a fucking parade; voices in the rear observe more accurately that we're a fucking disaster. Some earnest souls try to stamp feet in time to the drums; most of us simply shamble. Achilles tendons are scraped, metatarsals crunched, a sense of the ridiculous blooms like an evil fungus. We're a millipede new to thousand-footedness, a creature that contracts and expands irrationally.

Happy chance: the Roosevelt-hater is marching ahead of me. I'm able to keep step with the drums and he isn't, and I keep stamping on his heels.

A colonel, regular army medical corps, speaks to our seated attention. Notebooks are poised, pencils out. Here we go.

Welcome to the army, we hear. The colonel has the same brass-drum whiskey resonance that I heard at Fifth Army headquarters. Does the regular army have some consistent effect on vocal cords?

"Now you're probably wondering what you're here to learn. First thing is that you're not here to study medicine. You're all graduates of top-notch medical schools and top-notch internships, otherwise you wouldn't be sitting here. We don't have to teach you medicine; you know your medicine. We're here to teach you about the army."

There's the silence of disbelief; then a sounding of nasal Texas fills the hall.

"Ain't he the optimistic son of a *bitch!*"

We strangle; we hardly hear the colonel for the next hour as he tells of schedules and drills and proper wearing of insignia and tables of organization and where the Coke machine is, and how officers and gentlemen act in assorted crises.

Learn about the army, the colonel said. What the hell (runs the consensus), we're here to staunch the wounds of the United States Army; maybe the colonel's right; we should study its parts and movements. We're skillful students; we attack the curriculum.

1. How to inspect a mess hall: Look for spots on plates, dirt on fingertip when rubbed over anything. Smell the meat.
2. How to inspect latrines: We emphasize flies.
3. Close-order drill: After a week most of us can move a platoon front, back, and sideways; par for your average cretin.
4. Encyclopedias and eternities about requisitions, reports. We slumber; our incompetent, unpleasant lecturer snarls; stupor triumphs.
5. A superb course in map-reading. (On many a dark night in Germany I blessed Captain O'Brien.)
6. A spot of medical sunlight. A visiting epidemiologist lectures on typhus, malaria, dengue, in incisive German-Jewish accents that recall many of our great medical school teachers. "It was a sad day for the louse, gentlemen, when it decided to harbor *Rickettsia Prowazekii* in its gut...." Sanity, cheers.

Third day of training we had an hour film about "the machine gun in defense." The tactics were right out of 1918: apparently the army hadn't heard of tanks or self-propelled guns. Later in the day there was another film about scouting and patrolling. Some Rover boys went dashing about the woods, slitting sentries' throats and cutting demolition wires. From what I knew of stalking big game, the tactics illustrated would get anybody killed within an hour.

It was entertaining waste motion for most of us, terror for the Hater. In the barracks this evening he was waving some sort of right-wing lunatic-fringe rag.

"Machine guns! All that shit about machine guns! What are we doing around machine guns?"

"Killing time, looking at a stupid movie to fill up a schedule."
The Hater grimaced with the scorn of inner knowledge.

"Look what it says right here. Roosevelt hates Republicans, he's sending them out to get killed. Doctors are Republicans, right? Make cannon fodder out of us. Dead, we can't vote, right? See! Look!..."

The paper was the kind of effluvium put out by Father Coughlin or William Dudley Pelley or Gerald L. K. Smith. I thought they'd all gone to ground since Pearl Harbor, but this was a dying effusion. There were columns devoted to the communist-Jewish international conspiracy, and editorials with scummy cartoons about the Jew Rosenfeldt, and the way he was sending all the conservatives out to get killed. Like MacArthur.

A hand reached from over my shoulder and snatched the paper. I looked up to see the New Yorker, Scher, rolling the thing into a tube. He walked up to the Hater and began smashing him across the face with it, hard, deliberately, repeatedly.

"Jew-hater, huh? You ready to hate a Jew when the kike can punch your fucking teeth in? Stand up, you goddamned coward, so I don't have to hit you sitting down."

The Hater was so frightened it was embarrassing. From behind shielding hands he mumbled that he hadn't meant anything personal, he hadn't realized, and anyway how could you tell when someone had blue eyes?

We howled. Scher threw the paper away and shook his head.

"Sure, I'm a mutant. The blue-eyed Jews. Next thing we'll get nose jobs and you'll be in a hell of a shape. One of us might marry your sister."

(Guilty remembrance of my own school, Northwestern, where four Jews were admitted by quota out of a class of a hundred and twenty.)

I hauled Scher off for a beer; as we went out the door I could see the Hater gathering the scraps of his paper.

Day five: the Mourner and the Hater have discovered each other. Let me not to the marriage of true acquisitives admit decency. Tonight they were huddled over papers adding yearly totals: if a guy did so many major surgeries, and if so many of them were complicated and you could charge more, and if you kept your office nurse's salary down and charged for extras like dressings and bandages ... Money, the drug, the intoxicant, they're sniffing and rolling in it.

Day six: by God, we shut the Hater up. Iowa and I began it spontaneously this evening. We told him there were a couple of guys looking for him, a major and a colonel. Something about intelligence.

The Hater clearly didn't know whether to look flattered or alarmed. We settled it for him.

"It was something about all this crap you keep saying about the President. There's a regulation or something."

We passed the wink and a circle formed.

"You guys heard them, right?"

"They said it was about how the President is your commander in chief and you can't go around calling him a traitor. That oath you took, remember, all about true faith and allegiance."

"Something about a court-martial, one guy said."

The Hater fell into real terror; he looked frantically from face to face hoping for frivolity, but we were stone, nodding, tragic.

The rest of the night was blessed.

All we heard from the Hater were whispers; he kept plucking elbows, babbling, telling us how he loved his country.

Rumblings of mutiny: spell of strangeness woven of uniforms and saluting and drills and calisthenics is worn thin in a short week; segments of the millipede resume eyes and rational thought; perception of reality returns.

Over beers in the Molly Pitcher Bar ten days out in training: "I wonder if it's occurred to anybody else these guys don't know what the fuck they're doing?"

"I spent three hours last night drawing up march tables for a horse-drawn column, for chrissakes!"

"It's eighteen sixty-four and we got all these horses, see. On to Richmond!"

"I mean, this is no shit, you guys. I've never been in a war before...."

"Neither have these guys."

"Well, there must be a hell of a lot of stuff we ought to be learning about battle casualties and high-velocity wounds and evacuating people and logistics. When the hell are we going to learn something we can use?"

"Matter of fact, I'm not sure what it is we're going to be doing. Is anybody?"

"Don't ask me; so far I've learned how you hold your hand when you salute and who ranks who in the army general staff and how I shouldn't catch VD."

"Tell you what we'll do. We'll ask Snout. Snout's our boy."

The tables roared. We already had an enemy, a buffoon, and we had named him Colonel Snout. Like most medical administrative corps officers who are commissioned to help doctors run the medical corps, he hated physicians, and to this unpromising substrate he added a dense mind, a small soul, and a galloping insecurity that twisted his face in grotesqueries with the effort of conveying the time of day. We already had a collection of Snoutisms, and we were shouting them around the room when a couple of us saw Snout's long nose and close-set eyes rising like an evil moon over a booth. With nudges and kicks we conveyed the situation. Snout had a silent audience.

"Want to know what it is you're going to be doing?"

The voice had a British precision, and a feminine delicacy.

"Come to class Wednesday, gentlemen. I'm going to tell you all about it. Ten hundred hours."

At ten hundred hours on Wednesday, Snout for once faced a room full of attentive, concentrated faces.

We muttered, surprised, apprehensive, that the son of a bitch really looked happy; and so he did, or as nearly as he was capable of it, standing there on the platform, leaning on fingertips; his face had stopped drawing itself into exaggerations. He began gently.

"The field medical service, gentlemen," sonorous, long pause.

First Snout guessed he'd better tell us just what the field medical service was *not*.

A series of slides showed us where we were *not* going. Lowry Air Force Base Hospital in Denver, Walter Reed Hospital in Washington, assorted hospitals in London and Noumea, various university medical school units, hospitals under tents in places like Australia, field surgical units (called M.A.S.H. in later wars). Snout showed us pictures of a green, remote Cockaigne, where physicians worked as physicians, where young doctors could pick up unparalleled experience in reasonable comfort and safety and even in ease, where there were, by inference, nurses to screw and booze to drink.

Not, we gathered, by us.

Snout swelled his chest and struck a pose. "Now the *field* medical service. Next slide, Corporal."

We started with the medical support of "the fighting units, the divisions," from the rear forward. We noticed a clearing company under tents several miles behind the lines. Here the wounded would be stabilized, hemorrhages checked, splints and plaster applied to fractures; there would be sorting and evacuation. The clearing company would be out of range of anything except heavy artillery. Dull, no significant definitive medicine or surgery practiced, but at least safe.

We were taken the next step forward to the collecting company, again under canvas, maybe in a building a mile or two from the front. This, we learned, was the first level of real medical care the wounded would encounter, the first chance to immobilize torn tissues, treat shock and hemorrhage, and sort the casualties in terms of severity. Here we would be in range of medium artillery and, of course, planes. The collecting company should be sited with great care for maximum shelter and protection for the wounded.

"NOW, Corporal" — Snout really yelled it. The slides went off and the corporal pulled the curtain from the wall behind Snout; on the wall was a huge mural on panels of plasterboard, obviously a standard prop. The mural showed a first lieutenant, medical corps, wearing a helmet with red crosses on it; he was crouching in a shallow depression in the field with two aid men doing something to a bloody casualty. Shells were lifting the earth in shreds a few yards away, soldiers were running in the distance.

"BATTALION AID! THE REAL ARMY!" Snout dropped his voice from ululation to low-sinister and for the first time in a Snout lecture, I began taking notes.

"Every fighting battalion — infantry, artillery, tanks — will have a battalion surgeon. The surgeon marches with that battalion, sleeps in the mud and snow with it, suffers fire and hardship with it. He commands some thirty medical soldiers who will work in the aid station or march as company aid men, right among the riflemen and gunners. The battalion surgeon will set up the aid station in combat in the first available defilade. You may remember, gentlemen, that defilade means a place out of the line of direct fire of machine guns and small arms. It means in the first ditch or wall or depression in the ground you can find. You are going to spend your professional lives within a few hundred yards of the enemy and you'd better learn to dig holes quickly and deeply if you want to live long enough to be promoted. Artillery, mortars, patrols, cold, wet, mud, snow, and misery; these, gentlemen, are the facts of life in battalion aid."

Silence.

"Ha, ha, ha." The noise came out of Snout. The face didn't go with any sound of "ha" I'd ever heard.

We were going to be real soldiers out there, we heard. We were going to be part of a fighting battalion, and there wouldn't be any prancing around operating rooms being a bunch of civilians in disguise the way most of the goddamn doctors were when they came in the army. No sir. We'd better pay attention to what we were being taught if we expected to live.

"Doctors!" Snout laughed. We were going to be up there for morale, we heard, and that was all. We weren't going to be functioning as physicians; we'd be glorified aid men.

At the back of the room the commanding colonel coughed. Snout shook himself out of his euphoria and toned everything down. Of course, that was just the way some people put it. We were really going to be physicians — this with a cynical grin —

it was just that we were going to find ourselves in some extremely difficult and challenging surroundings that would call for the best in courage and initiative. . . .

The class, for once, was still: the facts of military life grinned out of the colonel's cartoon, and they didn't resemble anything we had imagined.

That night, in bars and barracks we calculated our chances like condemned men drawing straws: who among us would be the poor sods assigned to some infantry battalion? I listened, I nodded, I discussed benign alternatives, but a small voice told me I'd seen my future on plasterboard: throughout the rest of a month of marching and drilling and sleeping through frivolous lectures that mural exploded and flamed and I knew against all the comforting odds that that was exactly where I was going.

5

Biology of an Army:
A Parable of Dolphins

$\mathbf{F}$ROM CARLISLE BARRACKS I was sent to the headquarters of the Twelfth Armored Division, then assembling at Camp Campbell, Tennessee. For two years we marched and trained and maneuvered from the Kentucky border to Texas, clear to the end of patience, and then one windy September day in 1944, I found myself standing in the bow of a wallowing bashing tub called a victory ship, on the way to England, to France, and to war. My fellow passengers included some headquarters personnel and a tank battalion and we all said a hearty thank God.

Diary resumes: September 10, 1944, the North Atlantic. Conversation at the rail.

FIRST OFFICER: "Glad we made it to the Gulf Stream."
SECOND OFFICER: "Best part of the ocean. Look at that blue."
FIRST OFFICER: "Fuck the pretty blue. What's good is it's warm. It's steaming."
SELF: "Flying fish, sargasso weed: it supports an amazing amount of life."
FIRST OFFICER: "Including us, if we have to get in it. That's the point."

SECOND OFFICER: "What the hell do you mean 'get in it'?"
FIRST OFFICER: "Like if we just happen to have to jump over-
  board, stupid. Like for example torpedoes. Keep your life belt
  on, you could swim around for hours; back in the cold part
  you'd be soon dead."

Our Canadian corvettes quarter about us like furious whales,
hunting for the wolf pack that's hunting us. Last night in the
mess we felt the bang of depth charges from our feet through
our teeth: intimations of mortality rattled our steel. Warm water
is very much to the point.

Bronc, the signal officer, wanders to the rail.

"Submarines or not, Gulf Stream or not, I'm glad we're out
here. They finally let us go to war in peace."

Nobody laughs.

September 11: Bronc said we were glad, and he's right. We're
sailing to fire and mutilation and death with idiot grins: we exhale
relief. What's the army done to us?

The wind's up and a light colonel stands beside me, doubled
over the rail, his face very like a boiled potato.

Colonel (between retches): "Your Gulf Stream, Doc,
it's...ahhhh!...LUMPY!" He doubles again.

The lumps are impressive; they come hissing in amaranthine
walls, blotting out the sun, pure roller-coaster fun for a happy
few: it's important not to look smug, or the heavers and gaspers
will find us intolerable.

Colonel (breathing *hah*): "It gets easier when you're empty."
He inhales freedom from nausea, normal arrogance resumes. I
notice a book in his hand.

"What's the book, Colonel?"

"Fuckin' Jew book it turned out to be. I was going to throw
it over, but I remembered about submarines. Started out okay,
about this guy and a psychiatrist and what he remembered but
then it got to this Jew shit, I said hell with it."

I looked at the book: it was Koestler's *Arrival and Departure*.

The Jew shit the colonel referred to could only have been the scenes describing gassing of Jews in German death-vans.

"I hear that stuff is really going on," I told him. "Killing people, gassing them, burning them, shooting them. Nazis, you know."

"Jew propaganda. Goddamn Jew book." The colonel drew a few stabilizing breaths.

I couldn't resist probing.

"Apart from feeling sick, I'll bet you're glad we're out here. On the way. Finally."

"Goddamn right. Get the hell into the war."

The colonel drove a fist into a palm to show how much he wanted to get into the war.

I tried again.

"Great battalion you got there, Colonel. I talk to your boys, you know, a lot, at sick call and around in the field. Great morale. They act like guys that know what the war's all about. You talk to guys like Sergeant Stein, over in Baker Company, and they'll tell you what they're going to do to those fucking Nazis, all the shit they pulled."

My words were butterflies against stone: all the colonel heard was flattery. He told me what a fine battalion the eight-seven-four was and how hard they were going to fight, to please him. Then he wobbled to a companionway and sank below sight, still clutching his loathsome Jew book.

September 12: Sick call's done and I'm sitting on some kind of nautical box, out of the wind, happy in the geography of the upper deck. With submarines about, the nether spaces shriek of entrapment: here it's a short sprint to the rail. The ghosts of two years past come prancing: my diary ruffles its pages: it's time to write.

Touching the human condition, sir, what's the news? Any dispatches from within?

Of course, and full of significance, too, but here comes an echoing question as old as papyrus: what's the audience? For whom does one write?

Mankind, millennial culture, *die universal Weltseele* and ur-consciousness?

Not bloody likely, mate.

For whom, then? Answer, with brightness: for the kids.

Bears, seals, otters, humans, we survive on our instinct to teach the young: left to itself a little seal would drown and a bearcub would starve because there's no instinct to swim or grub. Teaching our young means continued presence on the planet.

Okay, kids. In case something silly happens to me (as a Hemingway character once put it) here's some required reading. Try it about the time you leave for college.

For the past two years your mother and I lived, like millions of other young Americans, a wandering life in back rooms and sagging houses in army-camp towns. Penny and the other battalion wives pulled homes and lives together on the run; there were Saturday-night parties where we played charades, picnics in Tennessee swales, box lunches lugged out to maneuvers, a very tender domesticity on the edge of the whirlwind.

Susy, you were born two years ago in Tennessee, and Hank arrived a few weeks ago in Texas. We agonized and sweltered through three days of wartime railways to get you home to a leafy-and-green refuge near Lake Michigan with barely time for good-byes before I flew off to catch my division as it entrained. I certainly hope I see everybody again.

During the past two years I've held almost every job open to a medical officer in an armored division, and as we sail for France, I'm the surgeon of Combat Command B. When an armored division gets ready to fight, it breaks up into war parties, just like the Cheyenne. The commanding officer of the combat command is the equivalent of Dull Knife or Yellow Hand: he takes over when it's time to start the killing.

A combat command is a third of an armored division; it includes a battalion each of tanks, armored infantry, and self-propelled guns. This fighting core is supported by a reconnaissance troop and a company each of medics, ordnance, and engineers. We'll have to call outside for air strikes and heavy artillery, but otherwise our three thousand bodies contain all the requisite deadly skills. We're self-sufficient.

There's going to be bleeding; that's where I come in. I'm in charge of the medical network that starts with the battalion aid stations, practically on the front lines, and stretches back through a platoon of ambulances to the treatment sections of the medical company, great trucks equipped as mobile operating rooms three or four miles back.

Armored divisions are expected to move fast, often behind enemy lines, and we're expected to keep up with them. We've practiced enough to know this is easier commanded than done; our elements are going to be groping for each other through night, storm, confusion, and enemy fire. I'm supposed to see that the groping succeeds.

When casualties are heavy, I'll help out in one of the battalion aid stations. (I remember being concerned about battalion aid as a career back at Carlisle Barracks; now it's a day at the office.)

September 15: Reminiscence resumes.

Today I heard someone end an argument by pointing out that orders were orders, and I watched the predictable resignation, frustration, and blotting of thought that gripped all the listening faces. Recollection took wing toward the night of the Allied invasion of French North Africa and fluttered to rest on the bar of the officers' club at Camp Campbell.

In preparation for a night of officers' classes the bar was jammed: to fortify is to survive. All of us except a few hard-core drunks were crowded around the radios, and as word came of the landings at Fedala, Oran, and Algiers we cheered.

Then we heard of resistance. We were baffled.

"They got some Germans down there? Italians?"

No, we heard, it was French resistance. Killing Americans. From reserve officers, medics, and graduates of officer candidate schools came the response of recent civilians — disbelief, outrage, speculations of treason, wonder at the stupid officers and men who obeyed orders to kill their friends on behalf of their enemies.

When do you stop obeying orders? We wondered.

Voices grew louder: someone guessed it was the French regular army, kissing ass to the Germans to keep their rank and their pensions.

Turn them over to the Free French, hang them: our solutions were strenuous and reasonable.

At the words "regular army" and "orders," some weathered faces condescended.

"In any army you obey orders," a bird colonel was lecturing us in a tone of two-plus-two. "Those French officers were only obeying orders. Too bad for us, but how could you trust them if they didn't?"

"Look, Colonel," Scher stood our ground. "Those Germans they're fighting for are murdering Frenchmen, torturing them, shipping them off to those camps, wrecking the country. So the French army gets an order from a senile bastard like Pétain, does that justify them fighting for the enemy? Killing the guys that are coming to liberate them?"

I felt Scher deserved support. "Aren't they supposed to be able to think?"

"They're supposed to be able to think about how to carry out their orders. That's what an army is all about, Lieutenant."

Scher was courageous by two drinks.

"So if you and I were officers in a French infantry outfit and someone gave you orders to shoot Americans, would you do it?"

"If I was a French officer, it'd be different. What if I gave you orders, young fella?"

"I'd disobey them. I'd probably shoot you because you'd be a traitor."

Three lieutenant colonels, an eagle colonel, and a straggling of majors and captains struggled with apoplexy: I longed for a blood pressure cuff. Scher plowed ahead, out of restraint.

"You say orders. Okay, what if you gave us orders to murder women and kids? To rape people and torture them?"

"Lieutenant, are you implying your superior officers are rapists and murderers?" The eagle colonel resonated with drill tones and authority.

Scher threw up his hands and turned away. The colonel seized his arm and spun him around, shouting.

"I asked you a question, by God!"

"It's not a rational question, Colonel, and I don't have to answer it. People's superior officers have been known to commit treason, and if that happens, you're supposed to know which country is yours."

"What superior officers? When?" The colonel, an older man, had gone an interesting shade of purple. I was hoping he might have a complicated stroke with elegant neurologic findings.

"How about Benedict Arnold?" Scher asked it quietly, weighting each word. "He tried to sell West Point and he was a general. According to you, his soldiers should have helped him out."

"Aggh! History!" The colonel shouted it like a dirty word. Obviously Scher had cheated.

Three young West Pointers, captains, had been listening. Now one of them spoke with an effort at loftiness.

"You can't be a traitor when you're following orders. It's not possible."

Time had run out, and we all left severally. Fortunately.

Next day our colonel called us in.

"Colonel Lapham complained to division about you guys practically stirring up a mutiny last night. He said you called him a murderer and a rapist, said his soldiers shouldn't obey him."

I was able to speak before Scher recovered.

"Nobody called anybody anything. We were talking about abstractions, like if your commanding officer went crazy or was a traitor. Like those French guys fighting us, is what started it."

"There are some people," the colonel spoke thoughtfully, "who cannot conceive of an abstraction. They can't imagine anything that's not directed at them. You are surrounded by people who will take anything you say very literally."

Scher put on a mock-solemn face. "Maybe Colonel Lapham's right," he intoned, "maybe we're just not armored division material. Maybe we should be punished, shipped off to something awful like an evacuation hospital."

Both sides of the desk grinned. The colonel told us to watch our big mouths around neurotics and we saluted yes and left.

We always referred to the episode in the bar as the French Confrontation; it was that same evening that I met Mike. He was one of the West Point captains who had been listening, and he caught up with us as we left.

"About orders," he said, "I see your point, but what if everyone felt they didn't have to obey orders unless they approved of them? If every soldier felt free to make judgments? I mean, can you imagine an army where every private understood all the issues and obeyed orders on some kind of moral basis? What kind of an army would you have?"

"Best army in the world. Cromwell's. You just described it. Unbeatable."

Mike grinned. "Touché. But in the U.S. Army . . . ?"

"Sand Creek, Colorado." I was ready for him. "A regular army officer refused to fire on a bunch of unarmed, helpless Cheyenne. He disobeyed the direct order of a colonel of Colorado militia, a murdering scum named Chivington. A court-martial condemned Chivington and praised the officer who ignored him. Precedent."

"Well, we don't obey criminals or traitors, but how about just stupid?"

"If stupid's going to get you killed, you'd better disobey. You owe it to all the people from you on down. Balaclava, for instance."

Mike finally introduced himself. "Schofield," he said, "Sixty-fourth Tanks. We should talk some more."

I looked into quick brown eyes as he nodded and turned away.

"That guy," Scher noted, "is thinking hard. Something's eating him about all this. Not just tonight."

I met Mike many times after that as he rose to major and then to lieutenant colonel, commander of a tank battalion. We chatted in dispensaries while I stitched his lacerated soldiers, we drank coffee on the firing range, we lounged around tables at the officers' club, and it was a rare occasion when he didn't revert to the theme of November 12.* We analyzed the charge of the Light Brigade, Passchendaele, Abercrombie's half-witted performance at Ticonderoga, who the fool was each time, the piles of corpses that sprouted from incompetence, what intervention might have been possible, who should have intervened.

One evening over drinks Mike surprised me with a round of insistent medical questions. If a mortar fragment went through somebody's belly, what would it tear up? Where was the liver, the stomach? If a fragment went through a spine, was a man paralyzed? Where in the spine? What did high-velocity missiles do to muscles and bones? Did they kind of explode? I'd treated lots of burns, hadn't I? How did people stand it when they were burned all over?

The questions began to trip over each other, manic: I looked up to catch a window in Mike's eyes, an unguarded view into shuddering space. He stopped abruptly and made a pretext to leave.

Two A.M. of a cold morning, on my way to guard rounds, I found Mike in his car, parked in barrack street, dead drunk, so I slipped in beside him and drove to a quiet area. For over an hour he mumbled half-coherencies. Eight hundred, I heard, eight hundred men. Tank battalion. Letters from mothers, fathers, wives, girlfriends. " 'Take care of my Tom,' they write to me, 'he says you're a real good commander. We sure want him home.' " Mike asked me, leaning into my face, if I knew what was going to happen to Tom. "Dead, blind, crippled, that's Tom. That's how I send him home. But I'll save more of him than most people. Know that? I'll save more of him." He gripped my shoulder and waved a finger under my nose. "If. They. Let. Me. For chrissakes."

Then he passed out and I drove him to the dispensary. With the aid of a trusty sergeant sworn to secrecy, I got him onto a cot in the back room. During the night I checked in often; once I heard a mumbling denunciation of the West Point honor system.

*November 12, the invasion of French North Africa and the sanctity of orders.

Turned in his almost best friend once, got the poor bastard tossed out, broke his family's collective heart, made him a drunk, but that's what they were fucking ordered to do. Ha ha.

In the morning I gave sedatives and helped him around vomiting: he drove away trembling but set, and we never discussed the episode.

A couple of months before we sailed, I met Mike's new wife, a fey, lovely girl with long hair that floated when she drove up in a convertible. She tripped and caroled like a bird, artless among steel slabs and shell cases.

"I think," Mike said, "my wife is a little bit nuts. She has no idea what this is all about."

"Not nuts, Mike. Charming. No part of a world where you carve people up with white-hot metal. Some ideas you don't want her to have."

"God willing," said Mike.

September 20: To stir memory I recommend a Spartan ocean voyage: there's something about the isolation, the indifference of the watery masses, the endless rocking and rising and liquid booming that quiets triviality. The dark spaces have their say, and the wise man learns to regard what emerges: when something recurs powerfully in memory, it's probably important, a fragment of something larger.

Whit, the headquarters company commandant, was in sick bay today with a sore throat and he asked, half-joking, partly anxious, if I had had a lot of practice taking care of the kind of stuff that was going to happen. I thought of two years of accidental shell-bursts, limbs crushed under tank treads, burns, wrenched backs and broken bones when paratroopers fell in trees, bleeding bodies in wrecked vehicles, hepatitis and pneumonia: I told him yes, I thought the practice had been adequate.

Practice: with the word an image blinked and I was standing in a tent, in the Tennessee hills, in the rain. We were a year along in training and our medical soldiers were deft: when we went into the hills with a regiment on maneuvers they could pull the surgical truck under cover, stretch a tent over it, and have every-

thing ready for casualties in ten minutes, generator running,
gasoline stoves and lamps burning, instruments sterilizing.

As I looked around the tent, filled with the usual clutch of
casualties, I realized that everything we were doing depended on
equipment and procedures we'd improvised. The United States
Army field medical service was a joke beyond travesty, still deeply
involved in the Spanish-American War. They sent us chests filled
with drugs like jalap and rhubarb and senna, that hadn't been
used since 1910; they issued silver bullet-probes admirable for
use in frontier saloons, because, as some wag put it, the X-ray
hasn't been invented yet.

On one litter lay a soldier who had scraped an arm on some
machine: a physician was dressing the wound with vaselinized
gauze, using packs we made ourselves and had sterilized at any
hospital we could cozen. Two men were badly burned from the
idiot practice of starting fires with gasoline, and the scorched
skin was being covered with pressure dressings we had contrived
out of wadding and gauze.

In a corner, Sergeant Leone, a short, profane North Woods
guide, was turning the crank of a wonderful wooden machine he
had built himself to pull bandage through powder and provide
us with plaster of Paris, an item never contemplated in our tables
of equipment. Thanks to the sergeant we were able to use the
closed-plaster technique of Trueta, the great surgeon of the Spanish Civil War, for transporting shattered tissues without motion
or infection: our superbly treated burns, wounds, and fractures
were the talk of the rearward hospitals.

I felt a sudden wild happiness: the tent seemed to fill with
light. Cult of Maimonides, Jenner, and Harvey, I thought, we're
part of something ancient and honorable.

Like a sad echo came the memory of the boy we had sent to
the station hospital two weeks before with contusions on his abdomen where some recoil mechanism had caught him, out on the
range.

He had been pale, and sweating, and in great pain, and we
agreed with the aid men that something was broken inside.

Ruptured abdominal viscus, we wrote on the tag, and we went

to the hospital some days later to see what surgery had revealed. There hadn't been any surgery. We found an arrogant major, who sneered at our diagnoses and pointed out the absence of gas under the diaphragm, to convince us the bowel hadn't been perforated.

I quoted some great surgeons I had worked with to the effect that perforations farther down the gut didn't produce free air: we cited the white blood count of 20,000, the fever, the distended silent bowel, the pain, we even brought our colonel to intercede, but nothing touched the major. He glowered in splendid isolation for a week until the boy died. Every physician from the armored division stood around the autopsy table and watched with sick sorrow as the pathologist pointed out a neat round two-millimeter hole in the jejunum that looked as if it had been punched in a ticket. Two stitches would have stopped the discharge into the peritoneum and saved the boy's life.

The major simply stared and walked off. I couldn't see any emotion on his odd slabbed face, and his walk was arrogant as ever.

That rainy afternoon I dissected the tragedy with Bob Orr, a valued colleague. We agreed the major was a self-propelled two-legged disaster: it was our clear duty to pray that God strike him dead.

"Also light candles to your patron saint so you'll never turn into that kind of a prick. Bob," I went on, "I realized today for the first time I love this. Who we are. What we do. How we do it."

Bob grinned and pretended not to understand.

"The rain? The twenty-five-mile march tomorrow? A first lieutenant's salary?"

"I'm not kidding. Think back. Medical school was a grind that wiped your mind flat: you ran yourself to exhaustion just to survive. Internship we were serfs, twenty-four-hour-a-day slaves, shivering in our shoes for fear we'd fuck up or some attending would even think we fucked up. Now we're different human beings in a different world: it's like a metamorphosis. We're physicians: we own certain kinds of competence, and nobody can take that from us. People come to us hurt and sick and we know what to do for them. My God, it's exciting: I feel as if I should pay someone for the privilege of doing all this. How can anyone not feel it? Could we ever end up like the major?''

''We could. Anyone could,'' the Mississippi accent came from Robbins, a quick, thoughtful medical officer. ''Vanity is how it happens. Make a diagnosis too quick because you think you're so damned smart, then you defend it and you get irrational because you're too cocky to admit you made a mistake. Humble pie is more important than vitamins. A good doctor consumes his share every day. Get your ego too blown up, you can be a murderer. Like the major.''

We spoke of medical officers we knew who resented the sick, abused them, who loafed in back rooms with comics while their sergeants apologized for them, and I realized what poor devils they were. They'd never see the light that flooded the world for me that afternoon. (Thank God it's never left.)

September 19: ''Fore and Aft!'' I'd been looking for the words all week and they burst into speech during a checker game below decks.

The room was a silent question.

''English regiment, famous one, the Gloucestershires,'' I explained, ''they had to fight to front and rear at the same time in some battle, and that's how they got their name, the Fore and Aft. We've been looking for a division nickname and I just found it.''

Bris, the S3-Air, grinned and expanded the notion.

''We're the All-Arounds, maybe the Four-Square. We've got the Wehrmacht in front of us, the Kriegsmarine all around, and back behind . . . ,'' he pointed west. Everyone groaned or said shit.

I left the game and walked the deck, thinking about the enemy behind. The notion pulled a lot of fragments together.

In 1942 we had no trouble seeing the enemy to the fore. He was a stain, spreading swift across the world, and we practiced killing him, hard and seriously.

When our tank gunners squinted down sights on a range, they were training themselves to hit the few small spots where heavy German armor was vulnerable to the weak American missiles, because if they didn't hit those spots quickly, they knew they'd burn to death in the answering German fire. When we blacked out our tents in the forest on maneuvers, we swore at any fool who showed a crack of light, because soon that crack of light might be guiding a Japanese patrol or a German bomber. When our aid men were worked to exhaustion dragging simulated casualties under imaginary machine-gun fire, when we learned the skills of navigating by platoons and battalions and regiments on moonless nights following compasses across country through rain or sleet or muck, when we swung hand-over-hand through obstacle courses or dug holes in Tennessee clay, we refreshed our tired brains and aching muscles with soldierly bitching and cynicism, but under that froth there was the strong and real current of dedication that came with knowing that our several and valued necks were going to be on the block.

At the end of a year we began to feel the power of another kind of dedication: friendships connected battalions and companies, our columns marched with guidons that were fluttering pennons of proud identity instead of limp nuisances on sticks, and our division patch became heraldry, flaunted in bars and streets.

Mike put it best one day when I stood panting beside him, having just led my company through an obstacle course in competition with one of his.

"Pride. Listen to them yelling. Anybody goldbricks, he gets his ass kicked tonight. That's the real discipline, from inside, the only kind."

I nodded between gasps.

"Nobody ever won a battle feeling apologetic about himself or his regiment."

"Or his horde or his legion or his gaggle," I added. "How it's always been."

Mike was thinking out loud.

"You drive them like hell. The real stuff, not the chickenshit.

They survive, most of them, and something else emerges. Something so strong men will die for it."

The companies had formed columns and were marching off shouting cadence. As Mike turned away, he seemed struggling to put something in words.

"There are people who don't understand all that, Doc. They can wreck any outfit. Sometimes I think they're possessed. You have to do more than train your men and lead them. You have to guard them. Watch out."

In the next year I learned what Mike meant. Clouds of neurotics hovered over us, fluttering out of higher headquarters, venting their obsessions and justifying their opulent nests. We had to stop training to scrub wheels with brushes and sweep new dirt from old dirt on roads in the forest. Generals descended with glittering outriders and eunuchs to watch while we went through well-rehearsed pointless fandangos.

Someone on high, we heard, hated our general, and one screw-faced weasel spent days in every battalion combing files and hunting for whispers of incompetence.

Descendents of Titus Oates responded to any criticism of equipment or procedure. To suggest that the M4A3 Sherman tank was a ridiculous thin-walled undergunned piece of shit — and we often did — was to bring down savage attacks that questioned one's fitness to be an officer or even one's patriotism.

(The phenomenon wasn't local. Back home on leave I talked to a friend in the navy who told me the best submarine commanders in the Pacific were breaking their hearts trying to tell someone the damned torpedoes didn't work. They conned their subs right into Tokyo Bay and saw their fantastic bravery wasted because the torpedoes were duds. When they reported what happened, they received official reprimands for criticizing NAVBUORD.*)

Dunces, fierce clowns, were the secret of our heavens, secure behind stars and eagles: claws and beaks and screeching awaited any who lifted the veil.

---

*NAVBUORD was one of myriad dazzling acronyms the navy came up with. It meant "Naval Bureau of Ordnance" in plain, almost-forgotten English.

As soldier-physicians we studied the phenomenon, and after much thought we invoked Darwin. We lived at the cutting edge of the army, working in a pitiless light where incompetence was instantly apparent and swiftly dealt with. We might sympathize with the stupid or the neurotic, but we couldn't tolerate them. They were sent off to havens where we hoped they could do little harm. (Military government schools were a favorite dumping ground.) In higher headquarters, free of selection pressures, un-challengeable, the breed of the incompetent and the twisted ran wild, like herbivores in a world without predation.

For a year our lines held against the witless, but Texas finally made us vulnerable. It was the second year of training that did it, the boredom, the sterile rituals, the repetition, the constant seeking for some other war play to keep the edge on our units.

Somewhere in the twenty-five-mile marches in hundred-and-ten-degree furnaces, in the weeks of blue northers raising freezing dust to snarl at sagging wooden barracks, somewhere in the officers' club smelling of stale booze and disinfectant and in the whining, miserly town, somewhere in all that dank we dropped our guard, and we paid for it.

A true relation follows. In June I was promoted to be combat command surgeon. Penny and I celebrated the prospective rank of major and the increased salary for what would soon be a family of four. A second pleasant surprise waited at Combat Command B headquarters: instead of the mindless reactionary politics of the medical battalions, I found a phalanx of New Deal liberals. Bronc, the signal officer, came from Wisconsin, trailing clouds of La Follette progressivism. Cooper, the intelligence officer, Bris, the assistant S3, and Whit, the headquarters company commandant, were rock-solid Democrats. Around campfires, with bourbon and cold canteen water we drank confusion to Wendell Willkie: in idle moments we wished the *Chicago Daily Tribune* and the Hearst press in hell or in Berlin. We assumed they'd find either congenial.

In July we heard the great news: the division was to move into the hills of our West Texas reservation for the final combat test that always preceded movement overseas. We balanced notepads and scribbled while the operations officer produced details. A combat command of another armored division would march to our area and dig itself in. Our troops would go through a prescribed series of maneuvers — reconnaissance, development of the enemy positions, frontal and flanking assaults, pursuit. There would even be an episode of firing with live ammunition by our artillery. Our job as staff was to see that the wheels and gears of Combat Command B whirred along smoothly.

At the mess there was exhilaration, with some sober second thoughts.

"Anybody thought what something like this costs?" Whit was curious.

"Hell, we're all sitting around getting paid anyway. Doesn't cost any more to have us on a maneuver."

"No, but gas. How many gallons of gas does it take to move an armored division sixty miles? That other outfit's coming from a hundred miles."

We talked of the war around the globe, and the way gas was gold. From the hedgerows of Normandy to the surf of the Carolines gasoline meant victories and its lack meant defeat. We guessed this final combat test was important enough to suck up all that fuel, but there were grounds for doubt in July 1944.

Through the furnace of a July day our division marched into the hills. Boredom had done its job: officers and men alike, everyone was so frantic to get on to combat that they performed incredibly.

I watched infantrymen dissolve in sweat while they dug holes in iron Texas earth. Umpires standing in thin shade nodded approval while men dropped from exhaustion lugging base-plates of mortars and machine-gun tripods. The metal of our tanks was too hot to touch, and the dust they raised choked the men who ran beside them, ducking and crawling as if they were in real combat. Maximum realism was the umpire's demand, and our soldiers responded with devotion. Anything to get the hell out of Dismal, Texas, and get on with the war.

We were drinking coffee under trees in the cool of dawn when Bris came from division headquarters with the news we couldn't believe.

"We've got to stop the maneuver." He shook his head as if he didn't believe his own words. "Some people came to inspect the camp and they say it's dirty. From Fourth Army headquarters. They're administrative, so they didn't know anything about us and this maneuver and going overseas. All they know is the camp's dirty, and we have to stop and go back and clean it."

We still didn't believe him: we were waiting for him to laugh.

"No shit," he said, and he buried his face in his hands.

During a long choking day while tanks and trucks jammed dirt trails, we heard the whole story from one of our liaison officers.

The commanding general of Fourth Army in person had led a team of inspectors to our camp after we had moved out. Since we had left at dawn, in confusion, beds were unmade, windows were heavy with Texas dust that had blown on them in our absence, and floors were littered with shoes and shirts. The general saw all this with noisy indrawn breaths and whews of disgust, but the real license for lunacy came when the general opened a large refrigerator: a fuse had blown and three days of Texas summer without refrigeration had turned a mass of food into a gangrenous stink.

Our liaison officer had a good eye and a retentive ear. "In his face he went red, like a turkey gobbler, only gone insane," he said; "that general went right out of his fuckin' mind, started screaming so hard he had spit all over. Stuff about how our man was a dirty son of a bitch all the way back to the Point. 'Get them back,' he said, and all his aides said who, and he said, 'Whole goddamn dirty division, get them back and clean up this mess.' Didn't make a fuck all the aides told him about final overseas test and army ground forces and high priority and our twelve thousand guys and those other three thousand and all the gasoline and money. That general didn't give a shit if we were on the moon, he didn't care who waited and how long, he wasn't going to send dirty soldiers to fight a war. So here we are."

We looked across miles of Texas backcountry, alive, serpentined, crawling with the moving shapes of tanks, trucks, self-propelled guns, and monster tank recovery vehicles, interspersed with the gnatlike shapes of jeeps and weapons carriers. Clusters of men, swearing, sleepy ants, covered everything that moved.

The supply officer had a little portable adding machine on his lap: he was computing miles per gallon per vehicle, multiplying it by all the vehicles he could see and then shaking his head and whispering. When I came closer, he turned to me. ''Thing about lunatics, Doc, they're so expensive!''

We worked on the camp all night. Full colonels blinked, unbelieving, at majors as dazed as they, scrubbing opposite sides of headquarters windows. In an infantry barracks I watched men who had been trying to pretend they were shooting machine guns at the Wehrmacht disgustedly sloshing buckets across floors and mopping away like muscular hausfraus.

All the role and thought of warriors and foreign wars was squelched out of sight in cleansing powder and the wringing of rags: morale was swept across the new-splashed floors and into dustpans. The offending refrigerator was purified until it smelled sweetly of disinfectant, and finally, in the heat and grogginess of dawn, our thousands of men, in columns of vehicles burning more hundreds of thousands of gallons of priceless gasoline, marched thirty miles back into the hills and tried to pretend they were at war. I watched the results. A platoon of men, without sleep for twenty-four hours, were told to attack through a blast-heat morning toward a grove of cedars where an enemy was supposed to lurk. They wandered, upright, listless, trailing their guns; when someone reproached them, they replied that the fucking cedar trees were dirty and that nice clean soldiers wouldn't go near them.

On a rocky ridge, soldiers scratched a little dirt and tossed shovels away. Those marks, they told an umpire, are foxholes. From here on you do it with mops.

Officers pretended not to hear songs about the perversions practiced in higher headquarters and our division's new role as a gang of castrated housecats.

In brief, nobody gave, or could give, a particular damn, and of course the umpires flunked us and concluded we weren't ready to go overseas.

Our commanding general, who had known us since our first fumbling days in the army, was relieved of command. A replacement utterly strange to us came along, and we were retested, in lower Texas, against another regimental combat team. This time we were not invaded by psychotics: given the chance to perform normally, we passed.

Interesting note on tactical awareness of the American army in 1944: Our combat command concluded the exercise with an armored raid around the enemy's flank, running over his artillery positions from the rear at dawn. At the official critique, a visiting infantry division commander referred jeeringly to this movement as "what the armored force likes to think of as a typical tank maneuver." He obviously thought we should be used as mobile artillery for his infantry, and note that this was in July of 1944, a week or two before the American armor went streaking across France, tearing the Wehrmacht into flaming shreds by exactly such raiding tactics as we had practiced in this maneuver. I muttered to a fellow sufferer that the classification of West Point as a third-rate engineering school had never sounded more appropriate.

We were loaded in troop trains to be shipped to the East Coast with another general, strange to us, whose only mission was to see us to embarkation; we supposed that overseas we might pick up a new commanding officer.

Sometimes the gods are kind: the day we entrained a forlorn little clutch of officers wandered up to the yard where tanks and trucks were being lashed on flatbeds. Their leader was a light colonel; he blinked through glasses as he explained their mission to our executive officer.

"We're" — he paused and looked at the uproar of the emptying camp — "supposed to inspect you."

"Inspect how we're getting on the train? We're leaving. We're going to get on some ships and go fight the war."

"Oh, well. No. I mean barracks and so forth." The colonel's

voice dwindled as his insignificance became clear to everyone. "The general was emphatic ..."

"You're Fourth Army?"

The colonel nodded and his troupe waved clipboards in little fluttering motions.

Cooper leaned in. "Don't they let you know what's happening in the war? Don't you people do anything except go around looking for dust?"

"We're administrative ..." The colonel tried to sound brisk.

"Noncombatants, like the WACs," we heard from a voice behind a tank.

By now the soldiers on the flatbeds realized what the visitation was and voices rang over steel.

"Fourth Army's here!"

"Hitler's secret weapon!"

"Tell them we ain't gonna fight no dirty Germans! We'd rather lose the war!"

"Stick their heads up this manifold!"

"Toilet bowl brigade! Self-propelled!"

"Fuck OFF!"

The colonel flushed, impotent; he and his uniformed housewives made gabbling noises as they left through grins, guffaws, and scatology. Catharsis!

Well, here in the bow of the victory ship, the air's chiming with words like escape, freedom, relief. It's true: they finally let us go fight our war in peace. What if there's nothing up there at the top? What if irrational dwarfs are kicking their heels in the thrones of power? We can't let it matter: this is a war for the world, and, for the rest, we still have the strengths that sustain men in battle — our respect for ourselves as soldiers, our pride in our battalions, and a profound, if unspoken, commitment to the cause a number of us will die for.

And to certain green, sleek shapes leaping in the bow wave, I take your point: you've made it all quite clear. For days I've been condescending, charmed to see how a dolphin can loaf and frolic in a man's apocalypse, and all the while you've been splashing significance under your tails. Proust and his madeleines, me and my dolphins.

You're telling me you are what you are because you can't be anything less, the ocean won't permit it. There's a dark force inside all living matter that never stops fermenting: it throws out a wilderness of behaviors and anatomies and it's only checked by the thrusts and bites of the world around it. Uncurbed, it's fearful: it can drive any species into nightmares.

You, my swift leaping friends, are perfect, but that's not cause for arrogance. Don't be smug because you're clever or because your fins and tails are incredibly propulsive. You're perfect simply because you're hammered into perfection. The ocean does it; the needs of life do it; it's the only way it ever happens. Your liquid shape, your dazzles of speed are forced on you by the fish you catch and the sharks you kill. Your challenges are your life: they shape you, you're totally dependent on them. Leave you alone in overfed tidepools for a thousand millennia and you'd be fat, fronded, fit only to survive in a bathtub backwater where the food floated into your mouth. Fourth Army headquarters.

We sapiens, without the innocent guide of instinct, need the pressure of survival from day to day simply to keep us sane. Deprive us of the life-shaping need to provide life's supports, give any of us unchallenged and unchallengeable authority over our fellows without the daily need to prove superiority by fang or skill, and the transition from gray-green leaping velocity to sullen eyes peering from cavern writhings is as certain as death.

Biologist's footnote to the human condition: It is the lion, said some Darwinian, that gives the stag its brightness and grace and speed and strength: terrifying knowledge, and as usual, Shakespeare said it better:

You all know Security [said a rebel leader to some wavering fellow revolts]
Is mortal's chiefest enemy.

✳ 6

Enter the Colonel

OUR NEW COMMANDING OFFICER came to us in the afterwash of the Great Cleanup Fuckup. Nothing about him bulked or loomed: dimensions were medium, attitude quiet. A tight mouth, pulled to one side when he tried to smile, and eyes that seemed consciously narrowed suggested a man crouching with effort in the slight security of reserve. His half-bald head made him seem closer to fifty than forty.

I suspected subsurface forces, and they erupted for the first time when our motor officer in the mess in Texas one morning muttered, "Oh shit," in response to some teasing; he was ordered out of the mess in disgrace, a colonel-tantrum blue around his ears. Later he stood at attention and was harangued about his own shortcomings, the inadequacy of officer training programs compared to West Point, and the length of his hair. After what seemed a calculated uproar, pleasant crouched reserve resumed.

All across the ocean and into England, winds were mild and seas were calm until our tanks went on the range near the seacoast with the new long-barreled 76-millimeter guns. Geyser the second: Our gunners and tank commanders weren't using the right formal fire orders.

"Left a little," they'd say; "down, steady, fire." They'd been doing it for two years and they were dead shots, but it appeared that somewhere in the waving, papered heavens there was a formal ordered ritual of statements about mils and degrees, and ready on, and fire, and by God, said the colonel, they would use that ritual and none other, and Christ look down on anybody who deviated. This was enriched by memoranda and table thumping, the pleasant, quiet face drowned in red suffusion. Rage over minutiae? I wondered.

Dinner in our mess in the old British cavalry barracks on Salisbury Plain was made unforgettable by a visiting West Point colonel who used words like *fuck* and *shit* right out loud in front of all our mess, both chaplains, and the colonel. Our colonel couldn't meet our eyes. We hid grins underneath the manners of soldierly reserve.

In combat the gunners and tank commanders forgot all about formal rituals and statements about mils and degrees.

"Up a little," they'd say. "Right, steady on, fire; you got the bastard, give him another one...."

Midmorning tea, Red Cross shelter, Tidworth Barracks. Headquarters staff, finding itself alone, launches an evaluation-dissection.

BRONC: "Can't tell about these West Point pricks. Half the time I don't think they know who they are themselves. The army kind of shreds their personalities."

BILL COOPER: "Poor little bastard's just trying to be someone he read about somewhere. He thinks he has to scream and pound so we'll think he's mucho tough son of a bitch."

BRIS: "Insecurity, like the psychologists say. We're his staff, we gotta build up his tiny ego so it has muscles. Make him think he's God; that's what we're here for."

AVERY (Ops. chief; New Hampshire vowels): "Who's perfect? We all have our little bitty flaws. Same boat, fellas; us and the colonel, here we are together. He's the guy we live and die with.''

I concluded in silence that our colonel was a complex man, worth study; I saw at least two people marching under that hardly maintained serenity.

7

A Small Detachment

OUR HEADQUARTERS UNIT included a tiny medical detachment — four of us, to be exact. There was a dental officer, named Davis, who took care of all the toothaches among three thousand men; he did a remarkable job of it, with a bag of instruments and a drill that turned by means of a foot pedal. The pedal was pumped by a large corporal who hummed a parody of "Pistol Packin' Momma" while he pumped — "Push that pedal down, babe, push that pedal down" — and drove us mad with tragic reminiscences about a dive called Powerhouse Pete's, in the slums of Pittsburgh. Until he was officially ordered to shut up, we heard every day how he wished he was back at Powerhouse Pete's, opening up the joint with a shot and a wash before setting forth to collect nickel and dime premiums on cheap insurance. The dental officer was always called "Doc," as I was, but somehow we always knew who they meant. When there was shelling close by, and casualties flooded the aid station, Doc and his helper dragged in wounded and tied dressings over blood like any medics.

Jack was the medical aid man, ambulance driver, and general expediter. We were almost constantly together in combat: I see his dark face and quick smile against a backdrop of fiery landscapes with running figures, exploding skies, starlight, snow, and sleepy dawns. Jack was a quiet man: I never heard him swear with anger or fear the way almost everybody else did. When circumstances were terrifying, he simply set his mouth with a peculiar backward grimace and looked to me for ideas about driving faster or jumping out of the ambulance to run for it. Jack was a Mormon, from Montana, and that was a godsend for my breakfast. The patriots who made millions selling K rations squeezed out a few extra dollars by substituting lemon extract for soluble coffee in some of the morning rations. As a devout Mormon, Jack didn't drink coffee and how often, through chattering teeth, did I bless Joseph Smith with every gulp of the life-saving stuff while Jack, uncomplaining, gagged down a decoction of hot chemical lemon-water. He didn't drink alcohol either, in spite of the gallons that washed around him, but one night he made an exception. The artillery of the infantry division that supported us had blown our radiator full of holes under the impression that we were the enemy, and we spent the dark hours being dragged around behind a self-propelled gun at the end of a chain, so far behind the German lines that the gun flashes looked like distant lightning back on the horizon. When we passed a bottle of brandy around, Jack took a long pull; he said he felt the situation outweighed theology.

✳ 8

Finally, Blood

IMAGINE A SEAT, secure in dark air, high over the borders of France this November night of 1944. Below, a snaky length of fire writhes tortured, from the North Sea to Switzerland, erupting all down its coils with jewels of flame.

Start with those Dutch seas, where the Canadians are fighting for a port at Antwerp to let supplies flow into the Allied armies; the explosions there are mirroring great flashes over water, because the Canadians are crawling through dikes and polders along the estuary of the Scheldt in wet, violent misery. Follow southward along the rim of flame where the British lines curve east through Holland on that salient pulled forward by the men of the airborne army, and south again, where hundreds of miles of dense, gloomy, packed fir forests sparkle with the orange pencils of machine-gun fire and bloom with the white of shellbursts while the American First Army fights belly deep in mud and snow and tangles through the Hürtgen forest and the Schnee Eifel; look farther south again to where Third Army is crunching the outer bones of the Siegfried line; heavy flashing of guns here, much reflecting from low clouds; and finally, from Metz to the Rhine, see where the veterans of Seventh Army, the old ones, have broken the Vosges passes and are marching north along the flanks of the mountains, pushing desperate Germans with supreme irony back into the old forts of the Maginot line.

Darker than the dark, just here you can see a trail of ants moving from south to north. These ants will now struggle into history where they will perform acts of slight but measurable significance. The Twelfth Armored Division bows on stage.

The bowl of night flashes and growls; explosions run along the horizons, swift lightnings, trailing thunder. The dark is alive; it blinks repeating images of torn trees and crumbling houses, tanks and guns and helmeted figures around machine-gun barrels, silhouettes of high drama against repeating, winking flares.

In the back of vehicles, men hear the roars and thuds and see each other's faces in flashes; they joke nervously about bowling alleys, and they wonder inexpertly which shells are leaving and which are approaching, and protagonist, like thousands of his fellows, struggles with absurdity, with a sense of the ridiculous and the familiar. All old hat, says a tiny, mocking voice. He's escaped up onto the screen of the Bijou Theater, of course, where he always wanted to be. Finally he's busy being a hero, and out there in the dark an infinity of small faces nervously grind popcorn as they watch him in his role as possibly Richard Barthelmess in that classic of World War I movie folklore, the Night March to the Front; the booming, the cold, the insane dark these men are marching into, yield to and heed the charm of the defined. It isn't all that scary, see — it's just like in the movies.

From Hagar's Falls and Evanston, from Portage and Prairie du Chien, we're marching right off the edge of that complaisant galaxy where we used to cross streets and lock doors. We're marching into the night of ancestral myths, and every man looks at his neighbor in the light of flashes and flares, and thinks, "My God, I'm really here! It's really me, erstwhile knotted-tie clerkface, being a soldier in a war!" Millennial echoes fill the dark.

Headquarters, Seventh Army, November 16, 1944
To: Headquarters, Twelfth Armored Division
Mission: Remove the German army from certain fortifications along the old border.

Enemy attitude: desperate. They've run to the end. Retreat now means fighting in their living rooms: they'll back into kid sister's dollhouse and slip on Mutti's *Zwiebelfleisch*. A few have the privilege of an Uncle Louie in Milwaukee and a fingertip on sanity, but the rest really believe we'll send all the German males to Siberia as a first step toward relieving the German females of their shreds and tags of virtue. Some of the less deluded would prefer dishonor to death, but there's no choice. We're in front and the battlefield police are just behind: German lampposts are heavy with deserters.

Enemy capabilities: substantial: plentiful artillery, heavy fortifications.

Local conditions: a dark mood by Dante. Freezing mud for infantry to squelch through, to drench in, for tanks to sink in. Rain with some hope of snow.

Ambiente generale: violent. (Our first weeks on the Lorraine front recur in flashes and roars: afterimages of explosions bloom around everything we did.)

November 17. Night. Command post in a schoolhouse. The Germans used the place too: their compulsive slogans march across the walls in gothic lettering.

"*Wir sind im feindes Land!*" When were they not?

"*Mit Pulver und mit Blei kommt eine neue Zeit herbei.*" The mind shatters to recall the reality of the new time all that powder and lead were going for, a world under the stamp of well-drilled savages driven by perverts and guttersnipes. The literal truth of history scampers past belief.

(My fluent German is in demand here on the border between Alsace and Lorraine. It's often important to talk to the men of the FFI, the resistance army, and West Point French makes them wince. The trilingual Alsatians find me a comfort; I'm an invited fly on command post walls as our division coils for its first attack.)

We're relieving the Fourth Armored Division on the line. That's lucky for us, because the Fourth Armored is brave and famous and skillful. The Germans fear and, of course, hate the division very specifically: they call the men of the Fourth "Roosevelt's

Butchers'' and they chill one another with rumors that the division was recruited entirely from criminals who had killed their own mothers. It's a fact, history, that the Germans tell and believe such tales. Why not? If people can believe in Adolf Hitler, they can believe in anything.

More luck: the commanding officer of the task force holding our stretch of the line is a legitimate hero, famed on both sides of the front, a man who's outfought, outflanked, lashed, and burned the Germans from Normandy to the border.

Creighton Abrams is the hero's name. He's a tank battalion commander, a legend in a division of great warriors. We've heard that when his battalion was cut off in the autumn fighting he turned to his infantry commander, one Major Cohen, and said, ''They've got us surrounded again, the poor bastards,'' and then proceeded to mangle all the Germans within range.

Abrams draws a finger across a map.

''Krauts have eighty-eights here, here, here. Lost four of our tanks yesterday. Damned careless, we were, but at least we made the Krauts give themselves away. We know where they are, so they're dead. They have Panthers, Mark Fives with eighty-eights and long-barreled seventy-sixes and they've got them down behind the old Maginot line forts with twenty feet of concrete in front of them. Plus all that armor.''

Taking his helmet off, running his hand through steel-pale hair, he shakes his head a little with the effort of emphasis.

''Charge head on into something like that, it's committing suicide. Some dumb bastard orders it, he commits murder. I can't tell you that loud enough or often enough.''

Abrams has a trick of compressing words and meaning around his listeners and then pausing, watching for penetration. He pulls out one of the cigars that precede him into battle, we hear, like a baton between clenched teeth. He lights it and the glow pulses against a face of finely seamed metal, wrinkling a little with the effort of puffing.

Around smoke, he talks more quietly. ''It's about people learning. Two plus two, sure. War, usually no, or so slow whole countries can disappear in the process. Nineteen fourteen to nineteen eighteen. Four years. Everybody finally learned you can't run men against machine guns and barbed wire because most of them die. Western civilization almost got wrecked because that's how dumb commanders were.

"Okay. We now have tanks to get us through the machine guns. One step forward, but now there are antitank guns, German ones, that can shoot holes through our tanks as far away as they can see them. Back to square one. Kindergarten logic, but it took the British two years in the desert to figure it out. Damned near lost the war while they learned. So, smart Americans, huh? If we could read and hear we should have learned all that, but in nineteen forty-two, at Faïd Pass, we sent a tank battalion on parade against Kraut guns in ambush. Lost the whole battalion and the commander in twenty minutes. It's almost impossible to learn about combat before you're in it. You get in a battle, there's a crazy force, it grips you. You have to fight for logic, you have to claw for it. Sometimes, most of the time, most people, they can't find it."

Attention around the room is at the limit of intensity; battalion commanders and staffs are being coached around sudden death and they know it and feel it, right to the edge of dread. At this point the angel of the grotesque directs my gaze to the senior officer present. General George Beaky, commanding officer of the unit that's going to make the attack, is inspecting something fascinating but invisible on the ceiling.

Creighton is swinging his eyes from face to face, forcing understanding, when he rounds on Beaky, where he holds the silence suspended, while Beaky continues to admire the junction of two beams. Finally starred remoteness twitches out of reverie. The snout resonates.

"Thank you, Colonel," we hear, "thank you for, uh, putting us, uh, in the, well, picture."

Faces turn away, embarrassed. Many seek relief, by spontaneously turning to Mike, who pretends to study his nails. Mike's assigned to Combat Command A: Beaky's his boss for the rest of the war. Tonight Mike is wrapped in the ultimate layers of career and self, wound tighter than any bobbin, a young West

Point commander leading his men into their first battle, his whole career on the *Schwerpunkt,* here, now : it's hard for him to nod, impossible to smile. He caught my glance at Beaky and our eyes met with the speed-of-light exchange of total understanding that's possible at desperate times. Then persona and identity snapped tight, but I could see Mike swinging those hard intelligent eyes from Abrams to Beaky, willing comprehension.

Creighton sits in judgment behind the rhythm of his cigar, studying Beaky, assimilating him, assigning his parts. Then he turns to the rest of the room and talks with passion.

"An American tank battalion is a lot of concentrated violence, but to use it you have to go back to Indian fighting. Sneak, stalk, flank : pull the bastards out in the open and hit them before they know you're there. Sucker them, fool them. Modern fighting is backwoods fighting : nobody charges anything in lines anymore. Our tanks have thin armor and weak guns, Christ knows why, but that's how they are. On our side we have speed and a fast power traverse to get our sights on the other guy first. They have to crank those big guns around by hand and it takes time. We are committed to two things, speed and brains. Sneak, stalk, bang, you win. This business tomorrow. Do not — repeat, do not — attack those positions head on. You know where they are and that makes them helpless. Shake them up with heavy artillery, drop smoke on them, flank them. You'll have them out and running in an hour.

"Brains and speed, that's how you survive." Creighton faces Beaky and exhales a sigh full of smoke. "Speed and," he pauses and almost shakes his head, "brains." The word echoes tragically : the hero seems to shrug as he turns and walks quickly through the blackout curtain.

Abrams was a mote of history, glittering in that command post. He went on to lead the tanks that broke into Bastogne at the climax of the famous siege. He survived the war and the doldrums of peace to end his career in command of the last stages of the Vietnam disgrace, bringing whatever soldierly decency and honor could be evoked in that morass, punishing military murderers and disciplining hoodlums, salvaging a little of the reputation and honor of the United States Army. He was a rare soldier who served the Republic with courage and intelligence.

November 18: Our battalions moved to the attack through the animal horrors of early winter fighting. Nobody in a battle ever sees what the historian sees: there's a mosaic: there are flakes and chips and flashes. I heard the stories of frightened, tired aid men and the gasping of the wounded; I saw flashes and dots through field glasses and heard the air sighing overhead into explosions.

The commander of a tank company swung his long-barreled 76-millimeter gun swiftly to the east and rested his sights on a Panther, fifteen hundred yards away. The gunners sent three rounds that hit the German swiftly and accurately, right on the front slope-plate. Each round bounced away, harmless, from the massive angled steel. Men heard the screaming over the tank radio net.

"Ping-Pong balls! Goddamn fucking Ping-Pong balls!"

The men were screaming in an agony of futility and fear because they had done everything they'd been taught, done it perfectly like competent brave soldiers, and they'd just watched the United States of America betray them while their death swung around on them in the form of a long high-velocity gun. The German shell went through the length of the tank, taking the bow gunner in a shower of bloody shreds. Oh God, the screaming anger for fools in high places who send men into battle impotent!

"Ronsons, you know." Propped against the wall of the aid station, the German shakes the massive bandages that cover his face. He holds out a cigarette and points to it with a blackened index finger. "Ronsons, yes, like for a cigarette. Our gunners see your tanks coming, all running over with that gasoline, and they say to each other, 'Here comes another Ronson.' Why do the Americans do this for us? Bang! and it burns like twenty haystacks. All the people in, my God." Most of the German prisoners are men of a famous panzer grenadier division, men who have fought on the Russian front. They're so relieved to be captured alive and by Americans that they become chatty, confidential.

"Those funny tanks with the little guns, and so high and straight we can see them from a long way in our gunsights. Those square sides, and thin, the armor. We know if we hit one it goes up." They're honestly bewildered: why does the country of Detroit send their men out to die in these things? Maybe because, like the Fords, they can make so many more so quickly. "Yes, but the men inside." They all shake their heads. Yes, the men inside.

Ronsons. The men inside. Bill Cooper and I walked through the mud to a burned tank. After a couple of disasters we've learned to approach burned tanks from upwind because after the smell of charred metal comes the roaring odor of dead flesh, cooked humans. We opened a hatch. The bow gunner's mummy grinned through a mask of cinders. The helmet rocked on a small charred ball, and the whole body was a blackened pygmy with scorched talons. The teeth were so white the grin screamed. Cooper pulled his hands from the hatch as if it was hot or foul to the touch.

He stared the way a man might stare at something from another dimension or a foreign galaxy, some sounding of stimuli that couldn't be caught in human synapses.

I slammed the hatch and marched him away while he kept grasping at terrible specifics.

"So little, all there was left, out of a whole person. I knew him. Friend of mine named Kenny. Why is it so little, what's left?"

"Water," I explained, "we're mostly water so there isn't much left when you burn."

"Kenny, like a tiny black, old mummy, and the teeth white. The white teeth make it much worse. Why aren't they black too?"

"They're different stuff, enamel. Last thing to burn."

"Those teeth were screaming the way he probably screamed."

"Must have been quick, actually. Shell went through his abdomen."

"I guess that's better. I couldn't look."

"Millimeters, velocities, map coordinates, they're for that, what you just saw. We're the only ones that see it, not the generals or presidents or the clowns blowing bugles. Us, here, in the butcher shop. Now we're veterans."

Epiphany in the mud.

Cooper was our liaison to CCA. He told us what happened in the attack. The very day after the briefing by Abrams Beaky ordered Mike's tank battalion to attack head on across a thousand years of bare plain, against German tanks sheltered behind Maginot line pillboxes. It was, said Cooper, like standing in a bad dream. Everything Abrams had warned against, everything we had heard from British liaison officers about disasters against Rommel, a maneuver that would have guaranteed a flunk at the armored force school, they were hearing it ordered. "Nightmare," said Bill. "Pinch yourself."

Mike argued with great force for a flanking movement. The enemy positions were thin, vulnerable, easy to get at, but Beaky's cerebral functions were blocked by a line on a map. The flanking movement would take our tanks through the zone of the Forty-second Infantry Division on our right.

Beaky lifted his nose in the air, the way he did when he tried to look intelligent and superior, and told Mike that corps had ordered that we stay within division zone, young man, and that is where we stay. Orders.

Mike broke out of West Point and argued to the edge of disrespect. The Forty-second Infantry Division line at that precise point, he explained, consisted of a few lonely riflemen, pathetically happy to see our tanks. No question of using their roads, getting in their way; all we have to do is run some of our tanks around through an empty meadow and catch the Krauts on the flank. Finally he shouted, "We're in the same army, dammit, sir!" Mike was fighting for his men's lives and everyone in the room except Beaky knew it.

He retreated into furious isolation. He was like one of those creatures mathematicians imagine, living in a two-dimensional world, who crawl up to a line and think it's a wall, uncrossable. No dimension to do it with; that was what Beaky lacked, the third dimension to take him over that line and into reality.

Finally Mike heard the direct order. He and his men were to attack in broad daylight, across a thousand years of bare plain, against the German guns snug behind twenty feet of concrete. No further discussion.

As he walked out Mike turned to Cooper and said, ''This is it, Coop. Good-bye.'' He was prescient.

We heard the next day how the line of tanks went slithering through mud against the pillboxes, the young commander standing in the turret waving a map case because the radios weren't working. Orange light winked from behind concrete across the wide field and Mike's head was torn from his body; his trunk slid kicking into the turret, spouting incredible volumes of blood. The carotid arteries and the jugulars were hosepipes. Crimson drenched the young soldier inside the tank, who screamed and screamed and pounded with his fists and pushed away at the windpipe and the twitching cervical muscles and the scarlet geysers that filled the air where his colonel's head had been.

Some of the tanks burned and the others fell back.

Next day I sat in an artillery observation post high in an old grain tower and watched the attack go in as it should have. Through the spotting scope I could see the line of forts, gray lumps in the whale-shapes of the Lorraine ridges. Since they were old Maginot line forts, they were marked precisely on topographic maps.

''We got them on a map, they're sitting ducks.'' The observer was a short lieutenant with a face that was made of upward curves, smiling with anatomy, until he began calling fire orders. Then the curves pulled into ferocious clenched lines, a proper mask for the death and fire he was invoking.

He chattered professionally. ''What're we shooting?'' he asked the radio. ''Eight-incher? ALL RIGHT. Got an eight-incher, Doc, couple of two-forties for backup.''

I remembered the enormous tubes I'd passed, back in corps artillery. The observer called map coordinates and the first round raised a swift thunderhead of smoke and flame, just beyond a pillbox. ''Hundred left, hundred short''; the lieutenant's teeth were bare, he was really snarling with the commands.

The next explosion was a few yards short of the target, and the third and fourth seemed to burst exactly on the pillbox. When the smoke cleared, a darker shape was separating itself toward the rear, scuttling.

"There's the Kraut! There's the tank! Get him, you guys! Get him!" The observer's fist was pounding with the excitement of the game in view. Our tanks were waiting in flanking positions: three violent sparkles of flame erupted all the German's hull and it stopped and began to smoke.

In a half-hour, three more pillbox-armor positions had been blown out of the way and we could see our tank battalion moving forward over the horizon.

The observer's face resumed its pleasant arcs and we smoked.

"Technique, see." The observer liked the word. "In a war nowadays, it's all technical and that's what you gotta use. Technical. Brains. The old slide rule, to kill people. You can't get overwhelmed by all this shit and go running ah-hah-ha at the enemy like you were Indians with tomahawks. First thing you gotta have brains and next you gotta have some kind of very strong stability to keep on using your brains when everything's screaming and blowing up. Like a gyroscope in your head keeps you steady. Ninety percent of your average guys can learn the crap officers learn in a classroom, but maybe one percent can use that stuff, keep on functioning, out here in a hurricane. That's a different kind of a brain. Unusual."

I felt history nudging. "Alexander, Napoleon, Caesar, Frederick the Great. They all had that gyroscope. Keep on doing the reasonable, steady, logical stuff in an earthquake or a typhoon. Makes you a genius. In nineteen forty, the French could have stopped the Krauts, if they'd used their brains and their artillery and their tanks. They got beaten in the head."

"They got beaten by a bunch of Beakys." The observer's insight was tragic, savage.

"Hell of a way to go."

The colonel's face was suddenly and surprisingly calm in the basement command post. Heavy German shells were blowing the building overhead into showers of brick and fire, but the colonel had just snuggled into a category.

"We're being shelled, gentlemen; I guess we're just being shelled."

By the end of the second sentence the colonel was almost smiling in a tense small mask. It was clear the words were magic, taking him by the hand, marching him from panic toward composure. Shelling was what was supposed to happen, official ... okay ... expected. I contemplated the colonel's happy file drawer, but it had nothing to do with where I'd just been; it made no kind of sense. I'd been looking out across the field when the first shell exploded next to one of our half-tracks and I'd run out across the field to the shouts of "Medic!" A wounded man was lying across an aid man's knees. His face was streaming red and I foolishly concentrated on it, mopping blood with an aid packet, looking for the lacerations, ignoring the frantic stammering of the aid man. Finally he connected words. "He ain't got no back on his head, Major. It's all tore off at the back." As we turned the boy over his brains slid out on my lap and he died with a couple of agonal gurgles. The occiput was torn off as neatly as if a neurosurgeon had been sawing and chiseling.

The sound of the next shell ripping the air in our direction sent us flat: I sprinted in bursts back to the command post, diving under tanks between explosions, furious, raging with impatience to get to a radio to call appropriate authorities to deal with the criminals who had just torn a boy's skull off.

Old murder was one thing; the cooling dead were something a mind could imbibe, given a shudder, but seeing somebody killed for the first time, actually seeing the body's parts sundered, sent reason squalling into outrage. Since when were people allowed to get away with murder? Before I could shout it at the colonel the question crumpled under the appalling swift answer from subterranean knowledge. Since forever. Since the first primates pulled themselves into clans and began social killing. The truth reared on its hindquarters, waving the bloody claws that only soldiers see, roaring what's only learned on the killing grounds, that murder is what is expected, enforced, required, legal, proper, rewarded. Someone, somewhere, was being patted on the back by appropriate authority for tearing the bones off a boy's brain. To refuse to commit murder, to disclaim any part as an accomplice, is to suffer the punishment of one's proper, God-invoking, white-papered, courtroom-bounded governance.

The world changed forever.

The colonel might be happy in his file drawer, but I was groping in the dimensions of bloody anarchy.

Six Ukrainian adolescents, slave workers from a border farm, had run and crawled through the lines all night; in the morning they walked into our motor park. They ranged from fourteen to sixteen, but otherwise they were six stamps of a die, wheaten hair, water-blue eyes, and grins that closed only when they spoke. There was no official place to send or order them and, more to the point, they had no intention of being sent or ordered anywhere. They wanted to be exactly where they were, with the fabled Americans. I made a speech about the official channels that would be opened to take them home, but when I did the grins vanished. Six heads shook like six little automatons. Jeepski, they said, Willyski, pointing to wheels and tracks, stay here. "*Bleib mit Amerikanski. Sei Soldat.*"

They might as well *bleib mit uns,* we found, because there were no official channels: nobody was prepared for the tidal wave of uprooted humanity washing across Europe and Asia. The mess sergeant put them to work on pots and pans and they chattered the afternoon away like a flock of starlings, just alighted.

That night we were shelled and hit. Most of us had run for the cellar when the first two ranging shots sizzled through the dark overhead and exploded a couple of fields down. The third shell hit the building someplace high up and the foundations shuddered, for it was a very large gun. As the echoes diminished, we heard high-pitched childish screaming, *Aiiii, aiiii;* we ran up the stairs to meet the Ukrainian children staggering down out of smoke, doll figures that had been whipped across with a brush of red paint. One boy was holding his crotch, slipping on his own blood.

In the basement, by lantern light, on litters, I took care of our half-dozen wounded. The Ukrainian boy was much the worst, lacerated in the buttocks and crotch, with the skin of the scrotum

torn away, leaving the testicles and cords dangling. Even while
I stopped the bleeding and bandaged shuddering tissues, there
was great comfort in the knowledge that nature, seeing us pri-
marily as engines of reproduction, grows skin back around testicles with extraordinary swiftness and completeness. As long as
the essentials are intact it's very easy to provide cover in the
most primitive operating room, and my sterile vaselinized gauze
and bandage packs were a kindly substitute for epidermis. Morphine had begun to ease the pain, and the youngster's eyes were
searching mine, asking the obvious question with the terror that
only another male could understand.

I held up two fingers.

"*Zwei,*" I told him, "*Sicher. Prima. Kein gefahr.*" I gave a
swift recital of all the simple German words of reassurance and
the youngster nodded.

"*Zwei.* Okay. *Prima.*" He let a wide grin slide under his Slavic
cheekbones as he fell back into opium.

The shelling kept up most of the night. I sat in the cellar with
the wounded while a candle danced monstrous shadows on the
wall and I sought refuge in a paperback murder mystery from
the boredom draped around terror that I was beginning to iden-
tify as a war.

In the morning I rounded up the four remaining Russians.
Now, I asked, didn't they want to go back, to someplace safe?
Until they could go home? They didn't have to stay here, it was
dangerous. They had certainly seen that.

The boys were already wearing helmets casualties had left behind, and from under steel brims I saw four faces that had hardened in conclusion. They repeated what they said the day before,
but now they said it with determination that could only be as-
sessed against the knowledge of agony and laceration they were
facing.

"*Bleib mit Amerikanski! Sei Soldat!*"

The words were a universe removed from the childish giggles
of the day before: now they were a small hymn of courage.

For a refreshing draft of assurance about the human species
I recommend standing in a muddy motor park watching four

children deliberately choosing to face terror and agony that most grown men would shirk if there were an acceptable way to do it, simply to be true to some image of courage and manliness that was part of their bones. They marched off to the mess truck, touching vehicles as they went.

"*Amerikanische,*" they said, "*Jeepski, Willyski.*" America was enchantment. They had reached the magic forest and there wasn't a wizard in the world who could make them leave, even if he waved death and torn limbs at them.

(N.B.: They did stay with us, to the end of the war. They acquired American uniforms piecemeal from casualties, and, finally, guns. They worked in the motor park and the mess and they often stood sentry, never flinching under bombardment or counterattack, steady on the edge of disaster. Leonid, Sasha, Mikhail, Alexei, you brave little bastards. You were good men while you were still children. I hope Russia and life go well with you.)

In the part of Connemara my mother came from, the Sidhe, the Good Folk do a brisk business swapping miserable changelings for humans. That only happens with babies, if western Irish orthodoxy means anything; certainly the rules wouldn't permit such traffic among adults at five o'clock on a Lorraine morning. Possibly I wasn't hearing right; I hoped I wasn't.

I wasn't hearing anything very well because, shortly before, the Germans had thrown a 120-millimeter shell right into my aid station on the second floor of a ruined apartment building. The wall came down over us with the brightest light and the loudest sound anywhere outside the bowels of the sun.

Wake up! called friendly Wehrmacht. Smell the lovely cordite! Run!

We ran. Soldiers had already dragged casualties into the cellar; a sergeant from our communications section lay without motion or breath on a table. In seconds I knew he was dead and I spoke the word into the ring of lantern highlights. There were the sounds of breaths drawn in or expelled that men make at those times; there were mutterings of "Jesus." This was the first death in our small headquarters; the corpse and our own sense of decency called out for a few seconds of recognized sorrow.

The voice from behind me was a shivery little dog, yapping.

"All right, all right. You'll see lots more dead men before this is over. Move him, come on, move him. We need that table."

Nobody believed that was really the colonel talking. We all stared at the noisy little former human, trying to tell us to forget that this was our friend, lying there with a red space where the top of his head used to be. There was no hurry about the goddamn table and we all knew it, but the colonel had shouted shit right out loud in church, and now he seemed compelled to run on through all the other four-letter foulnesses to prove what a splendid idea it had been.

While I bandaged the other wounded and injected morphine, he fussed behind me, whining.

"Are you finished, Doctor? Aren't you finished?"

He never called me "Doctor" before; in the military a medical officer is always and officially "Doc." There were strange clanks and wheezes that morning.

After we carried off the last of the wounded, I turned to the colonel where he stood rolling and unrolling maps.

"The table's okay for those maps, Colonel; just let me mop up some of the blood."

Ah, Colonel, I thought, you're shielding some layers from the outer air, but what a hell of a way to do it.

Log, informal, action at Gros-Upflange. (After any battle, the intelligence officer is supposed to put together a log that bears some relation to what happened. It comes in clusters of consonants like "Cmpny eny inf engaged two pltns hvy wpns co: eny dispersed with arty fire, 105 mm, 2100 hrs." The Chge of the Lt. Bgd. drowns in a sea of abbrvtns.)

This is a log, in some different dimensions, about a battle I wandered into by accident.

1300 hrs. I flagged a ride on an infantry half-track, leaving Jack fixing our tires that had been torn by shell fragments. The platoon sergeant said, "Sure, Doc," they were going near the aid station, but after a hundred yards a hag screamed in a little tin box and the sergeant, bending over the radio to listen, shouted, "Counterattack!" and punched the driver into a turn that made us rock. The half-track swung into a dirt road, north; and as we looked at each other with the standard army expression that said, Oh shit, what now, I realized that most of the men in the squad had been my patients — the tall Oklahoman who wanted his back taped before hikes so as it wouldn't get sprang, the smiling, incredibly methodical Iowa farmer who counted his pills and checked his own medical records, the Wisconsin Indian who practiced noncommunication as a way of life. They looked at me through chronic fear and fatigue, the mask we called battle-stare, but they nodded and smiled, and one of them said it was a good thing Doc was along, right in the half-track.

The sergeant didn't share their sentiment. He shouted, "Shit!" and flung out a fist; "only people are gonna need Doc are the Krauts." He pointed. "You guys are gonna make sure they need him, real bad. We been waiting for this. They're gonna be the ones with their necks out today and they're gonna get chopped." He brought the edge of his hand down on the 30-caliber machine gun to demonstrate. "You are personally gonna eliminate a lot of pricks."

The men looked at the sergeant like disillusioned children trying to believe in Santa Claus: for a long time they had been following tanks through freezing mud, digging holes to find safety at the price of a night hip-deep in icewater, listening to companions screaming and dying, torn by machines from over the horizon, frightened spectators while steel monsters banged out decisions, and now the sergeant was dangling the prospect of real killing before them like an erotic picture.

Their response at first was timid, incredulous: they couldn't believe that anything they did was going to make much difference. Impotence is never pleasant, even in thought, and we lurched along in skepticism for a kilometer before the mood was torn by an irruption of swift shapes, half-tracks, tanks, assault guns, skidding and yawing into column, saturating the air with the peculiar maddening roar of bogies and tracks, forcing men to shout as they sorted tripods and bandoliers, lifting everyone on a tide of power and motion and excitement.

In three kilometers we came to a village where the company commander was standing in his jeep, pointing left and right, screaming directions; platoon leaders waved vehicles into alleys, where tanks and guns slammed through walls and broke out windows. In minutes the company was invisible, crouching, with nothing toward the enemy but steel snouts: we had made a fortress out of a village, on the run.

In a corner of what was left of a house I found the only aid man in town: he was trying to improve his shelter with bricks and stones. "Jesus, Major, I'm so fucking glad to see you." The boy's face was jerking with emphasis: he almost stammered. "I'm alone here and there's gonna be hell."

A cynic within reminded me that my usefulness extended to six aid packets and a dozen morphine Syrettes, but I did my best to look reassuring and the two of us crouched behind a wall where we found a couple of hand-sized peepholes. Rolling an eye carefully against one I saw a surprisingly wide view across three fields to a forest, and I was still picking out rocks and sheds when the Germans came stepping out of the trees like phantoms materializing, erect, walking slowly, a long wavering line glowing in a halo of pale winter light. Officers were shuttles, darting, waving, pointing. I was sure there had been some mistake.

"Can't be!" I was shouting absurdly at the aid man. "They're not supposed to be there like that, just walking around. It's wrong."

The aid man made more sense.

"Dumb shits: don't know we're here, is what."

Across a courtyard I could see a farm building where the company commander was part of a cluster of heads around a machine gun and I ran there, crouching. The gunner was facing the captain, arms flung out, with the outrage of an innocent victim confronting a traffic cop.

"Please, Captain, for chrissakes let me kill them! Look in my sights: I got them, they're dead already. What a fucking target, I've been dreaming of it, there'll never be a target like this, pleeeease." The gunner became a child, two days before Christmas, dancing around a tantalizing package, but the captain shook his head.

"You give them your muzzle flash, that's a gift, something to shoot at. They don't get our muzzle flashes for free."

I watched the even dark features I had known at the bar of the officers' club and on parade and felt through them the power of calm, ordered decision sorting through hysteria.

"Best way to kill them is invisible, Charley. Invisible they can't kill us back"; and as he spoke I heard the *PUNG* of a mortar somewhere behind. In seconds an explosion lifted dirt and smoke fifty yards beyond the Germans.

Someone called corrections over a radio and in three shots the mortars were right among the Germans: a voice shouted, "Ladder!" and before I could ask what the hell a ladder was doing on a battlefield the bursts marched along the lines, erupting left to right, a flashing ladder that left a sprinkle of forms on the grass, wriggling, kicking, moving less and less while the survivors ran back to the forest. Finally we watched a solitary officer, standing with his back to us, waving at the trees.

The silence was abrupt: across the courtyard I could hear men shouting that we taught them pricks a lesson, and by God, they got their bellies full and they wouldn't be back, but a vision begged to differ, a memory of an elderly Irishman nodding into his pipe with the statement that Germans learned slower than pigs at their Latin, and sure enough, in half an hour, light artillery began searching the houses, preparation for whatever was coming next. Those of us not in armor used a simple trick the French general staff learned after three years of slaughter in the First World War: we fell back to the second line of houses while the bursts racketed away harmlessly to our front.

"Two stone walls, it takes a railroad gun to hurt you," said a noncom, and we smoked for purposes of nonchalance while the artillery blew away stones. When the shelling stopped, everyone ran back to windows and firing slits and whistled and swore to see the same vulnerable lines march out of the trees again, parade-ground style, weapons held high, simple targets. This time the artillery observer had the 105-millimeter battalion on the radio and shellbursts made flaming clusters twenty feet in the air, swift blooms over the vertical stems of mortar explosions.

"Like trees, kind of, like an orchard," the aid man said, "some fucking apples."

When the smoke cleared we could see a few last Germans running back to their forest, leaving another stippling of forms on the ground, some writhing, some still. We watched with professional interest while German aid men dragged a few casualties to cover and then, reminded of my own duties, I ran along the line to check for wounded.

We had a few lightly hurt men, mostly from stone and wood splinters during the bombardment, but compared to the abattoir out on the field we were barely scratched: certainly there was nothing to justify the odd sense of unease I felt in myself and in the men I talked to. The captain shared it.

"You wonder what the fuck they're up to. There must be something more, something we can't see. They wouldn't just wander out and let us kill them like that. It's a trick. Keep an eye on that right flank."

We all shook heads; the words "ruse" and "maneuver" were becoming plausible when a tall rifleman across the courtyard cleared the air by jumping to his feet, swinging his helmet over straw hair, and shouting in accents that belonged on the east forty in a Minnesota farm.

"Hey boys! We got no worry! Over there they got officers, they're bigger dumb shits than ours are! Yah!"

When the right solution to a puzzle emerges everyone knows it: in the command post we looked at each other and began laughing. Men called the simple truth along the line, adding variations and emphasis, and I could see them whooping, pounding on tank hulls and gun butts, doubling over with the high humor of relief.

"Swede says it's they got dumber generals than we have!"

"Beaky hired out to the Krauts!"

"Fuckups! They're payin' us to kill a bunch of fuckups!"

By the time the next attack came everyone agreed that some career jackass in a division headquarters was ordering more counterattacks and shouting down objections for fear of his own neck:

now all we saw was a mob of victims driven by powerful dunces to the death Charlie Company was happy to provide. This time they came sane, as someone said, in squad rushes, twenty yards up and then to earth, but it only brought them in range of the small arms that were mad with waiting. Tracers were horizontal sleet; I heard the infrastructure of a battle as a noncom counseled a young gunner who was waving his weapon from one group to another.

"Keep your sights on where they go down. Like shooting birds. They gotta get up sometime and you'll be ready. Concentrate on one bunch of pricks." The gunner held his weapon steady on a spot where a squad had sunk below sight: when they rose the tracers tore across them, sending men sprawling and kicking, even cartwheeling when the force of their dash was cut off.

There was shouting from a strongpoint a hundred feet away, and I ran there, thinking they were calling for medics, but when I flopped into the yard I realized the men were yelling defiance over the roar of their weapons, howling and yahooing and chanting place names.

"Tuuulahooma!" a machine gunner was ululating with the burst of his gun; barking sounds came with names like Kansas! and Texuss! There was even dialogue: a BAR gunner howled, "Fuck Texas! Innnndiana!" with the long rip of his gun. The edge of frenzy was rising over the yelling, and the stammering roar of the guns: I had a mad urge to join in, but as a noncombatant I didn't feel qualified. Furthermore, I reflected ruefully, "Winnetka, Illinois" would be a pretty anemic war cry.

After that charge the captain came along the line, patting a shoulder here, shaking an arm there, calling around.

"You're beating a fucking battalion!

"You're winning a fucking victory!

"Keep your heads down and don't waste ammo!" He crouched off along the line, leaving words in the air around his men, telling them the shape of what they were doing.

The sun was cutting the rim of the hill when they came the last time, with four tanks. By now our observations were judicious: we watched the Germans step around and over their dead and decided they must find it very discouraging. The tanks weren't even serious: everyone laughed to see they were Mark IVs and we watched the long-barreled 76s swing on them like gods watching a well-organized doom. Our whole platoon fired together and three of the German tanks stopped in showers of sparks. With wriggles and turns the survivor tried to back to the trees but all four of our guns hit it in a pillar of flames and smoke and it burned. With the death of the tanks, the attacks stopped, early winter dark settled across the fields, and we assumed, correctly, that the battle was over.

The aid man and I gathered our handful of wounded in the warmest house we could find and I went searching for the command post to summon an ambulance. I found the captain in a remarkably intact living room with 1914 soldier portraits on the walls; he grinned when I asked him about a roaring of voices and a pounding that seemed to come from someplace close, underground.

"The boys are celebrating," he said, "in a cellar. It's okay. We've got wire and minefields and trip flares and outposts all getting organized so the guys off guard, they can raise a little hell. They've got it coming."

Through two blankets arranged for blackout I ducked into a roaring cave: forty or fifty men were moving in lantern light, shouting, laughing. There was the sense of arriving late at a large noisy party: I wandered through groups and knots and detected an odd formal structure in the gathering. One at a time, men were reciting something about the day, declaiming, chanting, while those around listened with complete attention, and laughed, or sometimes cheered. Often the conversation was technical.

"Traversing too fast is your problem. You swing that muzzle too fast there's room for them pricks between tracers. Slow. Short bursts. Don't leave any alive is the thing."

Bottles of schnapps and wine were passing around and the effects were impressive. The Iowa farmer held me by a button while he explained that he had not wasted a single bullet that day, you could count the clips. Every shot a hit, or reasonable, he said, no Maggie's Drawers* in all that uproar. That was . . . he paused and wagged his head searching for expression. Then he smiled and said, ''Efficient,'' as he slid toward the floor.

The pounding started again, two men thumping a tub with sticks and dancing about, hands to mouths, backyard Indians.

''Bullshit war dance, Doc.'' The Wisconsin Indian was breathing over my shoulder. I tried a few words of Canadian Ojibway on him and he grinned.

''Menominee, Doc. Almost the same. I can understand. Good day, huh? Good night.''

He tipped his head to the ceiling and interrupted the dancers with a long shivering screech that dwindled through octaves.

The room applauded. ''Real by God official Indian war whoop.''

''Show them, chief.''

''Official Indian bullshit.'' He was confidential. ''War whoop is anything you feel like yelling.''

In a small alcove-storeroom I found the lieutenant of the mortar platoon, a wiry abrupt youngster with a tough past as a labor organizer. He had been wounded slightly and I walked over to check the bloody dressing around his thigh. Handing me a bottle, he spoke as he always did, quickly, unpredictably.

''Know how you save the world, Doc?''

I knew his games, and I thought before I answered. ''You kill certain pricks, is how.''

''And how do you find guys to do that?''

I waited.

''You put an ad in, see, 'Wanted, strong, well-trained unbelievably motivated men to save the world. Applicants must expect to stand around in piles of dead bodies with shit and blood all over; they will also spend eight hours a day in icewater, and a certain percentage will be cut up each day by maniacs with white-hot axes. Those who survive will be permitted to use inferior weapons on a gang of lunatic murderers who positively have to be killed if there's gonna be any more world. Worth living in.

*Maggie's Drawers was the name given to the red flag that was waved on the firing range when someone missed the target completely. It connoted disgrace.

The dead bodies, by the way, and the icewater go right on!' "

"Salary, compensation?"

"Less than if they stayed home and shoveled shit in a barnyard. Compensation will be a little while of being drunk and warm and feeling happy and brave after which they will be required to kiss the ass of certain clerks who wear stars and eagles and do a lot of clerky junk that little girls could do better, right out of a convent, literally, no shit, do it better."

Our game had pulled us close to the edge of rage.

"They will have to keep straight faces and look humble while the clerks swagger around with forty-fives, presumably for shooting mice."

I heard the clang of the steel backstep of the ambulance; the lieutenant and I ducked out into the street where the wounded were climbing aboard. As I helped the lieutenant in, he leaned to me and said, "Worst crime would be to tell them. Where they are now, it's all they have. All they're going to get. Ever. All the thanks they'll ever get."

As we drove away, the wounded in the ambulance began talking quietly, gently, helping each other with cigarettes. Behind us, diminishing, we could hear the men in the cellar imitating the Indian, practicing war whoops.

The Cooper-Bronc Theorem, or

An observation to save the planet, not to mention the species, or

Conversation in the new dark, sitting on a target

Persona: Bronc, Coop, Whit, Bill, Self

"What's impossible to believe is we're really moving off the line: we're going someplace they can't drop shells on us. I don't really believe there is such a place."

"Many times as they've hit our CP it feels like it's supposed to happen. It's a mistake when it doesn't. Somebody screwed up."

"I can hear some Kraut getting his ass chewed. 'Herr Oberst Guberschnitzen, what is der meaning uf dis? Today you didn't auf CCB drop the required shells! You have upgefuckt! You'll be court-gemartialed and geschotten!' "

"Fucking convoy. Stopping right here, where they always shell.

Just when we're almost away. We're a hundred yards from being around the hill and safe so of course we stop here.''

"Shell here every night, for chrissakes. They call it interdiction. I don't care to be interdicted ten minutes from being the hell out of here.''

The edges of the voices are rising.

"Fucking last few hours, fucking last few minutes. Worst time. You're always sure you're going to get it at the last minute.''

"Hope proposed maketh the heart sick.''

"Geez, Doc. You and the words again. You think that one up?''

"Guy named Johnson. Sam Johnson. Different the way he said it.''

To talk our way through suspended time we begin comparing fuckups. We consider the infantry battalion from the division that was supposed to relieve us and didn't show up. Lost. Officers couldn't read a map. For two hours there was nothing facing the German army but a couple of our command half-tracks.

"Blessed be he that fucketh the least up, for he shall overcome him who fucketh up the more.''

"Wars, countries, empires. They don't get lost because the guy who wins does something right; what happens is the guy who loses does something wrong.''

"Screws it up.''

"Consider Mike.''

"Alas, poor Mike.''

"Don't be funny, Doc.''

"I'm not being. I mean alas poor Mike no shit. Mike was the best of that bunch and he died of an overdose of West Point.''

"Hell, he could easy have disobeyed Beaky and fought that battle right. He could have said screw you and gone around that flank. What the hell could Beaky have done? He was so far away back he wouldn't have known the difference until it was too late to change.''

"Not Mike, he couldn't have. Not any West Pointer.''

"He died of obedience.''

"Ever think what a serious crime obedience is?''

"Obedience to idiots. Obedience to criminals.''

"Makes you an idiot or a criminal too."

"Worst thing is that it was Mike."

> *He was likely, had he been put on,*
> *To have proved most royally: and, for his passage,*
> *The soldiers' music and the rites of war*
> *Speak loudly for him.*

Silence.

"That was pretty good, Doc. For Mike. The way you said it. Shakespeare, huh?"

"*Hamlet*, at the end, when they're all dead."

Pause

"You're quiet, Coop. You okay?"

"I'm trying to think in the middle of all this bullshit. Great principle I just figured out. Applies to the whole world, companies and divisions and corporations and governments. Everybody."

"Let's hear it."

"Sure, why not? I'd rather hear anything than sit here wondering when the Krauts are going to get smart and drop a couple of 105s on us."

"It's the principle of invisibility on account of incredibility. There's an inverse ratio between how stupid you can be and still get away with it and how high up or low down you are. You expect to see dumb privates and corporals, and when you do you bust them or chew their ass, accordingly. Now, the first part of my great principle is the higher you go, there's just as much stupidity, but it's harder to see. It becomes invisible because it's incredible."

"President of a big corporation, a country, general of any army, with the way we're brought up we plain cannot believe that someone that high up can be a complete gibbering, neurotic, incompetent horse's ass."

"Except he frequently is."

"And nobody can quite believe it even when they know it."

"You see four stars or gold letters on a door or a title and your mind turns off what you already by God know for a fact."

"Those stars and those titles are like magic, they make the real guy invisible."

"Tarn-cloak, the Krauts call it. Like Siegfried had when you couldn't see him. You can dance around being a drooling idiot safe behind your wall of incredibility. See?"

"Haig in the first war. So dumb he couldn't empty a waste-basket without directions, also a liar."

"Justinian, Nero, Caligula, lunatics, criminals, perverts. Lots of great brave guys persuaded other brave guys to die obeying them."

"The crime of obedience, see."

"We should spend the rest of our lives tearing the wall from around dumb bastards. Crusade!"

"Start with Beaky. He'll get court-martialed or busted or something. You can see what he did . . . all burned out and shot up. Nobody can miss it."

"Don't count on it. West Point Benevolent Protective Society. Best invisibility cloak there is."

The convoy started to move and long-held breaths eased. Five minutes, ten minutes, our column was around the flank of a long, sheltering hill. The fear of dissolution began to lift. Twenty minutes and the blue light of a flashlight on a map showed us we were out of range of anything except a lucky hit by a railroad gun. Luxury filled the dark.

Bronc moved his light on the map. "Lookit here, from Sarrebourg up here over the German border, all back in France courtesy of us, the Twelfth Armored."

"We're so busy with our particular jobs and not getting killed that you feel kind of self-conscious talking about the big stuff, that we're really here for."

"The SS and the Gestapo and all that shit is gone. People in the villages and the farmers and the guys we saw with their sheep when it was getting dark and their kids and I suppose their grandkids. All out from under."

"Hard to think about countries and places on maps and why we're here, really, in the middle of all that tearing up guts and screaming. Only after it's all over people come up with words like 'victory.' History. We committed some history. Is it always that bloody and shitty close up?''

The dark's filling with ease: we're drugged. The prospect of bellowing and mutilation has filled the air around us, without a minute's gap, twenty-four hours a day, for weeks. Now, as we fall away into the gentle night of childhood summers and fireflies there's a pleasure so intense it has to be savored, like foreplay. Bodies jerk back into apprehension and then slump under smiles. We're drifting, each of us, far from fear, far from each other.

Hey, hey, skip to my Lou, skip to the fish on a string!

Dear other Planet, with what pleasure do I renew our acquaintance, most delectable of spaces, where duty's dead and humans pursue pleasure for its own lovely ends!

Instance?

Instance, on the wall of the infantry aid station, on the shore of the Lac Dieuze, those six glorious pike calling happy hello from the North Woods of childhood!

We're voluptuaries: we luxuriate in the bubbles water makes in holes new-chopped in ice, in the flashing of minnows caught in open shallows, the undulant shapes of hooks and lines whistled up for cigarettes.

My God, what elegance there still is in the world when a man can think of nothing but the tug of fierce life under water!

This is the private preserve of a duke, the best fishing in France. Two hundred of our heroes are scattered across ice, lost in the promise of gurgling holes. Only in Europe would authority presume, and here it comes in cap and leggins insanely daring, sputtering in French about a "permis."

Brooklyn said, "The noive of the little prick," after translation, and Pennsylvania and Minnesota laughed too hard to be indignant: they only patted his head and showed him grenades and gun butts.

Tell him this is our fucking permis, Doc, and I did. The permis sufficed, but I could not resist sniping.

Where is the duke? Fighting in the First French Army, no doubt?

No?

Then of course he was in the Resistance?

No?

Of course. One remembers. Collaboration. Unfortunate.

(Excellent shot. Practically all the nobility collaborated to save their goddamn tapestries.)

Collaboration, word of fear. Eyes become anxious dark buttons.

All the Nazis who fished here, the high-ranking specimens. How could the FFI* fail to notice? The FFI, the organization patriotic and ferocious, that we of course worked together with, closely.

As warden, it was necessary to be specifically involved with the Nazis, to guide them, possibly? How painful for him! How easily misunderstood.

Authority dwindled into apologies, deprecations, whining sounds about employment and the need to feed children. We sent him off with cigarettes and a message to the duke.

There were lots of us *morts* and a lot more *blessés* fighting for the liberation of the duke's country; he could surely spare a few fucking *poisson* for heroes who had just escorted the Boche over the border.

Unfrocked authority twinkled away.

Perverted notions about the ownership of Earth's creatures by an undeserving few vanished into air, into thin air, and the afternoon sounded with unfettered whoops as great speckled-green bodies came flapping into view, angels from icy deeps, freeing men to talk of trout in the Rockies and bass in Arkansas, clearing the border murk, bringing sunlight that shone clear back to pine woods and hickory groves and friends and campfires and the life everyone now knew should be treasured like diamonds.

---

*FFI was the abbreviation for the Forces Françaises de l'Intérieur, an amalgamation of the numerous and sometimes disparate Resistance groups, whose cooperation had often left much to be desired. All during the border fighting the FFI men, identified by armbands, armed with carbines, and uniformed in old jackets and caps, held roadblocks for us, brought in useful intelligence, and set an example of bravery and loyalty.

✳ 9

Tribute to an Army

DECEMBER ON THE LINE, Alsace-Lorraine. Seventh Army was the elbow of the western front, crooked along the northeast frontier of France. To the right, south from Strasbourg to Switzerland, the French First Army looped around the Colmar Pocket. (The French First Army! I never quite believed it when I saw it; but then, how was a refugee from Middletown, U.S.A., supposed to stay in touch with reality when he found himself marching with a battalion of the French foreign legion, or possibly turning some foothill in the Vosges to come face to face with a column of Algerian tirailleurs, all done up in turbans and djellabas, tinkling with grenades and bandoliers, leading mule trains of mountain guns? From the world where the Germans and Americans glared at each other, drab and murderous, the French First Army was a whisk to another and brightly colored planet, where the war, if not exactly cheerful, was at least swathed in antiquities that made the whole affair a lot less depressing. French First Army tanks didn't clank and squeak at prescribed speeds, they zoomed like Maseratis in a cloud of fleeing livestock while red pompom sailor hats bounced in the turrets. Officers' messes poured two kinds of wine; smashing Parisienne mistresses lounged around regimental headquarters. More of this fascinating organization later.)

Third Army was the leaden echo to the north. The poor bastards paid fines, wore neckties, and died to make headlines for some late-Byzantine toads who lived in trailers and palaces and squabbled over press releases. Bill Mauldin captured the feelings of Seventh Army toward Third Army in a cartoon that stirred a typhoon. It showed Joe and Willie, classic, tired, filthy, efficient infantrymen in a jeep so hung with gas cans, ammunition, and rations that it looked like a mobile dump, staring at a large sign.

"YOU ARE ENTERING THE THIRD ARMY," screeched the sign.

Fines:
No helmet: 25.00
No shave: 10.00
No buttons: 10.00
No tie: 10.00
No shine: 12.50
No shampoo: 25.00
Windshields up: 25.00
Trousers down: 50.00
   Enforced: by order of Ol' Blood and Guts.

Joe's comment: "Radio th' ol' man we'll be late on account of a thousand-mile detour."

(Patton was livid; he ordered Mauldin's cartoons banned from the Third Army *Stars & Stripes,* thereby causing a near-mutiny. Eisenhower intervened and the cartoons reappeared.)

Along the Seventh Army front were some of the great divisions of American history. The Third and Forty-fifth Infantry Divisions had stormed the beaches of Sicily on July 10, 1943. It was now late 1944 and they had never stopped fighting. After Sicily came the shattering battles of Salerno landings, when the Thirty-sixth Division joined in, the grind up the Italian peninsula to Cassino, the unspeakable winter of 1943/44 along the Rapido and on the Anzio bridgehead, the heady violence of the breakout to Rome the next spring, the invasion of southern France in summer, the pursuit of the German Nineteenth Army up the Rhone Valley, the crunching bitter push across the Vosges Mountains in the fall, the savage brawls around the Colmar Pocket, and the final thrust up to and through the Siegfried line. There were men in these divisions, unbelievably, who had lived through all this. They were a steel-wire mesh in units whose ranks had been replaced two or three times over. These were men who did not smile at Bill Mauldin's cartoon about being a fugitive from the law of averages; they had no statistical right to be alive and they knew it. Behind them trailed an incredible record of endurance — days, weeks, months of unrelieved terror and shattering fire, wet, freezing, starving animal misery with no end in sight except for death or mangling. To these men Valley Forge would have been a frolic.

Seventh Army front ran from Strasbourg north along the Rhine to the Saar Palatinate; thence it marched west against the Siegfried line through the fir forests of the Vosges, out onto the whale-backed ridges of Lorraine, ending with us. We formed the junction with Third Army.

In the middle of the month the Germans crashed into the Ardennes in their last great offensive of the war. The Third Army divisions to our left disappeared to the north to attack the flank of the Bulge; Seventh Army stretched its lines and held in place while the killing cold of the worst winter in forty years settled down over foxholes and gunpits.

✳ 10

Christmas 1944

CHRISTMAS 1944 brought, as a gift, sunlight: the skies throbbed with the roar of our fighter-bombers flying north to attack the Bulge. Other *Geschenken* included food poisoning and the cowardice of the chaplain's jeep driver.

The food poisoning came from contaminated turkey delivered all along the line to remind everyone of Mom and gluttony. Deadly inflammation: the most terrifying moment of a soldier's life came when he had to crawl out of his foxhole to hunker in near-fetal helplessness, genital and buttocks bared to white-hot jagged steel. The magazine *Yank* once published a drawing of a soldier crouched over a latrine, labeled "The worst moment at the front," and the editors weren't being funny. We ladled paregoric, bismuth, sulfa pills, and hope all along the gun emplacements. Something worked: the epidemic ended in a day. Lethal nostalgia.

The jeep driver's flight put me on the business end of the old Sicilian proverb about revenge being the only dish best eaten cold. Whoever set up the tables of organization for an armored combat command was hell-bent for salvation but didn't care much about people's physical survival. There was a jeep with driver for each chaplain of any persuasion but no transportation at all for the medical detachment: we were supposed to hitch rides on half-tracks and flag ambulances for our wounded.

I tried to convince the chaplains it was their Christian duty to combine their ghostly functions and let me and my medics have a jeep to ride in and carry wounded on. They laughed in my face. Generosity from army chaplains? Blood from stones? The spirit of first-century Christianity burned low in their bosoms, and the army had stamped out whatever smolderings they brought from civil life simply by making them officers. You could hardly blame them: most of them had spent a lifetime begging a congregation to drop their salary in a tin plate. They had had to be humble for their bread and butter, but now they were officers, with entitled incomes, and their congregation had to salute them and say sir. They moved in heavens denied to their humble parishioners, and how eagerly did they frequent the officers' club, the officers' reserved section at the movies, the general's tightly exclusive parties! How swiftly they became the agents of rank and power, justifying the latest starry self-serving to querulous villeins!

They were, after all, only human: they suffered a contamination that began somewhere on the Upper Nile with the priests of the dog-headed god and seeped through recorded history. Religion's a perilous bloom: one whiff of power and it shrivels into claws and tentacles. We smile to see monks carrying kindness to the poor in a halo of doves: tomorrow they may be twisting the rack while heretics scream.

With a straight face, I once suggested to a set of chaplains that a true religious impulse would have bid them refuse rank, and further would have sent them out among the huddled military masses to share barracks and mess, hardship and persecution, bringing the word of God to the oppressed in the manner of Jesus. Reactions varied from paranoid to Vesuvial: hell hath no fury like a threatened benefice.

As a lifelong student of theology, I could at least chat with the agents of the older churches, if I skirted tactfully around exegesis, but the spewings of the fundamentalist Bible Belt seminary-factories were real horrors. I could hardly believe such ignorance, arrogance, and hate could cohabit in a human skin. One division chaplain was a flagrant specimen; he sprouted from some lower-case Baptist denomination, and a career in the army had encased almost total lack of learning in a cavalry-officer shell. He kept T.S. cards on his desk for soldiers who sought consolation. Tough shit. T.S., the card said, I have never heard so heartbreaking a tale as yours. This entitles you to the use of the towel for crying purposes. And so on. When the victim left, the chaplain would wander down the hall to guffaw with the other staff officers. He and his kind were, in fact, the spiritual godfathers of those Yahoos who today profane the name of Yeshua and debauch his word over radio and television.

There were rare and saintly souls in the corps of chaplains, but they swam against the tide and found salvation in loneliness. The Grand Inquisitor proliferated: Thomas Aquinas was damned thin on the ground.

Wheels for the wounded? Not, I learned, at the cost of Godly privilege.

Appeal to command to get our medical section some form of transportation was no help; the West Pointers had a grand old tradition of cowardice around chaplains, for somewhere they had absorbed the notion that chaplains could wave wands toward the home folks, and through them persuade Congress to chop the next military budget into poverty-sized splinters, a superstition that persisted into the flood tides of wartime funds.

"Chaplain's jeep is sacred, Doc" — this in nervous exhalations from our executive officer — and my argument that organizing the care of human life might be even more sacred died right there on the parade ground.

In England our division surgeon traded some extra half-tracks for some genuine Dodge cross-country ambulances, magnificent vehicles with heaters and an impressive carrying capacity; and so, after much bitterness, medicine, science, and human survival triumphed obliquely, and that Sicilian beatitude bloomed on the snow as I stood in a darkening village square in Alsace on Christmas night while a chaplain pleaded with me to take him in our ambulance to a remote aid station. He needed a ride out to the Ruhling farm, where Captain Rocky of the tank battalion was in bad shape. Ruhling farm was the aid station of the 812th Tank Battalion, and it wasn't on the round of visits I had planned for that day.

Why didn't he take his goddamned sacred jeep? With gratifying Christian humility, he admitted the truth: his jeep driver was frightened and claimed he wasn't supposed to go that far forward. It was a pleasure to point out that there wasn't anywhere his jeep driver was not supposed to go, and to ask, after all the fuss about his sainted jeep, why he wasn't capable of controlling the vagaries of one T-5 driver?

This particular chaplain was not without subtlety. With some flickerings of eyebrows and settings of mouths, we conveyed back and forth his enforced penitence, my decently suppressed triumph, and the mutual knowledge that Rocky's needs outweighed our civil strife by several universes.

Some miles out in snowy dark we saw four snouts projecting out of mounds, black against darkening blue, the assault guns of the tank battalion, and as we dropped below them, just under their muzzles, they all fired, splitting the night blue-white, dazzling our eyes, slamming us into our seats.

"Smart bastards. Wait until we're right under their guns and let go." Beside me, fighting the steering wheel, Jack was shaking his head, blinking his eyes, trying to see the road through the after-dazzle.

"Hell, they gotta fire when the battery commander says fire."

"Nuts. I bet they think it's funny" — I had to admit I had the same sneaky, irrational idea myself; it was hard to believe the small malignant accidents of war weren't planned evilly.

Through two blackout curtains I stooped into a farmhouse cellar; in the first blinking of light I could see only a wet, red oblong stuck with gleaming light-points. Vision cleared further to let me see that it was a figure face down on a litter, the skin torn off the back, the muscles punctured and ripped, the light-points hemostats that a surgeon was moving deftly to clamp what seemed to be hundreds of bleeding vessels.

''Booby trap,'' the surgeon talked while he clamped and sutured and peered for spurters.

''Rocky and these other guys were out on a patrol; they opened a door in a barn and the damn thing was booby-trapped: glass, nails, scrap iron, screws, hunks of torn tin. Goddamnedest mess you ever saw. Got him right in the back; tore most of it off.''

''Pretty shocky, isn't he?''

''No blood pressure, no pulse; this is our third unit of plasma. I've given him a slug of adrenaline.''

''Should we try to get him out?''

''Every time we start to move him, he starts to die; his pulse quits and he turns blue. It's a hell of a haul from here to the medical company; looks like we'll have to get him in better shape before we try moving him. What do you think?''

I thought of the miles of rutted, frozen, jolting road back to the medical company, and I agreed: moving Rocky would have meant arriving with a corpse.

The chaplain knelt by the litter, taking out his gear, and I looked around the aid station. It was quiet, in one of those still isometric periods before the diastole of wounded flowing in, or the systole of survivors leaving.

Detritus of the last passage filled the room: bloody blankets sagged across folded litters; used aid packets made scarlet gobbets on the floor; helmets and guns were in a heap near the door. Last, in a corner, I saw the tree. The medics had set up a little fir tree, a few feet tall, for Christmas. On it were bits of tin cans, cut and twisted into ornaments, and at its top was a tin star, hammered flat, that kept flashing a dull, small wink back at the mantel lamp near the operating table.

All the aid-station crew who weren't helping the surgeons gathered around me as they went to look at the tree. Each had something to tell about it — the one who had cut it, the one who had scrounged the tin cans from the 10-in-1 boxes back at the mess truck, the ones who had wrecked two pairs of bandage scissors cutting the ornaments.

The men talked quietly — good medics never gabbled when there were badly wounded men in the aid station; they lived too close to human agony all day to become hardened or cynical or frivolous about it — and yet as each man talked about his aspect of the tree, the voices became freer and — it is difficult to describe — affirmative. They talked of something they wanted to talk about. If they had said, for instance, ''There's a lot of shelling near Baker Company,'' they would be saying what they had to say and hated saying; but when they said, ''I cut this tin around in a ring and made it like a spiral so it bounces up and down and sparkles,'' they were saying something beautiful, something fit for human speech.

The surgeon finished clamping and tying. Aid men wrapped pressure dressings over the macerated flesh. Fingers still raddled, the surgeon touched an ornament. ''Hell of a tree, isn't it? The guys made it.''

The circle of faces glowed under helmets.

Across the room Rocky started making the sounds of an animal drowning, and the smiles blew out.

He kept trying to talk about the goddamn door, everybody told me. They were sure he wasn't really conscious, not feeling any pain; he was just mumbling that one word, blown into his brain.

We tried plasma again, but we had to be cautious because he was loaded with too much fluid, and his lungs kept frothing with pulmonary edema.

The quiet of that cellar was deep and tense for an hour as the aid men watched us work over Rocky, injecting adrenaline and caffeine, running plasma into both arms as fast as we dared. Finally there was nothing left but waiting, and we settled into that worst period a physician faces, when active intervention is spent, all's done, and one must watch a patient and pray that one's meddlings and fiddlings will start the movements of oxygen and fluids and ions to begin the slow spiral of life up and away from failing.

The radio squawked; the radioman's face showed the kind of news he was hearing.

''Send both half-tracks to Charlie Company,'' he told his fellows; ''they've got a mess.''

In less than twenty minutes the half-tracks had gone and returned; litters, blankets, bandages, and splints were ready when the steel back gates clanged and the litter crews staggered through the blackout curtains, but two surgeons can't really be ready for ten badly torn men — nobody can work that fast.

The aid men told us what had happened: a couple of tank crews couldn't stand the cold anymore (World War II tanks weren't heated; sitting still in the cold they were like steel refrigerators), and they had dismounted and started a fire. A couple of forward observers came over to get warm, and a shell came in, landing right in the fire, killing or wounding everyone around.

While I was clamping two bleeding arteries in a torn thigh, digging among shreds of clothing and splinters of bone to catch the spurting vessels, I could hear the whistling of blood bubbling in the breathing of a chest wound with pneumothorax — air sucking into the chest, collapsing the lung — on the next litter, and I knew that every second I took clamping those two arteries might cost the boy on the next litter his life. It was desperately hard not to become frantic with haste when the air was filled with animal groans and cries for somebody to do something. I wanted to do everything at once — close the chest wound, start plasma, catch the bleeders in a stump that I could see out of the corner of my eye — but this only meant fumbling and fatal inefficiency. One trained oneself to think with a cold, steely, ferocious concentration on each specific motion; one chanted to oneself: "There is nothing in this aid station except this one bleeder, and all I've got to do in the whole world for the rest of my life is to clamp it," and every skill one had focused on sponging the blood and torn tissue, finding the ripped end of the artery and sealing it with as much care as if one had all day in the finest operating room in the United States. This kind of savage exclusion of the terror and pain around us meant speed, and our speed meant men's lives.

When the major bleeders were tied, the aid men began bandaging and applying a traction splint — gently, because the bone of the thigh was shattered and the muscles were so torn that much traction could have pulled the leg almost off; and while they did that, I closed the sucking wound in the chest by putting safety pins through the skin. It was at that precise instant I looked up, and even while my fingers kept on working, sealing the air inside a chest, I saw the tree.

Wink! The tree spoke. Bright! I was deep in the smell of a balsam tree, warm in the age of ten, stroking the spun-glass tail of an unspeakably beautiful swan dangling from a branch, quietly nudging the packages with my toe. Kindness, the tree was saying; love and presents and yelling happiness.

By then the chest wound was closed and I helped an aid man strap tape over it, but for the rest of the evening I worked in two worlds: somehow, vision could include the star on the tree and the closing of blood vessels in the stump of an upper arm, but the hearing was all with the tree; the air was singing all around, quieting all that groaning and spewing, triumphant. There was a horrible head wound with exposed brain that I covered gently, and then a jagged abdominal laceration through intestines and stomach, and while I worked as deftly as I ever had, I was partly far out of myself and out of the aid station, reaching for the shining of the tree, because if it really was there, then all this wasn't happening; or if what I was seeing in the aid station was the truth, it couldn't be as bad as I thought it was, not in a world with Christmases. I had an absurd impulse to tell the wounded men to look at the tree to feel better; I was moving in a trance of Christmas remembered.

It was bad evening for the chaplain and me. He was, in fact, the best of the uniformed clergy; as a Catholic he combined a decent education with the aura of tradition, but we were both self-conscious about the jeep-ambulance schism, and we kept annoying each other without intent. He always seemed ready to rub things on foreheads just as I was about to do something to save a life. Even his excuses sounded too solicitous that night; he was too apologetic. When the last casualty was bandaged and secured, he was still bowed in his rites. I was standing against the wall, rubbing my bloody hands, when a voice next to me muttered, "That's what we pay taxes for, that shit."

It was the Professing Atheist. I had forgotten he was around. He was an aid man from the tank battalion, but in civilian life he had been a coal miner in Pennsylvania, a survivor against history from the days when there was genuine working-class consciousness and morality, and when there was a healthy workingman's irreverence for constituted authority. His atheism was thoughtful, intensely moral, and proclaimed frequently and critically to the horror of our devout, mostly hypocritical yea-sayers.

"What shit?" I hoped for a particular answer.

"That shit here. Our tax money is paying for that spook rubbing magic stuff on unconscious guys' heads. That's going to get them into Heaven? Even if there was such a place? Listen, if there really was a God, and I was Him, I'd let guys into Heaven depending on what they did when they knew what they were doing. I certainly wouldn't let them in on account of some guy pouring oil over their head after they were dead. If any of those religions ever really meant any of the things they say, that chaplain there, and everyone like him, should have been going around telling people what to do when they were still alive, so these guys wouldn't be lying here bleeding out on the horseshit."

Ah, Stan, I thought, the bitter history snared in your words! The great German Lutheran Church swooned into the Nazi's lap without a blush: Lutheran clergy had been shouting obedience to Hitler in the name of Christ since 1933. In colossal open-air rallies, Lutheran bishops gave their blessing to SS divisions marching off to stain Western history. A few hundred brave clergy were starving in concentration camps, or dead, but their numbers were a reproach: the clerical masses and the hierarchy supped with shame. And the Keeper of the Keys, the inheritor of Peter? Hitler tossed him a concordat in 1933, and in return the Vatican ordered — *ordered* — all German bishops to swear allegiance to the Nazi party. There were brave German Catholic priests who defied horrors to save Jews and condemn national murder, but when the Nazis haled them into court with torture dangling, the Church officially disclaimed them. No protection, no help. They had violated policy, and they were to be treated as ordinary criminals, said the bishops, and the archbishops, and the cardinals, and the Vatican. Concentration camps were good enough for them. The integrity of the German Catholic Church was saved by a handful of saints who died in Auschwitz and Dachau.

And my own church? At least one archbishop of the Anglican Church had blessed Hitler for his splendid preservation of order, and the Anglican clergy had been elegantly mute while the Jews of Europe were beaten to death. When, for that matter, had the Anglican Church ever invoked the wrath of Heaven on British colonial murderers and enslavers? When had it ever opposed the Word of God to the government that fed it and kept it in after-dinner port?

How would history have run if the Pope had pronounced excommunication on all Nazis and their accomplices? What if the Lutherans had thundered without let from every pulpit against the devils prancing in their streets? What power might the Sermon on the Mount unleash for the armies of light?

It didn't happen, of course. The churches of the Western world failed. The clergy failed. The hierarchies licked the spittle of murderers and perverts, and the keeping of the blessed truth lay finally in the hands of a few disinherited fanatics.

Christianity didn't fail, Stan. We failed. Us. Nobody believed in Christianity enough to put it on a spear-point and ride into battle with it.

I straightened from thought; the battalion surgeon was finishing a face wound with a white mask of bandage. Only a few steady groans came from the litters; we were finished.

I told the aid men to load my ambulance for a trip back to the ALP. The ALP was the ambulance loading post, where the wounded were put in medical company ambulances, dog tags double-checked, and casualty statistics maintained. It was always near combat command headquarters.

By this time two of the ten men had died; aid men were lifting the rest into the backs of ambulances. I asked the battalion surgeon how Rocky was; he looked up from his litter and said, "Worse."

As the last of the litters brushed under the blackout curtains, I walked back to the tree. The ornaments still sparkled into the lantern light, and they looked so like the tinkly glass and metal contraptions of the trees of my childhood that I couldn't help flicking one, as I always had the bells and Santa Clauses of other years, to hope for chiming. It was tin, of course, and it could only make a dead noise like *tink* or *tonk*.

On the way past the assault guns, Jack squinted at the dark.

"If those bastards let go now ... ," he threatened the snowy steel, but the dark was decent, the dark was still; under silent gun muzzles we hauled our wounded out through the snow. Late that night Rocky died.

Love in Lorraine

A THOUSAND RED-BLOODED AMERICANS were stunned with admiration, and fatuous with lust, all over a German. Love before duty, even in the cannon's mouth.

It happened in a ruined town hall where blankets covered shell holes: it happened especially when she lifted her skirt to expose her black silk stockings to the limits of military censorship. Marlene, *du schöne!*

Bob Hope and Bing Crosby and gaggles of other entertainers wandered about that balmy world where the quartermasters stacked boxes on bales and stole from the combat troops. (The warm jackets and shoepacs that were supposed to protect our troops from cold and slush disappeared by the millions among rearward soldiers who never wet a foot or froze a nose. The men on the front lines shivered in thin field jackets and lost their feet to the ice that congealed through their leaky boots.)

I never met a combat soldier who had his morale lifted by any of the expensive, frantically publicized troupes that danced and sang and recited jokes in the world of comfort and safety far behind us. In fact, I never met a combat soldier who even saw or heard them.

Virgo intacta, without stain of publicity, Marlene Dietrich toured the front lines for the sole and defined benefit of the men who fought. She came to us in a shattered Lorraine town; soldiers clanking with weapons crowded an old school hall to hear her.

Her troupe consisted of herself, a helper who played the guitar and cracked jokes, and a speaker that ran off a truck battery. She appeared first in battle dress — slacks and an Eisenhower jacket — but even in olive-drab, her golden hair and her magnificent lines under cloth and her endlessly seductive voice sounded the music of everything any of us had ever loved in a woman. She was witty, she was brilliant and kind, and she possessed a voice that raised glandular hackles. All this was very pleasant, but as far as we were concerned the evening would have glistened if she had simply stood there and recited the Greek alphabet.

For the last part of her performance, she changed to a nightclub outfit with a spangly skirt and black stockings, and when she sang about Johnny's birthday and what Johnny was going to get for his birthday, she put one foot on a chair and lifted her skirt to a frenzy of howls and whistles and happy snarls.

There was an emotion close to furious tears when she sang good-bye and drove off in her truck through snow and ruins to the next division.

For days, the delightful specifics of Marlene hung like a string of sparkling lights in our troglodyte world, glowing in cellars and holes.

Best words came from an infantryman, looking up from the parts of his BAR:

"That was a real nice lady. It's different now because she was here. It ain't so fucking lonely."

Take great care, Marlene! Never die!

✳ 12

Herrlisheim:
Diary of a Battle

THIS IS A JOURNAL I kept during the battle of Herrlisheim, to try to record three weeks of the heaviest, bloodiest fighting in our division's history.

One might reasonably ask how I had time or inclination to keep a journal, but the truth is that boredom is one of the sensations that dominates any modern battlefield, hard on the heels of fear and loneliness. Between eruptions of violence stretch vast deserts of empty time when there is literally nothing to do. Idleness during combat is not the happy idleness of flower-picking; rather, it is often tense and fearful, and the fascination of trying to transmute sensations and events into words often filled one's mind with a grateful surge of activity.

The account starts on New Year's Eve, 1944.

December 31, 1944. Our combat command this morning went on one-hour alert; this always means we move out within twenty-four hours. Where? Usual mystery: much pondering of lines of black boxes on the map, German divisions bulging at us from three sides.

Twelve noon: Prospect of action and we move in charged air; reactions vary inversely with possibility of being killed. Our liaison officer to division headquarters has a somewhat safer job than leading girl scouts through Central Park, and consequently he goes swanking about with some quartermaster corps cronies, slapping his holster, making what he thinks are military noises. Headquarters staff is thoughtful, much quiet letter-writing. God knows we lead a posh life compared to the infantry, but our headquarters has been a favorite target of German gunners; we have lost dead and wounded on each trip into the line. A certain angst is reasonable.

Out in barns and ruined houses, the men of the infantry and tank battalions who are really going to do the suffering and dying are doing what I suppose fighting men have done in all times and ages: they are concentrating on the small, suddenly illuminated kindnesses of life. Nobody says it, but everybody knows that this is the last New Year's Eve a lot of them will see, and this New Year's Eve will be celebrated with schnapps and wine miraculously hidden from the Wehrmacht and traded for cigarettes and K rations, with dough pounded flat and cooked to what an Italian sergeant swears will be pasta *al dente,* with a number of fascinating alchemical mushes of snow and powdered milk and chocolate and sugar that I am assured will be ice cream, celebrated with an intensity of tenderness that is almost painful. It's as if each man were looking at a woman, lovely, deeply loved, for what might be the last time.

January 1, four A.M.: Gust of cold, space of night. In the open door a monster, helmeted, darkness against dark, spindrift of snow. Vision clears: it's the runner from the command post with attack orders: we're attacking something, somewhere. Goblin disappears.

Through Arctic dark, through mists of drink and sleep, we pack, we slam, we dispatch; within the hour I stand in the black before dawn, in a world of frozen metal, where hatches clang and tracks squeal, and I think wistfully of the heady warmth of our aid-station party a few hours earlier, of the magnificent broiled pike, of the lashings of grapefruit juice and gin, and above all, of the aura of kindness that enfolded everyone from the colonel to the medical soldiers to the sick on their litters, all of us watching the rim of gentle drunken euphoria rising over the night. Auld Lang Syne, we sang in the world we had almost forgotten. Happy New Year, we shouted, defiant.

Now, in the cold steel dawn, I squeak my boots in the snow to make a slight human noise.

January 1, midnight: Severne Gap, the Vosges Mountains. What the hell is the Divine Willy doing in this war? "A moonlit or a starlit dome disdains / All that man is, all mere complexities." Yeats goes drumming, clanging through sleep as I squint out the ambulance window at a little city of domes, many domes, glistening under starlight. Outside, blinking, awake, the domes are infantrymen's helmets sparkling with frost; under them the emperor's miserable soldiery draped in blankets, streaked with snow, numb. I start to encourage the men, to tell them there'll be an end to the ride with warmth and food, but I realize that for these men the end will come when they dismount into the snow to attack into machine-gun fire and shellbursts, and then, those of them still alive and unmangled, to chip holes in frozen ground and huddle there through an eternity of cold and terror. No end for them. As the column winds on through the starlit forests, I fall asleep inside the ambulance thinking about the mire and the fury of human veins. Frozen fury, I meditate; compelled, reluctant fury in the young veins threading the border mountains.

January 2, early A.M.: Corps headquarters is in an old mansion laced with telephone wires. The corps staff officer is drunk.

"A few thousand Volksturm in there, home guards, old men, kids, cripples." His mumble is rich with brandy and his finger wanders over the map. "Take your tanks and run 'em out."

He turns to leave: our colonel has to hold him by the arm.

"Few thousand? How many thousand?"

"What units do we know of?"

"AT guns? Armor?" The colonel and Coop fire questions, but the staff officer's attention is a blob of mercury, skittering.

"Few thousand. People they scraped up."

When our colonel persists, he's patted on the shoulder, condescended to.

"Skirmish. Give your boys some practice. Talk about real fighting, downnittaly ..." The staff officer stares, silent, swimming in reminiscence. He escapes.

We gather uneasily around a map. The German attack has created a thumb on the French side of a river. The river runs north and south, the thumb points west. On the south flank of the thumb is a forest — the Stainwald. Circling the thumb, ringing it, a network of canals and a river; bisecting the thumb north to south, a railroad track–highway complex. In the center of the thumb, Herrlisheim: the road center, the commanding terrain, the obvious key to the whole area.

January 2, night: An Alsatian village; guns, tanks, half-tracks full of infantry whine through for hours. Friendly balloons float in the dark above us; white reassured townspeople's heads talking to me in fragments, hopeful.

"*Bosch schnell kaput, eh?*"

"*Jawohl; schnell kaput. Nichts zu fürchten,*" I reassure them. Our one battalion of infantry and one battalion of tanks with their supporting guns make a brave show threading down the single village street. After all, we face a few thousand Volksturm. . . .

January 3, afternoon: Snowy outside an Alsatian inn: the men of the infantry medical section passing around a bottle of schnapps, marveling at the recent sexual exploit of the buck sergeant.

"Fucked this broad right in the snowbank. Right in the goddamn snowbank. Broad daylight. How do you like that?"

Sergeant Bernstein pulls hard at the bottle, seems uneasy, embarrassed, actually ashamed; he is a sensitive, well-educated young New Yorker; coarseness does not come naturally.

"Don't know why I did a crazy thing like that." He mumbles it.

"Geez, that's a sin, right before you go into battle. You might get killed with a mortal sin on your soul and you guys can't go to confession." We have a pious Boston Irishman in our midst. Someone pushes *him* into the snowbank.

"What'd you give her, Sarge? Dough? C rations?"

"He give her the business is all he give her, huh, Sarge?"

The men facing combat are wrapping themselves in the warmth of improbable fornication; they are reaching back for life; they can't let it go. But Bernstein finds nothing exciting or warming about it; he seems to know only a combination of postcoital triste and fear. . . .

January 3, night: Command post in an inn. The colonel explains the attack. We were going to have help from the French First Army on the south flank, but they're committed elsewhere, they're overextended. They will demonstrate.

"Demonstrate? Wave their turbans? Yell?" Someone is cynical. We are offered a chance to attack through the French lines into the southern base of the thumb, our right flank secure in the river, but the colonel decides against it. Instead we will attack angling in from the northwest toward the town of Herrlisheim.

Looking at the overlay on the map, I feel unease again. The railroad and the high-banked road will dominate our left flank; as our attack moves from northwest to southeast, that flank will be out in the air.

How to evacuate the wounded? Road out of Herrlisheim parallels the railroad embankment under direct fire. I ask for light tanks but I'm told they will form our reserve. I see jeeps and thin-skinned ambulances loaded with wounded running a gauntlet of direct fire. The canal-riverine network looks formidable. There are only a few bridging sites and it seems logical that the Germans will have them under fire. I tell the operations officer my doubts. Look at the open flank. The Krauts can slice us off. Look at all the bridges; what if they're blown and destroyed? Why don't we attack from the south with no bridges and both flanks tied down and not worry about communications?

Condescension; reassuring hand on shoulder; advice to concentrate on the wounded and let the experts worry about the tactics. I stare at the map some more and refuse to be reassured.

A thought about the experts who ran Passchendaele in 1916 flits through my mind.

January 4, ten A.M. : Sun bright on snow. Everything seems possible, plausible, even exciting as we roll through the town of Bettweiler, headquarters of CCB for the attack. Past housefronts of pink and blue, past half-timbers and gables, past Der Gasthaus der drei Engeln, past Le Brasserie de l'Ange d'Or, through cobbled streets of improbable picturesqueness, we rumble and snort. Our long tank guns, our thickets of bayonets seem oddly appropriate in this ancient bloodied land in a way they would not in the world of hamburger stands and used-car signs. CP in an old stone building with thick walls; great protection against artillery. It was formerly an insane asylum.

Out on the edge of town, watching the infantry deploy for the attack, I look east across a plain of incredible flatness, where a gun fired horizontally would carry to infinity. Higher, from the top of my ambulance, I look toward the Rhine along lines of trees and hedges that foreshorten themselves swiftly into squares and parallelograms, everything glinting with a tracery of canals and rivers, all deep, swift flowing, barriers to wheels and tracks.

The Moder flows east and west here. Our infantrymen deploy to the north, across a wide, snowy field, advancing toward Rohrwiller, assembly point for the attack. A kind of beauty, I think, watching; an army with banners, the age-old Homeric grace of armed men. Clusters of men dismounting thin to left and right until they are lines of dots across snowy fields, the moving shapes emphasized and distorted by bayoneted rifles, automatic weapons, dangling grenades; I hear shouts from under helmets; I watch men waving, gesticulating, forming lines; I am seeing a strong, slow ballet with the dangerous appeal of violent history. I meet the infantry battalion medics with their half-tracks and jeeps. We drive along a road to the right of the infantry between the advancing men and the river, the Moder, to the right, deep, swift. No activity ahead; we fancy ourselves daring fellows and go belting along the road actually ahead of the infantry, waving and yelling, Red Cross flags fluttering, with the exhilaration of an army advancing on the enemy, still unhurt, banners intact, caught up in the sense of invincible power. Rohrwiller, the actual starting point of the attack, lies a quarter mile ahead, lovely, pink, white, blue, a cluster of gems edged with poplars, a travel-poster kind of village. At the entrance to the town the air suddenly erupts with time fire; slamming flashing suns with rings of dirty smoke, the explosions march toward us.

Heroic silly season ends abruptly; we stop; straining Red Cross flags are still. We confer, decide to follow the infantry across the field, find areas behind the village dead to shelling, look for a thick stone house. Those few thousand Volksturm suddenly seem to have a lot of artillery.

January 4, noon: Air at command post calm, confident, where our division general and colonel nod helmeted heads above maps, discuss numbers of prisoners to be taken. Everything cool, professional, organized.

Three P.M.: Ambulance loading post. The first casualties are coming back, soldiers groaning and babbling their glimpse of the battle, their particular facet of a fly's mosaic eye. "We went past this town and we were near some buildings and a lot of artillery come down on us."

"I hit the ditch next to the road and I felt this thing hit my ass and I couldn't walk."

A panicked white and blood-colored youngster keeps clutching my field jacket, babbling, "Am I gonna die, Doc? Am I gonna die?"

Since his abdomen is torn with shell fragments, the odds are very good that he will; we get him out fast.

Three-thirty P.M.: Command post. General departed, likewise optimism. Air tense, faces gray; radios crackle confusion; patrol reports bridge in — wrong bridge. Key bridges are out; river deep, swift, infantry teetering across planks, no way for tanks to follow. Heavy shelling, more casualties.

Captain Bowes of C Company wounded; Doc Zimmerman of infantry wounded. I volunteer to go after Bowes, check on Zimmerman, drive along the same road by the river, realize as I go that it bulges out toward the Germans. Nothing between us and them but river and snow; hope the ambulance looks a lot like an ambulance.

Road through Rohrwiller flashing with mortar and artillery fire; I bum a ride in the command tank of the infantry battalion commander. We learn that Bowes has been evacuated and the ride turns into a reconnaissance out toward the Germans across the snow. Explosions close around; the tank rocks; everyone closes hatches except me, and I am leaning out experimenting with the hatch release because I don't know about the new model, actually trying to see which way the steel turns while the loud, shattering bursts and cordite smell edge me toward panic. Gunner leans across, slams hatch. Beautiful clanging as steel closes over my head and shell fragments claw across armor. High explosives and mortars will only make our ears ring; I pray nobody out there has an eighty-eight.

Colonel shouts questions into the radio.

"Baker Company? Where are you? Phase line I? What? Not? Well then where? Where from me? Can you see me?"

The answers aren't what they should be: the colonel shakes his head and mutters.

"Charley Company? Sunray One, come in Sunray One...."

This is a command tank with extra headphones. I put on a set and hear the battalion network. Squawks and screeches predominate: voices are rattly, far, occasionally coherent.

Someone is calling for the weapons platoon. There's no answer, but the caller keeps trying, rising to exasperation.

Another squawk tells of artillery fire. "I can't get my men to the fucking phase line because they're taking cover. Shelling."

People begin to shout personal names in what sounds like frustration; the colonel gets on the net, shouts about procedure. More squawks, more buzzing.

"Sunray Six, what are you guys firing at?"

"Bunch of fucking Germans, over by those trees."

"Not our guys? I say again, not shooting our guys?"

The network explodes with a shout of "Shit!"

The colonel exhales, gives the driver directions.

We circle, followed by explosions, around where the attack is supposed to be. No attack. View through periscope of drifting smoke, snow, weeds, running dots of figures. Illumination in a tank turret: vision of modern war: no ranks and drums, no bayonets of the man behind making a man move forward; only sudden, shattering loneliness of men dumped in the enemy's face, men until minutes before controlled by godlike figures who fed, drilled, clothed them, moved them to the edge of danger and then left. Godlike figures suddenly shrunken to tiny voices, electronic dwarfs calling from the other side of the universe.

In this particular battle, the gods are not only shriveled; it seems the gods didn't know what the hell they were talking about. Decisions now up to lieutenants, sergeants, privates, organizing confusion, calling for artillery fire, siting machine guns, building defenses. No bridge, no mass tank attack, no disorganized German home guard running away, instead, determined German infantry attacking hard out of mist and snow. Our men hunker in the snow, shoot at blurs. The battlefield has stepped in and is shaping the battalion's actions; colonels and generals may as well bay their orders to the moon. The mosaic of the fly's eye is seeing the truth.

Back across the field and down the road to town; infantry crouching, running along ditches, explosions follow us awhile, then give up.

Five P.M.: I thank colonel for a lovely ride, look up the infantry aid station in stone farmhouse. Zimmerman, the battalion surgeon, limping about, bandage on knee. "Little bitty bastard didn't hardly hurt." He says fuck it to the idea of going back; for chrissakes, he might have to do paperwork. He's exhilarated, almost manic, puts his face in mine and grins. He's been hit, the thing we all dread, and it didn't hurt much and he's alive and not scared. He's drunk with courage. Images rage while Zimmerman laughs at his won blood; Hotspur plucking bright honor from the pale-faced moon, Hamlet setting his life at a pin's fee, profound Shakespearean truths living and breathing before me for the first time. I happen to know that Zimmerman signed two waivers of disability to get into combat service when he could easily have stayed at home or been assigned to something safe in the rear. I realize as he talks the difference between being brave and being fearless: brave men can suffer fear but the point is that they continue to function. Bravery is a chronic state, a life-long characteristic; the intoxication of utter fearlessness, by contrast, is something no one can sustain for long, but it's an illumination to see it while it's happening. I don't have the heart to order him back; rather, here in the cold, snowy farmhouse I commend to my patron saint the long and happy life of Randolph Zimmerman.

Six P.M.: Command post. What I saw from the colonel's tank is the hottest news in the CP. Fog of battle; attack floundering into the dark, much artillery, many casualties; battalion will hold in place and defend. Everyone dazed by failure of events to unfold; progress running backward.

"It's the goddamn bridge." The operations officer speaks. "Moder and Zorn are goddamn deep rivers. We need bridges. Important bridges are out."

And what, I muse, was I trying to tell everyone the night before? Not much satisfaction being right.

Nine P.M.: Infantry aid station. Spending the night here in case Zimmerman's wound gets to bothering him; we share a feather bed.

January 5, six A.M.: A peculiar night, heavy firing from out at the mill, three hundred yards away, automatic weapons, German and American, occasional blasts of cannon fire. Zimmerman snores, dammit. New discovery! I can sleep through all the shooting in the world but the rich, wet crescendo of Zimmerman's snoring keeps me jumping awake.

Through the night, infantry officers wander in and out, faces white and cold shining in lantern light. From frosty ovals we learn that what took place this afternoon was a meeting engagement, an unexpected collision of advancing forces.

"You want the maximum fucked-up fog of war, that's how you get it," a grateful company commander mumbles through a cup of hot chocolate. "Dark, they pulled back, we dug in. Now we've got a line, organized, wired in. In those buildings around the mill, out along the canal. Pretty solid.''

Zimmerman and I exhale relief. The German army's only three hundred yards away and there are, we now know, SS troops out there. A wandering patrol of Hitler's Worst would think nothing of lobbing a grenade into an aid station, red cross or not.

As the captain turns to go, another officer hurries in, a lieutenant platoon leader with a sprained ankle. He's a replacement, new to the battalion, and he speaks with that air of explosive, barely contained excitement that we all know means he's frightened.

As we inject novocaine and apply tape, the lieutenant talks to the captain, holding him by the arm, insisting on being heard.

''Attack. That attack, in the morning. Not just us over the footbridge. Not without tanks ...''

The captain obviously recognizes the symptoms. He speaks calmly, steadily.

''Of course, tanks. There's a Bailey bridge coming : it'll be in tonight or in the morning. We'll go in with the whole tank battalion.''

''God, naked infantry across that canal, no tanks or AT guns ...''

The captain applies a level of sternness.

''They'd get creamed and the command knows it. We don't have a bunch of idiots running things. Get on out to your platoon. Check the wires, make sure all the phones are working. See that there's flares. Rotate your men sleeping. ...''

The lieutenant nods with each command. He limps out, controlled, directed, calmed.

Finally, near dawn, we hear an uproar of deafening firing, slamming, popping from out at the mill, then a rush of our own artillery shells coming in overhead, slamming of the barrage, dwindling of firing. The wounded come back ; the first man in is yelling loudly, happily, the only laughing wounded man I've ever seen. He whoops like a drunk in a Western saloon, even while we pull together ripped flesh in a thigh. ''I killed a son of a bitch with that son of a bitch.'' He waves his M-1 rifle around ; he won't let it go. "Two years I carried that fucker around and I cleaned it and I drilled with it and I marched with it, and today I got this Kraut right in the ring-sights and I squeezed down and I killed the son of a bitch. I shot him; he fell down; I killed him." His yells rise to hysteria while he pounds the floor with one hand, but he leaves us no doubt that his is a happy hysteria; he is a profoundly happy, fulfilled man. Savage elation, berserk screaming, how many thousands of years have warriors ridden over pain and terror on their wings? Infantrymen spend most of our war being ground up or burned by long-range machines; simple pleasure of killing an enemy rarely experienced; heady stuff.

Uproar of last night is finally explained: it seems there was a heavy German counterattack with tanks three hundred yards from us. Someone knocked out a tank with a bazooka, and our lines, scattered, held more by luck than skill. Desperate chance courage of some half-frozen men stood between us and death or capture while we snored in our feather bed. The human condition? Are we all lumpen, snoring away while a few heroes save us from starvation or disease, death by fire, death by water?

Eight A.M.: Combat command CP. Good news. Bailey bridge on the way after every conceivable disaster: trucks off mountains in Vosges; equipment lost in snowdrifts. Bridge should get here this morning; a relieved excitement, much shoulder-slapping, everybody pictures the tanks rolling in a coordinated attack, infantry riding on tank decks, guns blasting.... Colonel asks me about casualties, genuinely shocked to hear numbers. (Medical facts of life: five percent casualties per day, battalion gone in twenty days; ten percent casualties per day, battalion gone in ten days. Line officers usually do a progress from stunned disbelief through grudging conviction to an irrational tendency to blame the casualties on the medics who report them.)

Nine-thirty A.M.: Bad news. Division G-3 and chief of staff closeted with colonel. Raised voices through doors and three grim, clenched faces emerge. Colonel salutes them out, calls us together, sends runners to infantry tank battalion commanders. We listen, disbelieving, as he tells us division is still convinced we face a handful of home guards. We are to attack, now, this morning, without waiting for tanks. Corps headquarters is fuming. General X concerned about his relations with army. Personalities involved.

Silence. Finally someone points out we're sending seven hundred–odd infantrymen against some thousands of Germans who have tanks and self-propelled guns. Our tanks are stuck on our side of the river waiting for a bridge that may not be put in for hours, maybe all day. What's going to happen to our men when they get run over by German tanks in the snow? Bazookas? Grenades? What's the hurry about the damn bridgehead anyway? We have the Germans locked in; they're not going anywhere. The plains here are a shooting gallery; whichever side sticks its neck out gets shot up. We could just sit here, dug in: let the Germans beat their brains out against our positions.

The colonel puts on his harassed-into-a-corner face; mouth closes, a trap; his voice becomes brittle; the parade ground is with us. West Point visor clangs down, reasoning human disappears within. We have our orders; higher headquarters has a better grasp than we have. No further questions. Phase line I. Phase line II. Column of companies. Mortar fire, artillery support, tank fire from across river. The bridge will be here shortly, we can count on it. (The colonel is talking pure drivel and he knows it and we know it, committing a stupidity that may be a disaster, driven to it by some bitchiness in a corps headquarters.) We file out, praying for a miracle.

Eleven-thirty A.M.: Infantry aid station. Attack going on across fields to Herrlisheim through fog, searchlight fingers of sunlight gold on serried thundering explosions enveloping our infantry. Flickering gun flashes along high road embankment; men running, disappearing, bobbing. Fog closes down. We go back to the aid station and wait: in half an hour the first casualties come back and in minutes the aid station is jammed; Zimmerman and I work frantically, sending casualties back to rear aid station to let us work on badly wounded. Must be a meat grinder out there; incredible number of casualties from B Company leading the attack. (Later I learn half of B Company has been killed or wounded crossing the plain.) The British taught the Scots a

tactical lesson at Culloden Moor, Napoleon taught the Russians the
same lesson at Friedland; the lesson is as old as firepower: don't
advance with a flank open to enfilading fire — and for God's sake,
here we are doing it. . . .

One P.M.: We make a swift run to the mill to pick up wounded
and we see the last of the infantry moving out through mortar
and artillery fire. Men run doubled over; explosion shatters a
squad a few yards from the mill; six screaming bloody remnants
sprawl on the snow. I watch the faces of men crouching to start
their run and realize why they look different from any other
faces. It's the eyes: they're either narrow, painful slits or wide,
staring, frantic; never a normal simple forward gaze. Squads,
platoons run doubled up, tinkling, clanging, into eruptions of
flame and smoke. The officers are yelling meaningless commands
to carry rifles at the port, anything to give the men a sense of
ritual, of order, a sense that the terror they're charging into is
the accustomed, the proper, the appropriate. Go, go, go, the officers scream. The men run.

Three P.M.: Infantry companies have disappeared into fog and
noise; radio contact gone; sudden quiet in aid station after last
of bloody groaning burdens loaded into ambulances. I head back
to combat command and here, for chrissakes, at disastrous long
last, comes the Bailey bridge, monstrous out of mist. Colonel of
the tank battalion literally dancing up and down at the edge of
Bettweiler, ignoring shouted excuses of white-faced captain who
leans out of truck to itemize catastrophes. *Get that fucking bridge
in.* The colonel can't hear anything but his own frantic need.

Five P.M.: Command post. Desperate, our engineers are fighting
failing light and time fire to get the bridge in; heavy casualties.
The Krauts know exactly where the bridge has to go, and they
drop shells down the engineers' necks. Our colonel's face is a
study in molded rigidity as he watches the worst happen. Slowly
but inevitably the mistake of judgment squeezes a bloody hand
on our infantrymen: no bridge today; they're trapped in that
village without armor or antitank protection.

Eight P.M.: Dark. Tanks won't get in tonight. I drive up the
canal road to Bettweiler, stand with the infantry medics looking

across the half-mile to Herrlisheim. The fog is glowing; Herrlisheim's burning. In clear spaces between snow squalls we can
see tracers as they spurt, flung sparks dwindling up into the dark.
Radiomen in infantry battalion headquarters fiddle knobs desperately; no contact. A scant half-mile separates us from the
infantry; they might as well be on the moon; total electronic
collapse; we'd do better with tom-toms.

Ten P.M.: No wounded coming out. We sit in the farmhouse
aid station wondering. Any infantry left between us and the
Germans? Any of the battalion left alive?

Eleven-thirty P.M.: A patrol goes out to try to meet the men
in Herrlisheim, sees a German patrol silhouetted against the burning town, kills them all except one, brings the survivor back for
questioning. The prisoner stands at attention in the battalion
command post, young, frightened, talkative; he tells us the same
story he told the patrol: all our men in the town are dead or
captured. The Germans counterattacked in the dark, and the
Amis are wiped out. From his pockets we fish American chocolate
bars that he claims he took from some of our dead. His story
can't be entirely true, for we still hear firing and see tracers, but
it is unnerving, in a sense of the word I never thought of before,
to hear this enemy soldier calmly telling us our men have been
slaughtered.

January 6, one A.M.: Combat command CP; radios are chattering, phones are ringing, messengers from division are in and
out. Cooper's repeating the German's story to the colonel, but
back here it seems less convincing. The colonel's surrounded by
order and process and he's clearly having a hard time believing
that all that official planning and clanking machinery could be
scattered, dead, wounded, destroyed: all that organized profes-
sionalism couldn't be blown into bloody shreds. It isn't reasonable.

"What about our own scouts?"

"They're sure there are still Americans fighting in there. They
can hear our machine guns."

"Never believe the first rumors, good or bad." The colonel is talking to himself. "That's true but it's hard to apply it in a battle."

He tilts his head and looks at us in a way that defines us as strangers. We leave him but stay near enough to be useful.

Nobody talks to the colonel. He doesn't invite conversation and what the hell is there to say? He stands with fingers tapping between reports from the bridge site, staring at the map, at the disaster he was ordered to order. Everybody concentrates on the bridge now; officers are in and out with reports of progress and delays. Through the night the engineers fight snow and shelling, and reports keep coming in of maddening accidents, of parts lost in the dark, of more wounded. I look at a clock on the colonel's field desk and can almost hear it jeering as it pronounces ticks, pushing us through the darkness toward the dangerous light when the Germans can drop shells on the engineers with the accuracy of marksmen on the range.

Four-thirty P.M.: A wild and wavering day: tanks got into Herrlisheim under smoke at dawn. Our infantry had been fighting off Germans all night, at first wouldn't come out of cellars and holes; precious hours wasted. Attack to the rest of Herrlisheim, launched after noon into smothering artillery and small arms, went nowhere. Wounded hauled out on light tanks were often wounded again or killed during the run past that railroad embankment right under the muzzles of the dug-in guns. Artillery barrages came down on us in thunders, with an intensity unimaginable, indescribable, large-caliber shells bursting with density of massed machine-gun fire. Lying on the floor, feeling the aid-station building rock under a torrent of high-caliber explosions, waiting for a white-hot fragment to hit and tear, I automatically put my helmet over my crotch; so, I noted, did everybody else.

Five P.M.: Infantry aid station. Thoughts after two hours of frantic work, sitting still now, staring at bloody hands. The wounded are instruments, singing pain. A monster strums steel claws across them; this is a general-monster, with three stars on its shoulders. It loves consistency and order; and it clacks its beak and nods its head in time, happy, approving, as the proper resonances of agony fill the room, each man tuned by the pegs of childhood and culture, by heroes and scoldings and shaming, each with his own fixed pitch of despair or fear.

The claws pluck, testing, one string at a time. Highest pitch, tenor, E-string, the Germans. Germans always scream; surprising, considering Germans. Listen to this youngster while we pull his shattered femur back in line; masses of bloody splinters, the bone ends sink back through skin as we tighten traction.

AAAIII. MUTTIMUTTIMUTTImuttimuttimuttimuttimutti- muttimutti. AAAAHHHHH. Note diminuendo with final hoarse shudder in larynx. Very consistent. Multiply him by ten, keep them all screaming.

Middle register, Americans, cowboys all; men don't scream or cry; grunting, groaning, swearing, all the fashion. Pain fantastic, grunts and groans of intensity unimaginable.

AAAAHUHHUHHH, Jeeeeesus, GOD GOD, OOooooh, AAAAAHUHHUHHUHHUH; hands move feebly, incredulously over shreds of abdomens holding entrails, red caves where faces were. Note broad middle range from shrills of screaming to throaty snarls.

Wind section: universal, pancultural, noted in men too weak, breathing too fast to form words, only with each windy exhalation, oooosssshhhhooooohhh, conveying all the meaning they are capable of; how can anything hurt like this; how can part of me be torn away like this, the inward breath short, aahh, a quick gasp for air, the outward breath oooosssshhhh, the only intelligible sound these man can frame. Words couldn't do it even if they could talk.

Base and rhythm section, lowest pitch: subhuman sounds, bubbling of blood in air through torn chests, feral exhalations of the dying.

Chords signaling end of each movement, the steel clash of the half-track step, intolerable, with the next burden.

Finale: when sounds have quieted a little with morphine and splinting for some and death for others, shellbursts make the walls dance and send flakes of ceiling down; sounds rise again, edged now with terror, screaming of seagulls, grunting of bears, squealing of spitted rabbits, the last defenses of brave men ripped away, all down to the simple crying of terrified children: "Oh God, Doc, don't let them hurt me any more." "Jesus, I can't take any more." "Don't let them, don't let them." Men whose courage carried them past terror and pain have in this world of kindness and care let down their defenses briefly; now they find themselves totally helpless, crying, clinging, agonized, bleeding children, pitifully dependent on us, their physicians, and we're responsible for them; we are supposed to keep harm from them; and we can stop their bleeding and their pain some of the time, but we can't stop this dark, roaring insanity that keeps hunting them down to inflict pain on pain, an insanity that won't give up even when they're whimpering remnants on litters, and a voice inside my head is screaming stop, stop you fucking lunatics, for Christ's sake and the world's sake stop!

Six P.M.: I have just let out the longest breath of my life. Colonel Phelan, commander of the tank battalion, was wounded in Herrlisheim; would I go after him? Not really my job; there are two tank battalion surgeons, but I seem morally obligated. There are large chunks of ice in my gut as I stow gear in the ambulance and prepare for the run under the muzzles of the German guns, trusting to the Red Cross flag. At the top of the aid-station stairs I hear the S-3 call to me that division has ordered a retreat; hold everything; the battalion is coming out tonight, carrying the wounded on tanks. ExHALE!

Ten P.M.: Out with ambulances to meet retreating men; staff officer is giggling, half hysterical, won't give me rational answers, sends us to the wrong place. In the dark we hear calls, swearing from across the Moder. Recriminations, excuses, slipping and sliding on snow and ice; we meet the first wounded finally and load them into ambulances. Men keep materializing out of fog, white with snow, exhausted, matted with blood, hanging on to each other's ammunition belts in flashing darkness, stumbling out, walled off by a rippling, thundering box barrage. The battalion comes out, what is left of it, carrying its wounded, carrying its weapons, staggering, but still charged with purpose, still fighting.

Tank battalion aid station. Colonel Phelan, thigh shattered, talks quietly; he describes the same overwhelming artillery fire we caught in Rohrwiller. "They smothered us; it'll take a regiment of infantry to crack that place." He drifts off under morphine.

A young paratroop lieutenant, a replacement in our infantry battalion, slightly wounded, talks with an eagerness that sounds artificial. "Cowboys and Indians." His voice is cultivated, educated, slightly pretentious. "We were playing cops and robbers, for chrissakes, it was ridiculous. Here I was sneaking along the street, cracking down on Germans like kids playing bang-bang-you're-dead. Ridiculous! I saw this German and he saw me and we both shot except I shot first and he fell over. Play-acting, except he was dead." The lieutenant's manner is unconvincing, glib, bright; he sounds like a cocktail party, but he was, I found later, entirely genuine. Chuck Willis became my friend; as he sat in the aid station while I bound a minor wound we compared notes about Chicago, and he rattled on about his only living relative in the world, a rich uncle there. Everything Chuck Willis said in his party voice we all learned was absolutely reliable; he was the most fearless, deadly fighter in the battalion.

January 7, two A.M.: Official communiqué: "The battalion retreated and dug in on defensive positions." Jesus Christ, the insane meaninglessness of words. Just back from the line out by the mill. A hundred-odd men, the unwounded survivors, were all ready to march back to warmth and food, to keep going all the way to Milwaukee or Pittsburgh, Harry's Bar, or Aunt Sally's fried chicken; they had to be turned around forcibly in some cases and led to where they were to dig in through deep snow into frozen ground. The men are half starved, crazy for lack of sleep. Their shovels make a pathetic clinking against the ice. No shelling, thank God. Headquarters company comes out carrying sleeping bags, C rations, K rations. The infantrymen stuff the half-frozen food in their mouths, take turns hunkering in sleeping bags and shivering while comrades dig. Battalion command is disorganized; twice during the night the men are ordered to move elsewhere, dig new positions. Finally they give up everything, huddle in sleeping bags, shivering, exhausted, numb, asleep.

Verbatim conversation on the line:

SHIVERING PRIVATE (to his sergeant): ''Can't do no more, Sarge. I'm gonna get the hell out of here. I'm just gonna start walking back. What the hell will they do — put me in the stockade? They can't do nothing worse than this.''

SERGEANT: ''They can't do nothing worse? They just shot that guy, they'll shoot you. Dig your fuckin' hole. At least you're out of that goddamn town. You ain't surrounded. Tomorrow they'll bring up some hot chow.''

(Willy Slovic had been executed for refusal to fight, on our front, the Seventh Army front, a month before. His execution was reported in a two-paragraph item on the back page of the Seventh Army *Stars & Stripes,* but every soldier in Seventh Army knew about the man who had been ''done to death by musketry.'')

January 7: Sunny, thank God. Temperature up near freezing. Men rotate off the line for hot food and a night's sleep in a rest center we organize at the rear aid station. Talking to these men is an exercise in the incongruous; soldiers who have been on the other side of Homer, deep into a nightmare world of flame and sudden death most people can't even imagine, are suddenly pathetically ordinary.

''Remember the sore knee I had all the trouble with in Texas, Doc? Still hurts, right here,'' and all the man's attention is genuinely centered on his chronic sore knee.

Those who live, I think, will go back to grocery stores and assembly lines and dumpy wives and mortgages, and the Viking rage and the Scythian shriek will become unimaginable, something they can never communicate, something they can't really remember, something to recall only in troubled dreams.

January 10. Three days after the retreat: I haven't been able to write about what's happening until today. Must try....

Love conquers all, including us. Corps commander has a pas-

sionate affair going with his ego, will sacrifice any number of
lumpen soldiers to sustain it. Ego stakes all on original estimate
of our opposition — contemptible, a few thousand home guard —
and when reconnaissance and intelligence reports describe masses
of well-trained German infantry with tanks and guns, specifying
units, ego pouts prettily, hands over ears. Nothing gets in.

Ego is also murderous: after our frozen remnants stagger out
of Herrlisheim it gives them a generous twelve hours' rest and
orders them forward again: for three days the attacks go on, our
dwindling hundreds marching through a meat grinder of flying
steel to attack some thousands of Germans. None of the attacks
gets as far as Herrlisheim, wounded pour through our aid stations
in a bloody gasping stream; corpses stiffen in the snow.

Incident of the battle: January 11, afternoon, the aid station.

Training tells; the SS trooper is a dedicated, consistent swine,
even with his right hand blown off at the wrist. Has he had a
shot? Snarl, contempt. Does he hurt? Does he need help? Snarl,
grunt, glare. He'd spit in my eye if he wasn't supine. Fuck you,
Herman, we mutter, and we ship him off, bandaged. Half an hour
later Zimmerman and an aid man come in. Zimmerman screaming, carrying a Red Cross flag and a pistol. Where's the bastard
with one hand? Zimmerman's going to stuff the Red Cross flag
down his throat and strangle him, so help him God. Pico's dead
is why, and that prick murdered him. Not combat, not an accident,
murder. Pico, I breathe, not Pico, and they tell me yes and describe the killing.

The aid man was crouching in a ditch with Pico, a hundred
feet from a wounded man who was lying in the snow, his belly
all torn with machine-gun fire, crying. That was the worst, I hear.
This guy wasn't screaming or groaning or swearing, he was crying
oh huh huh huh, like a little kid hurt, his hands all red from
holding over the blood running out of his belly. He kept calling
for someone to help him. Isn't anybody going to take care of me?
he was saying, quite clearly, and then he'd cry.

Pico finally told the other aid man he couldn't stand it. The
machine gun was still firing random long bursts, but Pico said

that it was worse listening to that guy than maybe getting shot and, anyway, it was bright sunlight on snow, and anyone could see the red crosses on his helmet. He grabbed a Red Cross flag and ran out across the snow waving it. There was no mistaking what he was doing. He was kneeling by the wounded man; he had just given him a shot and was putting on a dressing when the machine gun cut him in two. The German was clearly having a lot of fun because he kept on firing long bursts into the wounded man and into Pico, keeping the bodies jumping and spreading red all over the snow. He'd used the wounded man for bait, an old SS trick.

All that time one of our patrols had been crawling up a gully, and they threw in a grenade; the German tried to throw it back but it went off in his hand. Why the hell had they saved him? The aid man hesitates — it was kind of automatic, you see a wounded guy, you know . . . He's embarrassed.

Riding back to the forward aid station Zimmerman and I talk about Pico. It's our memorial service. We agree you couldn't tell who Pico was by looking at him or hearing him. The dark squarish outside and the West Side New York accent were wrapped around a small Vesuvius; he erupted only on call. In training, his absolute lack of military tact made problems; we hid him when inspectors came around, but on maneuvers, when a truck and a tank were wrecked on a mountainside with men trapped deep in gasoline fumes, Pico had charged into a prospective holocaust, swearing, hauling, leading, saving, with a couple of gasps to spare before the vapors exploded. That was one instance, often repeated. Even before we left the States it was accepted that Pico's real physiology emerged in time of terror. Disasters released a strange happy violence in Pico: he plunged into them like an otter into cataracts.

On Hill 609, on the German border, when the Krauts were shelling hell out of our infantry, Pico was the first to sprint from behind the pile of frozen turnips where we were sheltering, running to every call for medics through flashes and smoke. Other men followed, dragging and carrying, but Pico was in charge of that exploding hilltop, running in his inner spell of invulnerability and an inhuman lack of fear that went with it, a tarn-cloak he put on when death or dismemberment were close.

That had happened so consistently we took it for granted, like his name. Now Pico and the cloak had been torn into bloody shreds by the subhuman grunter I'd sent to the loving care of an American hospital.

Shit, we said our prayers, goddamn, shit.

Would you really have killed that guy?

Thought from Zimmerman, then, yes, he was quite sure he would.

I wouldn't have stopped you either. War's war and murder's murder, and the more I see of war the more I know there's a difference. You hear civilians, who've never seen blood, yapping about total war, how logical it is. Kill everybody. Well, total war's a crime and the guy who thought it up is a goddamn criminal against the last definition of the word *human*, against a place that is really sacred, that we hold inside ourselves, away from the killing we all do because someone tells us we're supposed to.

Seems bizarre to worry about people killing unarmed medics when bombers are blowing whole cities to pieces, but even at the bottom of the night some idea of a code of human behavior, some sense of caring for sick and wounded and helpless, some feeling of man for man not dictated by utility or advantage or generals, is sacred, to be cherished, something to keep us from sinking into a fanged past.

January 11, third day of attacks: Men walking out holding up their hands, praying out loud to be hit in the hands or arms instead of in the chest or belly; wounded are hysterical with exhaustion or pain. One man, horribly wounded in the genitals, is simply giggling in sustained, agonizing bursts while blood drips through the hands he has cupped over his crotch.

I look up to see the colonel, standing behind me, staring at the wounded man, his eyes all a wonder and a deep surmise, the well-worn steely glint of command washed away, the feeling, thinking human painfully exposed, raw. He asks me some questions about the number of casualties, walks away silent.

Four P.M., infantry forward aid station: Yes, Virginia, dybbuks do happen. In Rohrwiller's main street in the last hour.

Antidisestablishmentarianism used to be the longest word in the language; Larisch, tough, small New Yorker, aid man in the infantry, just improved on it.

"Lookatthefuckin'brassinthefuckin'streetdon'tthemdumbbastardsknowaboutthemortars?" Bug eyes, spoon waving out the window, he communicated this miracle of compression around a mouthful of Quartermaster's Revenge.

Outside in Rohrwiller's main street all the brass in the world, division general, his staff, our colonel, some of our staff, two colonels from corps; stars, eagles, shiny boots, glowing scarves; division and corps types immaculate, preening, pompous. Napoleon at Wagram, give or take a few plumes.

They have the serenity of men who have never been shot at; clearly they don't anticipate upcoming mortars, staff-personnelwise. We smile nasty at each other; who are we to upset them?

I run across the street, shelter behind a light colonel, listen. Division general is telling our colonel what our combat command *will do. It will* take Herrlisheim today, hold it while the rest of the division comes through the passes. Staff nods, knowledgeable, marks things on map covers. Where they'll go, they say to each other, what they'll do.

Our colonel speaks with weary patience, with the force of a man spending his last strength: We're sending a few hundred infantry against thousands of Germans, he says, obviously for the hundredth time. Murder. No. The general barks yes, the colonel barks no; Ping-Pong begins, ends only when the general turns red and bellows. (Popular military myth: Turning red and bellowing, great way to make things happen.)

He guesses Charlie doesn't realize it, says the general, but he, general, is giving him, Charlie, a direct order. Attack Herrlisheim. That is a direct order.

(Service academy ethology: Direct order awesome towering ultimate force, never questioned; recipient of direct order is supposed to impale himself, order waves of men into furnaces, do absobloodylutely anything.)

The general waits for tense yessir, snap of salute. Not today, by God, not today! Today we have metamorphosis!

Before my astonished and delighted eyes, Colonel Charlie is taken over by a dybbuk; the ghost of his real self, long years ago buried under the sod of West Point, suddenly released, back in human habitation, happy, assured, delighted to be itself.

The dybbuk speaks with relaxed, commanding composure of one who does not give a flaming damn about any authority anywhere, as one cast in comfortable bronze after final, irrevocable moral commitment. Dybbuk explains to stunned brass the stupidity of attacking, when we can dig in on strong defensive lines, let the Germans shred themselves on our machine guns, artillery, and tank fire; let our air bomb them whenever the skies are clear, let the Germans go broke supplying this ridiculous bridgehead across a broad river. No terrain, says dybbuk, of the slightest military value in the damn thing. Their Passchendaele, not ours. Dybbuk concludes by assuring the general that he understood the direct order but that he, Dybbuk Charlie, had to refuse to obey it. End of discussion.

The general seems to shake himself; he has been under the spell of logic, of convincing heresy. With corps officers looking over his shoulder he finds refuge in a stereotype. Firmly, albeit kindly, he tells Charlie he is formally relieved of command. He is sure that Charlie is tired; he is not thinking clearly; he'll ask him to come up to division headquarters to help out for a while. A new commander will be arranged for this afternoon, should be on hand tonight. I sprint for the aid station with the news.

As I bang in the door, everyone has just hit the floor with the whistle of the first mortar shell. Larisch is still at the window, fascinated. He screams, joyful.

"Look at them asses! Look at that collection of self-propelled asses!"

I follow his gaze; final metamorphosis, brasses to asses. Domed, propelled at incredible speed by twinkling legs, the foreparts of the creatures bent almost to sweep the ground, the stars and eagles are a collection of dwindling behinds, crabs, ragged claws scuttling before the impersonal, flesh-hungry blast of the mortars.

Twelve midnight: the command post. The colonel's back is what I will always remember: he didn't turn around when he lifted a hand to us, leaving.

We hold heartfelt salutes while the small figure in the jeep dwindles into snow and dark. Stay with him, Dybbuk; animate him in a world where pity or love, ideals or altruism, are suspect, vices, not admissible as motives, where advantage is the pole star to men's acts.

January 12: Well, hell. I want to stop writing in this stupid journal. I want to write something funny. I want to write an episode from Saki about exquisite Edwardians being side-splittingly bitchy to each other: "You're looking much better than usual today, dear, but then, that's so easy for you to do...."

I want to write about lovers meeting in a winter twilight by the statue in front of the Plaza, while the city glitters about them, towers of jewels of affectionate light....

I want to see or hear or feel something — anything — trivial or amusing; one witty sarcasm would do. Aren't soldiers supposed to be funny? They always are in books or movies, like Mauldin's cartoon of Joe and Willie, hunkered down in an invasion boat, heading into a holocaust while Willie mutters, "Try to say something funny, Joe...."

Anyway, tonight is the bottom of the pendulum's arc. It's got to start up from here. Two days ago our new colonel, a decent enough man, with extreme reluctance ordered an attack, using a troop of reconnaissance reinforcing our infantry remnants. He believed what our scouts and patrols told him about enemy strength, but orders were orders. Units strange to each other tried a night attack, shot each other up in a cross fire, fell back to their old foxholes under a steel rain of German artillery.

January 13, six A.M.: Well, sir! Combat Command B wishes to thank their Oberkommando der Wehrmacht for rescuing its combined sanity. Thank you, Hans, Lothar, Manfried, and everybody. We had just about convinced ourselves that this enemy, this German army we have beaten the ass off a lot of times before, was suddenly some kind of monster, invincible. We were in the process of defeating ourselves (which, when you think about it, is how people usually get defeated) when, Hi Yo, Silver! Out of the sagebrush the human condition comes riding to the rescue! Universal stupidity! *Der lang erwartete,* der superkolossal fuckup!

At ten P.M. CP radios came to life, screaming about a German attack into Rohrwiller, calling for reserve tanks, medics, artillery fire. Jack and I tear through the town so fast we rock and skid on snow out to the canal road and then spend two hours stuck in a solid mass of tanks and guns moving toward Rohrwiller, watching the town flash at us in silhouettes, trying to judge the battle from orange, white, geographic dots, lines, angles, tracers drawing networks across the night, red pencils of tank fire, hearing comfort in the wickering of our shells high in the dark, friendly fiends erupting in orange, white, red.

Tank radio, after a succession of impersonal commands and responses, suddenly breaks into human noises.

"Jesus Christ," someone is screaming, "we're killing those pricks! Look at 'em lying all over the ground! Look at those bastards running! Get 'em! We're killin' 'em!"

Rebuke from company commander: "Watch your goddamn radio procedure; stick to business, this is a battle." Three of us collapse, laughing hysterically around the bow of a tank: a tank gunner wags his finger under a driver's nose. "That's right, you hear what the captain said? None of this bullshit about dead people, you see? You're fighting a goddamn battle!" The men whoop, pound each other on the back, laugh themselves silly.

Midnight in Rohrwiller. Bedlam, wounded Germans staggering along streets waving handkerchiefs, hands over heads; our men yelling, howling like wild Indians, actually laughing, jeering.

Zimmerman, in an aid station crammed with bloody Germans, stammers of hours of confusion, noise, and ends with the word *victory.* He seems astonished by it; it dangles in the air while we both contemplate it with pleased surprise. In battalion headquarters I hear about Captain X getting hysterical when the attack hit, ranting about everybody getting killed, and Captain Brown of the tanks, on the other hand, walking in, flat cool, handlebar mustache over grin, looking at a map, displaying that rare gift of great soldiers, the gift of using the same unhurried logic in the middle of a thousand-decibel nightmare one might use adding a grocery bill or solving a problem in geometry.

"Shit," he said, "we got 'em," and he stalked out to lead his tanks across the bridge.

Almost a feeling of kinship for the wounded Germans as they lie there cursing their commanders. Somebody in the German high command got the idea the Americans had retreated all the way to the Vosges, sent their infantry marching in columns of fours, rifles slung and radios playing, right into our machine guns.

"Like kids going to school," a German is gasping his anger between mouthfuls of bubbly blood. "All we needed were satchels with books in them — those stupid shits!"

An SS lieutenant is accusing, finger pointing, even while we put traction splints on his shattered legs. "You weren't supposed to be there. Nobody was supposed to be there; we were supposed to occupy your forward positions. There was a mistake."

We collapse again, laughing weakly, barely remembering to hold on to the ends of the poor bastard's legs.

Our machine gunners grin while they tell about the Germans marching, calling and chattering, right into our guns. "Like when our battalion used to march to a VD lecture back in Camp Campbell, for chrissakes." Our men felt funny, they tell me, shooting at people just walking around like that; they looked official, says somebody, as if they ought to be there; it didn't seem legal, another one tells me. Sitting birds...

Two tank officers at dawn over aid-station coffee: "Like we were the U.S. cavalry and they were Indians with bows and arrows; it was really crazy to be inside the machine where the other guy can't possibly hurt you, and then you just sit there and kill him. I mean it really got relaxed. I guess that's how the Krauts felt when they did it to Polish cavalry. By God, it was really fun." The officer's name is Czarnicky; I can't begrudge him his small pleasures.

Second officer, analytically: "When our tank treads were right on the Krauts, you could always tell it; they felt different under the treads than just plain snow; more give, you know.''

Well, I wanted something funny to write about, didn't I?

January 17: Quiet week, shelling, patrols. A few sunlit days, blessed among calendars.

Fun and games at the front.

Games I. We explain to distinguished rear-echelon visitors the difference between incoming and outgoing mail. Shells going out *BOOMwhoooo*, shells coming in *sssssCRASHBANG*. When we point out significance of latter (German artillery searching for the batteries in the woods behind us), imposing visitors lose imposure (word?), remember important appointments ten miles back, go bobbing away on the winds of fear, thistledown, slight men. Keep up the good work, disappearing voices call around corners. Sure, we tell them, the work will be kept up. Very consoling.

Games II. You tell me your dream, or, don't neglect your daily adrenaline.

Now I lay me down to sleep and I know that when I close my eyes I'll see that same colored movie sliding at me, uncontrollable, fast, the road into Rohrwiller screaming under tires, the poplars on either side moving from discrete shapes to a blur of speed and then the awful slowing when we come to the icy spot next to the Moder, right where the German gunners know we'll have to slow, where the German battery is zeroed, and we drive, hunched over, waiting for the slams and flashes that rock the ambulance and dazzle us, and then we speed out from under flying dirt and rocks, skidding the last thirty feet to the stone lee of the aid-station building. We run. The dream is so consistent, so accurate, that the actual daytime run becomes a convincing nightmare; reality goes all blurry around the edges. Nothing more serious than a few holes in the back of the ambulance; great sympathy for ducks in the shooting gallery.

Dream the Second: hallucination? Late afternoon, out on the last foxhole line, on the part of the thumb farthest west, where I haven't been yet, looking across the snow to Herrlisheim.

(Sneaking feeling I'm getting a little crazy. Following my guide, the brave, small reconnaissance captain, Bart, down a road exactly like the road along the Moder, complete with poplars, the dream switched on and I was absolutely convinced German gunners were tracking us on this road, ready to let fly. I got out of my ambulance and walked through the snow to be a smaller target. Shrewd of me, I thought, while Bart stared from his command car wondering why the hell I was plowing through knee-deep snow when I could ride.)

Herrlisheim at the end of converging lines of hedges, fences, small clouds of winter trees, an intricacy of cubes and planes and dying gold, a village by Courbet, lovely, lorn; hard to believe that it's packed full of German tanks, guns, infantry, and sudden death. Looking to right and left, sudden terrifying illumination : main line of resistance of the whole damned United States Army at this point consists of a ragged row of riflemen, machine gunners, BAR men. The line is so thin each man can hardly see the next foxhole. All our tanks and heavy weapons are away on the left flank; here, all we could do in case of attack was bounce thirty-caliber guns off heavy armor and get run over and killed. Hallucination? Waking nightmare? In the twilight I seem to see a ghostly eruption of German tanks, loaded with infantry, gun muzzles winking, shell-fire rolling ahead, tearing our tissue-paper defenses, blowing the command post out of existence, leaving all of us dead or mangled or running for our lives. The vision passes and I stand shivering in the early dark, wondering again about dream and reality. Walking back, I squint at the map; some kind of canal in front of Herrlisheim, but it doesn't look like anything that could stop a panzer division.

Command post: reassuring, condescending, pats on the back when I talk to staff about our naked central front. Uncrossable canal there; leave the tactics to us, Doc. Hope my Cassandra average falls off, but so far I've been dead right.

January 19: Hail, hail, the gang's all here; the whole division came through the mountain passes into the line this morning, launched a coordinated attack on the bridgehead. The attack's been going on a couple of hours, and while we wait for reports I think of Wendling Pinckley *und der Tisch.*

Wendling Pinckley III (he always signs himself like that) is an errand boy from division staff universally known as a prick, by which everyone means a self-serving, pompous dunce. His habit of rolling his eyes to heaven with pained but saintly patience, his labored Harvard Yard weary knowledgeable stare, his Himalayan condescension, make it hard to concentrate on what he's saying, it's so much fun thinking about throttling him.

We keep civil faces, but Wendling finally brings down the house when we state doubts about the division plan to have the Sixty-sixth Infantry clear the Stainwald in one day to cover the right flank of the Seventy-sixth Tank Battalion as the tanks lunge for Herrlisheim. Wendling contemplates the ceiling with the weary-patient performance, then comes out with an answer beyond price, an inanity I shall treasure to cheer me in dark, small hours.

"I can only tell you, gentlemen," His Eminence condescends from the snowy upper reaches of Heaven, "that when the question was raised last night, General Beaky pounded his fist on the table and said, 'By God, the Sixty-sixth Infantry *will clear the Stainwald.*'" Wendling makes a gangling little fist, pops it against the map a couple of times, tries to generate Old Beaky's parade-ground whiskey rasp. "He means business, gentlemen, and you know General Beaky." Knowledgeable, ominous shake of head. We stare. Wendling isn't kidding. He really thinks Old Beaky's pounding maps and acting determined is going to change something in the Stainwald. We launch an instant theater; we portray a couple of comic opera SS *Obergruppenführers* clapping hands to heads and yelling in panic, "*Gott im Himmel,* General Beaky is pounding *der Tisch* about us! Run everybody!" We collapse, laughing hysterically while our new colonel tries to shush us and Wendling stalks off, obviously thinking we're victims of combat fatigue.

Our decimated infantry battalion, we hear, will attack to the railroad in a "holding action." Crummy to get killed in a holding action; if one is going to die, one should die liberating the Holy Sepulchre or defending the last copy of the Bill of Rights.

Evening: Big attack under way. No news yet from the rest of the front, but our infantry put on one hell of a "holding action." Following their great new company commander, Salvo Gagliardo, B Company charged screaming across the bloody field, firing on the run, dropping grenades in the foxholes, ended right up against the railroad, yelling at the Krauts on the other side, lobbing grenades at them, only retreating when the Germans started to flank them because the other companies fell back in front of mortar fire instead of charging through it, leaving the men of B Company, after a superhuman effort, to fight their way back through cross fire from front and flank. Bad scene at the mill, Salvo screaming obscenities at the officers and men of the other companies, calling them a bunch of fucking cowards, a battalion he'd never fight with again. Worse, the groaned reproaches of wounded men from B Company as we carry them out past men of A and C: "Where were you guys, for chrissakes? We needed you on our right." "You let them Krauts come in on us." "We got all the way out there this time. If you guys would only have kept coming." Exquisitely painful when a wounded man points a bloody hand at a friend from another company, mutters, "Where the fuck was you, Tom?" In most of life love means coming to rely on someone else for detumescence or money or encouragement or company, but in battle friendship (God forbid we should use the word love!) means readiness to be killed or mangled rather than fail the other men in a squad or a battalion; it is a fierceness of love and dedication unknown anywhere else, and a betrayal is a thousand times worse than the agony of a wife learning that a loved, trusted husband has just fornicated off with a secretary. Under lowered helmets, shame, shrugs, muttered excuses, self-loathing.

January 21: two days of fighting. Rumors of a victory, rumors of defeat, rumors of rumors. By evening we learn that from Wendling Pinckley III to disaster is but a step — three steps to be exact.

Step one: Germans in Stainwald, totally unimpressed by Beaky's pounding the table, cut the Sixty-sixth to pieces with storms of cross fire from log bunkers.

Step two: Beaky pounds the table some more, sends tanks right past the Stainwald still full of Germans; 88s in the forest depths shoot holes through snow-silhouetted tanks: plain billows with smoke of their burning; radios horrible with screams of men burning to death.

Step three: Armored infantry charges into Herrlisheim without tanks, gets surrounded by a regiment of SS troops *with* tanks, remnants fight their way back out under the muzzles of tigers.

Absolute bloody total disaster. As dark falls, worse: the whole Forty-third Tank Battalion has disappeared out into the German lines. Last word from the tank commander fading on the radio, "Only thing that could help us is ten thousand doughfeet," then silence. A whole damn tank battalion simply swallowed up in the snow. What the hell's out there, we ask each other, the compleat German army???? This is getting eerie.

Nine P.M. Things getting eerier faster: prisoners beg to be sent to the rear; tomorrow, they swear, comes *der gross Angriff*: the big panzer attack right through here, right through where this headquarters is. They know all about this headquarters and they're coming to get us. Please, they say, remember the Geneva Convention, send us back somewhere. Everyone around here's going to get killed. Wounded prisoners all along the line give the same story: attack early tomorrow afternoon. Word flashes through the battalion; commanders dispose machine guns, plan barrages.

In the command post they're all looking at the old battleground over by the mill, and I talk myself silly — and unpopular — trying to point out the naked front toward Herrlisheim just two thousand yards away. Everyone feels safe behind preconceptions. "Canal there, Doc. Tanks can't swim, you know."

No, I think, but German tigers can wade damn deep, and German engineers can build bridges, and we're just plain naked.

I have a route picked out to get self, crew, and wounded the hell out if German tanks break into town: side entrance into the ambulance, down several strategic streets, into the woods that lead into the Vosges. No use us being blown apart because my colleagues are fatheaded.

Midnight: Our new colonel has left for division headquarters; some air of mystery. Is our colonel coming back? Four of us sitting, talking by candlelight; thump, we hear steps, and slam, the door opens, and there, for the everloving Christ, is our own colonel! We jump up, four of us in a row, stupid, silent. He nods, walks across to the table, plunks down his helmet, dumps his gear. He is clearly back and in command.

He faces us, standing at attention the way we are with the difference that his jaw is shut and ours are hanging open. Silence. We would all like, I suppose, to come out with some military equivalent of "welcome back," but we can't dream how to say it.

The colonel solves our problem.

"Next time," he says, and it sums up a world of agony and frustration, "next time the sons of bitches will listen to me."

Helmet back on, the small, erect figure marches out of the cellar to the command trailer. We whoop. We'll be collectively, happily damned! Somehow the attack seems less threatening.

Morning, January 22: Quiet all morning, jumpy. German artillery flicks explosions along the front. Outposts report half-seen masses in the streets of Herrlisheim, vehicles, columns of men running, disappearing again into ruins. I collar everyone and talk myself hoarse, pointing to the nonexisting line between us and that typhoon swelling to our front. Even our colonel can't really hear me; we mass our tanks on the left flank, on the old battleground; we fancy ourselves secure behind that ridiculous canal. Again the deadly preconception, the excluding preconception: my God, the awful power it has. It can make people blind even to sudden death.

Noon: Air strikes on the way; we watch from a top window as P-47s dip in and out of clouds through suddenly erupting strings of Christmas-tree lights, before one speck turns over and drops toward earth in the damnedest sight of the Second World War, the dive-bomber attack, the speck snarling, screaming, dropping faster than a stone until it's clearly doomed to smash into the earth, then, past the limits of belief, an impossible flattening beyond houses and trees, an upward arch that makes the eyes hurt, and, as the speck hurtles away, *WHOOOM*, the earth erupts five hundred feet up in swirling black smoke. More specks snarl, dive, scream, two squadrons, eight of them, leaving congealing, combining, whirling pillars of black smoke, lifting trees, houses, vehicles, and, we devoutly hope, bits of Germans. We yell and pound each other's backs. Gods from the clouds; this is how you do it! You don't attack painfully across frozen plains, you simply drop in on the enemy and blow them out of existence.

Even as we watch, even as we make noises about discouraging those bastards, it happens. Right from the base of the black smoke a swarm of black dots debouch, spread out along fan ribs, form columns, multiply. Good God, I think, we kicked the anthill and here come the ants, furious, armored.

"Krauts, Kraut tanks, a whole fuckin' panzer division," someone says slowly. Through binoculars I can see the tanks, twenty, thirty, fifty, materializing out of bomb smoke, low, long-gunned, black, hived with infantry.

Thoughts can race in a few seconds; history, I think absurdly, I'm watching the nightmare of twentieth-century history, the steel outriders of organized horror, the most magnificent machinery of war ever assembled, serving the ends of degenerates, the advance of a German Panzerkeil, an armored hammer, the waking delirium of a few twilights ago, right where I knew it was going to happen, right across the plain toward our line of occasional riflemen.

Forward observers in the tower are shouting fire orders, obedient flashes begin to sprinkle the tanks, ripples of fire where a battery is tracking a single tank, masses of black smoke and fire over fifty square yards when a battalion concentration finds a fatter target, enemy bunched up. Over, short, left, right, two observers are yelling frantically; the elf in the radio keeps responding, "On the way," and the shells hiss overhead. Through our glasses we can see some American Sherman tanks among the attackers; that's where some of our tanks of the Seventy-sixth

Battalion went, captured intact, turned against us. (Ironic note: Six tanks are burning from our artillery fire, and they're all captured American Shermans. Bitter commentary on American engineering, American slavish addiction to high-octane gasoline; diesel-fueled, heavily armored German tanks keep right on coming.) Tanks keep moving. Indirect fire is a poor way to hit moving targets but it's all we have; Jesus Christ, I almost scream, why don't we have some heavy antitank guns out there? Where are our tanks? When will we learn?

More resistance; tracers flash where suicidally brave infantrymen are firing machine guns; planes come back in for a strafing run; streams of tracers erupt from wing edges, fiery dots carom off tanks. German infantry run, scatter, fall. Two passes, eight planes, and the German attack is faltering. The tanks halt, naked without their infantry. Ammunition spent, planes arch up into cloud, whine away leaving us feeling fatally alone. Dots now are startlingly large, closer, and they begin their march in parallel lines with short twists and spurts to throw off artillery observers. Fifteen hundred yards: someone calls the range reading and I wake up. Fifteen hundred undefended yards between us and the SS panzers. Orange winks are appearing in tank muzzles.

I run to the basement to see what's happening; the colonel is shouting orders to the tank battalion to get the hell over in front of us. All my life I have had a childish lack of faith in machines; I'm always surprised when they work, and now I'm convinced that the radios can't possibly function; we're isolated. Our tanks will never come. The words ''Roger, coming fast'' sing out from the receiver like divine music. The unlikely, improbable machines are working!

Tanks on the way, but how long will it take them to get here? Germans a thousand yards away and coming.... Right then division headquarters sinks below the bottom of lunacy; some ass calls us and orders our colonel to send a company of tanks up the line to help the Xth Armored Division. Colonel goes hoarse, desperate, trying to explain we're being counterattacked; orders keep on being parroted. Colonel slams receiver and ignores it.

Beginning of the colonel's postgraduate education; illumination.

An explosion rocks the command post, and a second and a third. As I run upstairs following the cries for medics, I see that a vehicle has been hit outside the door; gasoline is exploding, flaring orange light in the courtyard, and out there we finally find two wounded men lying under a shed. I follow Davis's back as he sprints across the courtyard, right where the next shells are going to land. One of the men is lightly wounded; I kick his ass and tell him to run like hell for the command post; Davis and I pull the other man's arms around our necks and, as he cries in pain and fear, we half run, half drag him toward the black oblong of the door, miles, centuries away through leaping flames. We run to beat the next shell, to beat the German gunners' correction and reloading time, and as we run I feel the beautiful anesthetic of groundless fearlessness; there's no question at all that we'll beat the next shell; we're *supposed* to get through the stone door ahead of the next explosion; it has to happen that way, and of course it does. We're through the door and around the corner before the next shell explodes in the courtyard. Good shooting, chaps, I find myself muttering, a little late perhaps, but then that was how it was supposed to happen. Scenario.

Back from the ambulance loading post across the street, running with wounded on litters, doubled over under shellbursts, back in our own building, we hear frantic sounds of slamming and packing; we too begin jamming dressings and plasma into chests, stuffing packs, slinging gear in the ambulance, bumping into white-faced clerks dashing up the cellar stairs with full arms to half-tracks.

In the basement CP there's an attempt to look official and soldierly, a thin membrane over tension and near-panic while everyone rolls maps and gives orders to load equipment. (Mental image of a German tank gun poking through the window and blasting us all to bright red hamburger. My kneecaps are literally shaking in an interesting clonic motion; never knew what shaking knees meant before, but now that the wounded are taken care of and there's not one damn thing for me to do except sit here and listen to the radio screaming the progress of the German attack, kneecaps begin a frantic, uncontrollable twitching. Wish to God I had a gun or something to do.)

I don't have to wish long. Almost at once I have something to do and so does everybody else in the command post. What we have to do is go out and get ourselves killed stopping a panzer division; the colonel just said so. He turned from the map and started a series of short, breathy phrases that froze all the hurrying commas. The room looked as if it were filled with children, halted with one foot in the air in a game of "Redlight."

After the colonel said, "Stop," three times, loudly enough to penetrate the almost-hysterical air, he said:

"Stop this goddamn panic.

"We're not retreating anywhere.

"We're defending this command post; we're holding this line.

"We're soldiers; we have weapons; we're expendable."

The sentences came out in short bursts separated by single inhalations. They spoke of some irrational kind of determination inside the colonel, swiftly transmitted, for while he talked, the apprehensive commas dropped papers and gear and straightened themselves into exclamation points, facing him, standing at something like attention, listening to what might be their last commands on earth.

There were a couple of seconds of silence for purposes of percolation, and then the colonel said, more quietly, "You'd better hurry," and a couple of German tank shells crashing overhead said, No kidding, and here we go, scrambling mad as hares, up stairs and through doors and over walls, following the headquarters commandant's shouts and pointing, the armed might of CCB headquarters, thirty-six clerks and mechanics and cooks and staff officers, six machine guns, assorted carbines, M-1s and grenades, and one tank, deploying to stop the Tenth SS Panzer Division. I organize my three helpers as company aid men, crouching with litters, and as I watch men squinting down machine-gun sights and snuggling over rifles in nests of grenades in windows, I have to deny a panicky inner voice that shouts the phrase I used in a letter one time about "the predictably lacerated" and

listen instead to the more enthusiastic voice commenting that the
colonel is some little bastard, he is, with a propensity for getting
possessed at the damnedest times, all dybbuk and demon, and
he's kicked us all over some kind of cliff edge and here we go on
a wild-assed, uncontrolled trip clear out of any constructive concern for life or limb. Ballsout!!

Most Ridiculous Moment: Someone remembers there's a bazooka in the mess truck and two cooks fill the air with pots and
dishes looking for a bazooka and twelve rounds of ammunition;
out of domesticity the tube presents a snout; the mess crew run
with their spindling weapon to rest it across a garden wall. . . .

Machine guns rip long bursts, closer up the street, as our outposts fall back shooting; more shells screech just overhead; to
boom inside the building, and then, at the precise moment that
a couple of our fifty-caliber machine guns begin firing and our
bazooka gunner lets a rocket go on a long, high arc, comes a sound
more beautiful than birdsong or golden bells, the sound of life
shaking the stone walls, vibrations, rumblings; the first of our
tanks tears past and the whole blessed battalion rocks around
corners, knocking stones off walls, swinging hard left and down
to the battlefield. Our embattled few are frenzied, run with machine guns down the street between tanks; they jump walls and
bang at shadows, a small wave of shouting and flame, they meet
the retreating soldiers in yards and alleys and, with the power
of the tanks, everybody turns toward the enemy, savage with
relief.

American war cries, violent short sounds ring back:

Okay, you guys, now okay!!!

AwRIGHT!!

Comeoncomeoncomeon!!!

GET them fuckers, comeoncomeoncomeon!!!

Through the blue, frozen air, darkening, the cries and the rumblings fade forward, toward the plain; I run up to the fourth
floor to watch the battle. Our tanks swing into lines at the edge
of town, the long column breaking into clusters left and right,
advancing by bounds, covering each other with gunfire.

Just there, right at the point of eruption, the fog comes and puts out the battle. Rhine Valley fog is a dense, white curtain, pulled swiftly, whirling and boiling, leaving every tank, every soldier on the plain isolated in small worlds a few feet across, everyone out there straining to see a few inches into coiling blank. All that steel menace is suddenly invisible. Silence. Our tanks advance with fiddling caution into the white wall, but the advantage is all on our side now. When two tanks surprise each other in the mist, the rapid power traverse of our tank guns will always beat the Germans and at close range even our short 75s can kill Tigers.

Nothing to see; I go down to hear what the radios have to tell. Cautious wonder from the tankers. Sudden quiet. Question . . . Where the hell are the Krauts? Nothing to shoot at.

The whole headquarters is a *whew* of solid relief; rumors keep floating with fog that rolls up our street; German patrols on the edge of town, mysterious bursts of firing. At the aid station, the detritus of the battle, a few nearly frozen men from the outpost line, one youngster frigid, terrified into a fetal position, his limbs and skin icy to touch, shivering like a dog in agony, speechless, sunk to subhuman depths of bare survival, lying on our floor, incapable of anything but this convulsive shivering. Two weeks in snow and deadly cold and then a whole panzer division against his M-1 rifle; the boy is spent to the edge of death.

Down in the command post we hear wonder from the tank radios. The Krauts seem to have melted off, probably to the south. Nothing out there in the fog. The tanks probe, grope through whiteness, confirm the unbelievable. Some burning tanks, some dead Germans.

Later we found out where the German attack went: the German commander counted his losses, decided we were too strong, and swung south toward CCA where General Beaky did a Duke of Plazatoro; there were no dybbuks around CCA headquarters; intact epidermises and unminced viscera were high-priority concerns down there as our hero and his entourage hesitated not, but ran for the rear, the first of all their Corps-O. The more we hear about what happened at the other end of the battlefield, the prouder we are of our colonel; there was much close-in, desperate fighting by the combat troops down there, lots of heroism; final victory when a platoon of Shermans caught the German tank column on the skyline, broadside, knocked them out from rear to front, two shells to a customer. When the shooting stopped the German tanks were flaming in the snow and the Americans had used their last shell.*

Evening: A certain swagger in our line officers, tired elation, much passing of bottles of schnapps. Mood changes when prisoners and German wounded begin talking again. Tomorrow, they all insist, comes the *really* big attack, fifty Tiger tanks and a battalion of panzer grenadiers heading right here, right for this town, right for this headquarters. German prisoners, so anxious to get the hell out they sing like canaries, give us every detail of the attack.

A blow, but not necessarily fatal. The combat command puts on manly readiness with much hurried conferring, siting of tanks and antitank guns, pick-and-shovel work by engineers digging obstacles and gun positions. In combat command headquarters a battalion CO comments that we'll be a lot more ready tomorrow than we were today.

Then the great ax falls. The artillery commander and our supply officer have been arguing, swearing, desperate-voiced over the telephone. They put down telephones and tell us the news. Our artillery has exactly fifty rounds of ammunition, with no resupply this side of Paris; two minutes of rapid firing by our battalion and that's the end. Our guns are dead. For the tanks we find a half-day's ration of shells and machine-gun ammo, for the infantry about the same. Again, no resupply this side of Paris, and Paris, over four hundred miles away, is on the far side of the moon.

I leave the headquarters room where men are staring at each other with nothing at all to say. In an hour the word is all through

---

*The colonel's tactics were not as mad as they seemed; repeatedly during the Battle of the Bulge, and for that matter during the whole European campaign, little troops of headquarters personnel and engineers put on such a rousing Fourth of July with a few weapons that heavy German columns, thinking they were facing whole divisions, sheered off and actually retreated. Wild-assed, flat-out irrational commitment has a lot in its favor.

the battalions; men react with shock, disbelief, rage, and finally with a weighted, heavy fear. I now understand the cliché about "paralyzing fear"; on the line everybody lives with terror twenty-four hours a day, but this is the terror of complete helplessness. The power of our guns is our potency, our identity; it is the voice we use to challenge fear and conquer its source. That power will be gone and we'll be changed utterly. Fugitives. Survival. These are concepts that we can't live with; they freeze our will.

Conversation of an infantry platoon in a barn, the men toying listlessly with the catches on their weapons:

"All them goddamn factories, Pittsburgh, Detroit..."

"Nobody shooting at them; they got enough to eat, they got good places to sleep. You'd think they could make enough ammunition."

"It's the fuckin' rear echelon; 'course the people in Pittsburgh or wherever make enough ammunition. It's the guys that tell them where to send it and how much and seein' it gets there, and you know who does that. It's those bastards with their eight-hour days and their French whores and their black market...." As the sentence ends the sergeant stands pounding his fists against the wall in a rhythm of rage. "Them fuckheads, them fuckheads, them cowardly lazy fuckheads! After all we done, after all we've been through, after the way we beat those goddamn Krauts..."

"*Quintili Vare, legiones redde!*" In another German war the Emperor Augustus found a wall to pound on while he screamed at the folly of a political general who led his legionaries to slaughter in the Teutoburger Wald. *Plus ça change.*

At the command post the colonel talks about a "fighting retreat" and "hurting the enemy as we fall back." I check out sheltered side roads for the ambulances, shortcuts through forests away from artillery fire. We can all see traffic snarls, German tanks shooting up stalled columns, and we do everything we can to plan around catastrophe, knowing all the time that with the confusion of retreat added to the fog of war, we'll probably be running for our lives through the woods.

Ten P.M.: the night before Agincourt, a proper night to wander. From aid stations to gunpits, shapes of men and guns glow in black against fresh-falling, quieting snow; voices come muffled through flakes.

Forms cluster near a ruined shed; I hear voice one say that he has so many rounds of thirty-caliber machine-gun ammo.

Well, says voice two, that should be half that many dead Krauts if a guy's careful.

Yeah, from voice three, then dead us.

A soldier kicks something that clangs; he snarls in whispers that he doesn't want to lose to them pricks, not like this, see, not when we got them flat-assed beat; it ain't fair, see....

Shit, he says fair; he thinks in war it's fair....

Or anywhere it's fair....

Men laugh and start talking more cheerily about how if everybody kills ten Krauts each how many total would that be and what would it take to discourage them....

There's logic and there's what I can believe, and tonight they don't touch. Logic is convinced that this particular instant, people are warm and safe and drinking in places like the bar of the Kitchener Club off Berkeley Square; or they're laughing themselves silly watching Hermione Gingold down the street at the Strand; logic wants me to believe that Grand Central Station is all a murmur of voices and shufflings of people moving from offices to suburban shelters where they'll sink into soft chairs and hold glasses; past any belief, logic claims Penny and the children are asleep in New Britain, teddy bears and dolls and games on the living-room floor. Right now.

Belief says, Ha; belief says, Bullshit, they're gone, those other worlds, lost on the other side of time, bobbing away down some icy, devouring torrent. All that can possibly exist tonight is this cold end where men huddle over snowy gun barrels, tapping hands on steel, waiting for the dawn when they fire their last rounds.

A loneliness like the loneliness before death blows through the command with the snow; we've been deserted by everybody; we're alone, what's left of us.

Eleven P.M.: Bris hangs on the phone as if he's listening to God. He starts screaming in the kind of improvised code we always use to confuse the Germans and drive the division signal officer insane. "Cowboys?? The cowboys are coming? Tonight? They bringing their six-shooters, their big ones? They got lots of bullets for them?"

I never knew what the word *gibber* meant, exactly, but that's what Bris is doing right into the telephone. What he's gibbering about is that someone on the other end of the phone is telling him that a regimental combat team of the Thirty-sixth Division, the veterans of Salerno and Anzio and Marseilles, are marching up to take over the line. Three thousand men with artillery, tanks, and lots of ammunition. Here in two hours.

Bris actually tosses the phone in the air, slumps on the desk, face in arms. Everyone goes looking for something to drink. People are almost giddy with relief.

January 23, two A.M.: Clumping and rumbling wake us from dozes. We run outside, watch through falling snow smudges sharpening to figures under packs and weapons, infantry on both sides of the street, tanks, tank destroyers, trucks, caissons full of ammunition, the whole, beautiful, life-saving, life-giving tangle of men and weapons and supplies, more live American infantry than I thought there were left in the whole world. Irrational relief to find that we're not alone, that we're really part of an army.

We turn over our aid station to a medical captain and his aid men. While I point out danger areas on the map, show where ambulances can go safely, where shell-fire interdicts roads, I find myself describing the past three weeks at length and with feeling. With gestures. A small T-5 aid man who has been listening intently says soberly, quietly, "Jeez, Major, it looks like a real bitch. Reminds me of nineteen forty-three down at Cassino." As I look down at the small, narrow face in need of a shave, I see no sarcasm there; I see a completely sympathetic man, absorbed in what I've been saying, a man who has survived Salerno and Cassino and the invasion of southern France and the battles in the Vosges Mountains, our Herrlisheim battle twenty times repeated, and I am suddenly very humble and shut up.

Later, outside in the courtyard, we wait for the column to move. The ashes from the burned jeep of the afternoon are right beside us. For some lunatic reason we assemble our column on the German side of the courtyard, exactly where the shells were landing this afternoon. We are exquisitely vulnerable and there's the awful half-certainty that just now, right when safety lies a few minutes away, something is going to whistle in and blast us into screaming remnants. Danger can be faced when danger stretches to infinity, but when the end is in sight, it becomes intolerable.

Quiet. A jeep chatters and makes an outrageous gash in the silence. I stand on tiptoe watching for gun flashes from the German side of the plain, but there is only more silence. We settle back in the ambulance, chattering with the line officers who use any excuse they can to bum a ride in the warm back end. A lovely womb image, I think, dark, soft; Hah, Sigmund, says rational mind, lousy wartime womb you got here; wouldn't stop a thirty-caliber slug. . . .

Tick, tick, eternity, all clenched until a ghostly arm waves from the lead half-track and we follow, grinding steel, oh, grateful, around the agonizing first corner, out of direct fire, into the beginning of the world of physical safety that's been floating back there like Atlantis. Out the far edge of town, we wrap in blue-white luxury, starlight, moonlight, all without fear; we drift into the ultimate incomparable intoxicant, the sleep of bodies newly away from the danger of tearing. Floating, dropping, rising, the cat's eyes of the vehicles ahead are tiny blue planets swimming through a luminous sea, a sea rippling with crooked shadows all across its floor, a sea silent of explosions, strange to terror. Forests, villages, dark figures at crossroads, repeated wakings to touch reassurance, to feel silky brushing of silence and kindness, and, finally, plunging sleep.

One eye squints through a window to discover we're stopped. Well, the column's still, but something else is moving, and what's moving is light, lifting silver and blue along the street of an Alsatian village, touching the red and blue and pink of house-fronts until the street as far as I can see is glowing. I'm caught in that same bright velocity I've waited for on glaciers and in spruce boughs : this dawn's broken free of the slow crawl up across the rim of night, and it's racing now in tidal waves of gold and sapphire. The flooding light commands silence at peril of decency. Understood. I open the ambulance door with no more than a chirp and my boots stir soundless puffs of snow. The wizard of this morning will know what sounds are appropriate and when : until then, quiet.

I'm the only one awake. Every tank, every truck, every half-track is filled with exhausted men, slumped over weapons, huddled in whitened blankets all in a cold trance far below sleep, stirring the frost a little with their breathing. I'm floating in another life, past heaps and mounds of frozen survivors.

Now the wizard permits the first sound, a church bell at the end of the street, high in clear air, a voice flat and bronze. Well done : it's an interesting bell, modest without clang or boom : it sidles into the morning with a flat metal *whank* and then again *whank,* single tones with each swing of the clapper, spare, just enough to bring a few dark figures out through doorways and send them soundless across snow.

Quite suitable, even handsome, but nothing to what the wizard brings on next : the sound of a piano drifts into the street through a slightly opened window. I haven't thought about pianos or what they do for centuries; anybody playing almost anything would push feeling past words, but when I see through parted blackout curtains a little starched girl, possibly ten, leaning past braids to see notes in the half-light, anxious and precise, bending over twinkling fingers, and when I hear of all Earth's melodies "Für Elise" floating into the silence in simple jewels, why then I can only bow inadequate homage. It's one hell of a stage manager of a wizard we've got prowling this dawn.

I can't leave the window : that could be my Susy ten years from now and I'm looking into a chamber all glowing with love : I'm looking ahead into life and there's a desperate tender need to live long enough to get there.

"Give beauty back, beauty" : Hopkins and the Golden Echo are sounding in the rising light, and I'm wondering where my eyes and feelings have been all these years. Beauty has to be seen to exist and every perception is a beginning, like this one. It almost overwhelms vision to start seeing what was always there, the shining of shapes of happiness surrounding loving humans, of houses holding warm walls around sleepers, houses not blown into charcoal tombs, of men and women and children resting in kindness where there are no screaming wounded and no frozen dead. How can any place in all space or time be this beautiful?

I sit down suddenly on the running board, feeling a thousand years old, dry, hollow, like the emptied shell of some insect glued to a rock by a stream, fluttering quietly in the sun.

If I were about eight years old, I think I'd sit here and bawl.

✳ 13

Colmar

P UZZLE 1914/1940 (for students of politics, history, and human
inexplicability).

In 1914 the Germans invaded France and occupied a large part
of that country for four years. They shot innocent hostages, they
terrorized the populace, they looted under barely legal pretexts,
and they successfully alienated the people of France, for in all
that time no Frenchman known to history turned traitor and
none gave aid or comfort to the enemy.

In 1940 another German army invaded and occupied France;
this one was so much worse that what it did slips quite past belief
now, in the fading years of the century. You can read some certain
words or you can speak them out loud, but I don't think you can
stretch your mind around their meaning. Try it.

The 1940 Germans reintroduced human slavery to Western
Europe. In the most literal sense they made slaves of hundreds
of thousands of Frenchmen, along with people of other nationalities, and marched them away in columns, in truckloads, at
gunpoint, to work camps and slave pens where thousands of them
would die of tuberculosis or starvation. This is history; the Germans did it, in France, between 1940 and 1945.

When any patriotic French tried to resist their conquerors, the

Germans liked to retaliate by rounding up hundreds of innocent hostages, men and women and sometimes children, and killing them, often by mass machine-gunning, and sometimes by shipping them in trainloads to the death camps.

France reeked with German torture chambers, elegant, scientific, dedicated to prolonged agony. There was one in every major community and they were the scene of thousands of shuddering, terrible deaths.

To compress a nightmare into a sentence, the 1940 Germans looted France to the point of exhaustion and starvation, they murdered by thousands, and they broke every law of God, man, and the Geneva Convention. There had been nothing like them in morbid history since Tamerlane.

And how, you ask, did the French nation respond to this worst horror in its long and tortured history? Well, there's the puzzle.

You have to see things to give them any substance; try seeing what happened in Paris in 1942. The Germans decided that everyone with one Jewish grandparent would be classified as a Jew, should be robbed of all personal possessions, and should be shipped off to concentration camps for starvation and death by gassing. One expected that of the Germans, but one is baffled to find that the elegant detection work to find out about all those Jewish grandparents and the superb logistics and transportation to round up all the Jews in a great city and deliver them to one point at one time, why all this was done by the Paris police. With enthusiasm. With superb efficiency.

The French police in their natty blue capes dug through files and verified birth certificates; they practiced the roundup of Jews in every arrondissement until they had it timed to perfection, and then one awful day they crammed crying, terrified people into trucks and buses with whatever they could carry on their backs and drove them to a a great central stadium where they turned them over to the Gestapo and the Wehrmacht so that they could be crammed into cattle cars and shipped off to Germany for execution. The French police stood there, one must imagine, proud of their work.

Another picture: Truckloads of French militia, the Milice,

swarmed down every road in France to help the Gestapo and the SS hunt down Resistance fighters. The Milice were fascist French militia, sworn on oath to aid their German comrades in the extermination of their own nation, and they tortured, informed, betrayed, and killed in this incredible cause.

Another: In French North Africa regular officers of the French army and navy enacted anti-Semitic laws and enforced them with all the pious patriotism of a reactionary military clique; they penned Jews in concentration camps, they deprived them of property, they turned them over to the Germans whenever they found it convenient.

Another: The SS troops were the scum of the German armed forces, murderers, torturers, psychopathic to a man. Their own countrymen feared them. The Germans often commented to me, *"Die SS: das sind keine Leute mehr"* — the SS aren't human — and they were right.

On the Russian front, and this is hardest of all to credit, there was a whole *French* SS division, called the Division Charlemagne, fighting bravely alongside the very men whose organization was running torture chambers back in France.

Another: The senile Marshal Pétain, ruler of puppet France, entrenched in Vichy, smiled vacantly while his helpers organized youth groups with fascist symbols and stiff-armed salutes and bellowing of anti-Semitic slogans around bonfires.

Now see a small minority, the glory of France and of humanity, the men and women who resisted the horror when resistance seemed hopeless and when their efforts must have seemed the most pointless of gestures. Men like Louis Aragon, Camus, Sartre, Mendès-France, and thousands of other heroes never surrendered and never compromised; some of them died under torture rather than betray comrades; some showed determination beyond ordinary belief, like Leclerc, who started in French West Africa with a dugout canoe and twenty men to attack a Vichy outpost and begin a march that would bring him two years later to Paris at the head of a French armored division. The world and history, however, should know that in the words of a leader of the Resistance, the heroism was confined to the outside few, the nonconformists, the "odd ones."

By any reasonable estimate most Frenchmen didn't do anything to resist their conquerors; they concentrated passively on survival, while a large part of them, possibly half, actually snuggled right up to the monster, did handstands for it, climbed in bed with it, and kissed its feet while it planned their destruction.

What happened to the French between 1914 and 1940? Did too many sane, brave Frenchmen die at Verdun? Did an entire nation, or a very large part of it, turn criminal in twenty-six years?

In the battle of the Colmar Pocket as part of the French First Army, we found ourselves marching and fighting our way through a mesh of those questions and some of their answers.

The Colmar Pocket was the last French territory held by the Germans in the Second World War, a crooked half an *O,* dipping its ends in the Rhine, looping west through the foothills of the Vosges.

Guide Michelin: of interest to tourists, the city of Colmar with persistence of medieval stones: twelfth-century castle at Neuf-Breisach w/moat: site of Field of the Cloth of Gold (near city), Mathias Grunewald altar triptych (in city); profusion of monasteries, castles, villages, old before Caesar. Of interest to *military* tourists, a confusion of languages and cultures so profound that the inhabitants couldn't seek their loyalties in maps or laws or governments; their governments had been changed for them too many times for any legal pretense, and they had to make their commitments on the basis of the Ten Commandments, or the Beatitudes, or the Fire Sermon, or maybe only the whispered voice of God. City hall was no help.

The Pocket was formed in the fall when the Allies surged north to the border, leaving a mass of Germans behind on the right flank, on the Alsatian plain around Colmar. Sandy Patch, commanding Seventh Army, assured Eisenhower that the Germans trapped on the Colmar Pocket had "ceased to exist as a fighting force," but nobody bothered to tell the Germans about their demise and they settled down, heavily reinforced from across the Rhine, personally directed by Heinrich Himmler, to fight with sullen desperation.

Why did the Germans fight so hard for this useless bit of mountain and plain? Part of the explanation was Hitler's no-retreat obsession; the German soldier stood on his conquests, even if it meant being destroyed. The German army never left anything until it was pushed off, suffering a palsied rigidity that made it a lot easier to surround and obliterate. The German generals, mostly skillful, understood this and protested as far as their meager courage allowed, but the grand old principle of stern obedience to madmen was not to be violated, certainly not by the German General Staff.

Down in the psychic cellar, the battle of the Colmar Pocket made a murky, Germanic kind of sense, for in the winter of 1944–45 this was the last conquest of the disciplined savages, their last hurrah, the only place on earth where Germans could stamp and cow and terrorize a subject people in the grand manner once in vogue from Moscow to the English Channel. All around the rest of the German perimeter, from the Roer to the Vistula, the Germans were backed into their own country fighting desperate last-ditch battles for German cities, watching German refugees trundle belongings in carts through the snow, guiding their night marches by the fire of German towns. It was a squalid, depressing comedown for the conquerors of continents, and worst of all, direst hardship the Wehrmacht ever faced, they were among their countrymen and they had to be *nice* to people. This was a hardship hardly to be borne — and to be fair, in the case of the SS it was a hardship *not* borne; they hung Germans out of windows just as they had hung French, Polish, and Russians. Fair play, no favorites.

The French First Army was born around the Colmar Pocket. Fragments of French troops from Africa, Italy, and resurgent France coalesced here for the first time into a unified whole under French command. Foreign legionnaires, Algerians, Moroccans, sailors from French battleships, native French divisions newly raised, shreds of empire, tatters of the titanic army of 1918, undequipped, often undertrained, they dug themselves into the snow, barely containing the lunges of determined counterattacks.

After the German attacks in the north sputtered out, the Americans loaned the French First Army three divisions to help clean up what Eisenhower called "this abscess in our right flank" before the Allies began their great final attack across Germany.

The French First Army and its comforts: We drove into an Alsatian town to find billets on the heels of the Fifth French Armored Division moving out ahead of us toward the battle. I thought I saw a couple of tautly curved, magnificently shaped, glorious young women mincing through snow and manure piles in outfits that belonged on the cover of *Paris-Match*. Too many shells, I thought, too much cold; I knew that something, sometime, would push me over the edge past reality; I was hallucinating. We gaped, they giggled. "Americans," they nudged each other, but before we could say anything two furious French officers stormed out of the building behind them and hustled them out of sight; clearly they were not going to lose this last manifestation of their manhood to a gang of American peasants. We found that it was customary to bring mistresses as far forward as regimental headquarters — and what mistresses! Why do French women make most other women in the world look like piles of rags and old frumps? Who the hell would want to struggle out of a bed that held a creature like that to go shoot Germans in the cold of dawn? The lineaments of gratified desire don't make it on a battlefield; the best killers are hungry and frustrated.

During a night march forward through flashing, thundering silhouettes, we halted at a large building where German prisoners were penned. They were oddly menacing, a mass of big men, SS mountain troops looming light blond, wide, pale-eyed; staring, angry in lantern light, still murderous, even disarmed and under guard, conveying primitive fear, the image of the semilegendary killers who had ranged across a third of the world, defiant, barely contained, held at bay by depressingly average-looking Americans. I sensed for the first and only time the power of the death bone that the Germans had pointed at civilization, the incantation, the sense of irresistible evil that had held old civilizations bound with fear, unable to resist. Then came Brooklyn.

"This morning in that goddamn city," (the city was Colmar; the speaker was a short, wide Italian-American corporal) "I comes around a corner with my squad and I sees a dozen of them shits, those ones right there in the corner. They was carryin' a whole arsenal and before they could do anything with it I yells, Lie down, you pricks, and I yells at 'em some more, Lie down or I'll shoot your fuckin' guts full of holes." His voice rose, more Brooklyn, more intense, not shrill but full, happy, triumphant over many layers of fear.

Colleagues joined the circle, admiring, supporting.

"That's right, you shoulda heard Vito."

"He just talked those dumb bastards into surrendering."

The epic resumed.

"They looks halfway stupid when I point my BAR from the hip and I keeps on yelling, Down, you pricks, down, you motherfuckers, I'll dump your guts all over the pavement. I'll shoot you so full of holes the wind won't even slow down going through ya, down, down." He looked at the prisoners contemptuously. All through the recital other soldiers of his squad were nodding, grinning, approving, reliving a happy, triumphant moment. The corporal looked at the prisoners.

"Come on, you Kraut son of a bitch," he nudged a particularly menacing-looking one, "get the hell back with them other turds. I bet your uncle peddles sausages in Yorkville." He shoved contemptuously, and I thought as I watched him that this was not a little, vicious, angry man, but a small, wide Italian, used to the ways of peace, suddenly enlarged through the conquest of fear, taller, in that instant, than all the prisoners in the room. They shrunk away, cows, cowed. The menace fled; God bless Flatbush armed and angry.

At dawn we were strung along the highroad into Colmar: the rising light discovered the German mountains, blue-black across the Rhine, savage, remote, unattainable. P-47s screamed toward the earth out of streaks of red across frozen blue: corpses sprawled stiff along the roadside, an arm on one frozen, vertical, pointing

to the cold and unsympathetic heaven. (A psychiatric casualty
in the back of the ambulance, finger of one hand crammed into
mouth, mumbled, "Is them dead guys Germans? Is all them dead
guys Germans?" and fell back into a reassured fetal posture when
we told him they were.) The walls of the city were abrupt, high,
black across the morning snow; the old familiar freezing invaded
the belly as we wound through burned ruins, waiting for the first
flashes and slams, and then around a corner, our world lifted,
erupted in a sea of screaming, happily toothed civilian faces, a
street lined with almost uncontainable happiness, men, women,
girls, boys, thrusting into the windows of vehicles, draping us
with flowers, shoving bottles of wine into our hands, incompre-
hensible gurgled monosyllables in the middle of hugs and kisses,
our first liberation, delirious French all over us. We didn't deserve the ovation since other troops had really liberated Colmar
the night before — some had even caught Germans drilling that
dawn and shot them to pieces on their parade grounds — but we
did represent more security, more tanks, more guns, more infantrymen, to people who had forgotten what security and law meant
in a four-year nightmare.

Our column jammed the street; we threaded a maze in and out
of crowds, and at one of our stops we were in a curious still
backwater, facing a side street that angled to a tall stone wall.
Eight Senegalese soldiers faced the wall from twenty feet away,
leaning on rifles, their faces fixed with that curious rigidity men
have when they can't admit emotion. Carved West African masks
were looking at us from under old French army helmets.

Jack and I pushed out into the crowd, and I was asking myself
what eight Senegalese were doing standing there in a row, all
professionally remote, staring through us and around us, and
what all the tilted faces in the crowd were so white and still about,
and then the thought leaped into words: "Firing squad; that's
a Senegalese firing squad, for chrissakes. Who are they shooting
this soon, I wonder; they just took the damn city. . . ."

The answer came, murmuring from faces lifting over shoulders,
muttering sideways to faces next to them without ever taking
their eyes off the tall, black men and the wall. "*Verrater,*" the

word was breathed, not really spoken. *"Collaborateur ... geschossen."*

I translated for the half-dozen Americans standing nearby. "Traitors, collaborators, guys who worked for the Nazis. They're shooting them."

Most of the Americans looked stunned.

"Christ, we just took the place."

"They don't screw around with lawyers, these guys."

"Neither did the Nazis."

We heard voices approaching around the corner, one shrill, begging, others low and contemptuous, and I found myself squeezing my eyes against what I was going to see, and feeling relieved when the column began to move and we had to run back to get into the ambulance and drive into a main street again, into the yelling and laughing and kissing.

"Sure didn't take them long," from Jack. "How did they know who to shoot?" Our psychiatric casualty sitting in the rear of the ambulance, watching through the back window, answered with the clarity of the mad.

"When they have traitors for next-door neighbors, of course they know who to shoot. Wouldn't you?" Then he stuffed his fingers back into his mouth and went back to his frozen contemplation of the end of his litter.

While our tanks stabbed at the 88s of the German rear guard south of town, we watched a city go giddy with relief.

Any two men in uniform walking along the street were an instant parade, cheered and applauded; a French infantry unit made a formal entry, a general walking first, alone, doing his best to look like a symbol, staring firmly forward while men wearing Resistance armbands ran up to kiss him on the cheeks. In the city park girls hugged French soldiers in the turrets of their tanks and mugged for pictures; a squad of police in the afternoon marched down the main street in their old French uniforms while pedestrians clapped politely. (Considering the average Frenchman's attitude toward the flics, polite applause was miraculous, the equivalent of an ovation.)

At our temporary headquarters in a railroad station a whiskery gent introduced himself as a very important official of the postal service for that area. Very important, he insisted, puffing our cigarettes, a key personage. Why? Head cocked to one side, rheumy eyes staring up at me, tap of forefinger on my lapel, why, under the Germans he had worn *four stars,* and his four fingers sketched the sites of honor on his sleeve.

"*Ja, unter die Deutsche hatte ich vier Sterne!*"

"Under the Germans?" I loaded my voice with surprise. "You had four stars from the Germans?"

His head wagged no, so hard that his whiskers vibrated a half cycle behind the movements of his head. His eyes opened maximally, redly, to convey sincerity. I mustn't think he collaborated; someone had to deliver the mail; surely I understood, didn't I understand? He was most grateful for the cigarettes, he would be delighted to be of service, he anticipated remaining an important personage; he fled.

Late afternoon, the aid station: A peasant was brought in from the fighting south of town, one eye torn, almost hanging out on his maxilla, much of his face lacerated, shrinking from our aid men and from me. I explained that the eye might still be saved; the hospital would make every effort. Dangerous, I told him, not hopeless. Vast relief, an exhalation. He sat heavily.

His broad wife railed, "I told you the Amis wouldn't hurt you, you dunce, you fool. I told you they were all right."

All right? Hurt him? Where along this tortured border did people start fearing us?

Crépuscule dangereux: There I was in improbable twilight, lost in Vosges foothills, looking for missing ambulances in forests where the armies snaked around each other almost front to back, creaking over dark blue snow through possibilities of minefields and German outposts, straining out windows for explosions, exhaling relief when a shadow turned out to be a French sentry. He waved me to a hut that glowed through flimsy blackout under fir trees; across the snow it sounded with nasal voices singing to a flute, a high, wild, minor-key set of sounds made for deserts and shimmering heat. Inside two blackout curtains I faced a platoon of Algerian infantrymen; the singing was coming from

faces dark under crescents of old French army helmets; long
corduroy robes were swaying and bandoliers were tinkling as
bodies swung to dissonance.

In the center of suddenly silent brown faces I talked to the
young French lieutenant, who commanded remarkably good English.

The lieutenant showed me where I was on the map; an understandable mistake, a badly marked fork in the road, no problem.
I passed around cigarettes; I sipped coffee gratefully from a pot
at the fire's edge.

An older Algerian soldier, apparently a noncom, asked me in
pidgin French if I'd like to sell some cigarettes. Sell them, hell;
I was grateful to be alive and among friends; I was ready to give
away my shirt. I conveyed the idea that I wouldn't dream of
taking money, not from my friends and allies, and that I had a
carton outside in the ambulance they could have as a gift. Sudden
silence and sober staring away from me into firelight, until the
lieutenant took my arm firmly and suggested that we go for a
walk in the snow, and, walking, explained kindly, as one would
the facts of life to a teenager, that these were professional soldiers,
mercenaries. For them war was a business, it was how they made
their living. They went to war for a tiny salary, for good food,
for a chance to loot and a chance to trade. It was their way of
life, their career; they all hoped to make good at it. For me to
offer them a small fortune in cigarettes meant either that I held
the goals of their lives in amused contempt as an enormously rich
person, or that I was some kind of fool who needed a keeper.
Either way, they couldn't accept me as a brother in arms. I dug
out the carton of cigarettes and followed him back.

"Bargaining is polite, it's important. That carton is worth a
thousand francs and you'll have to make them bargain for it. Be
prepared to be hard-hearted; remember, not bargaining is like
spitting on your plate at dinner."

What followed had all the charm and ordained progress of
Greek drama. The Algerian noncom offered five hundred francs;
I clutched the carton to my bosom and looked sad. He threw his

hands to heaven. By depriving his poor wife and children back in Algeria he might go to six hundred francs — only because he liked me a lot. The circle of eyes swung to me, and I dramatized the poverty of my wife and two children in America, their utter dependence on the sale of these cigarettes, the disgrace in my family's eyes if I failed to generate a proper return on this enormous investment, even though I liked him very much and he was a sterling good fellow. The platoon's eyes kept swinging from the noncom to me and back again as we staged our tiny dramas, like a crowd following a tennis ball back and forth across a court.

After I realized how you did it, I considered my performance more than adequate, even, at times, inspired, and it certainly was a lot of fun. It was a great release from the sordid fears and tensions of our usual occupations: I understood perfectly what bad manners it would be to refuse or abbreviate any part of the performance. It would be, I reflected, as if someone came out two minutes on in a drama and announced exactly what was going to happen at the end of the fifth act so that everyone could forget it and go home. I thought my neatest touch came when I invoked my aged father, shivering, cold and hungry, huddled in a great city on the shores of a frozen inland sea. Approving nods, sympathetic murmurs.

We finally ended at nine hundred eighty francs; while I surrendered the cigarettes with great show of loss and friendship, alleging profound personal sacrifice in his interest, the Algerian winked slyly at his fellows, meanwhile assuring me that he was bankrupting himself.

Before I set off on the right road, the lieutenant and I had a sober, chilled conversation in the starlit, snowy space next to my ambulance. These were mercenary soldiers, he explained, they didn't fight for abstractions. "They're brave for me, they're brave for their careers as professional soldiers. They'll go exactly as far as I lead them; if I don't lead, they don't follow. I am paid more than they are, therefore I'm supposed to be braver than they are."

An unpleasant thought struck me. At the time of the Allied invastion of North Africa, I asked him, what did these troops do? The lieutenant looked uncomfortable.

"I don't know if these men were actually engaged in the fighting or not, but if they'd been ordered to they would have fought you. Orders are all that they know. I was lucky. I was away south somewhere. I didn't have to make a choice. I didn't bring my unit up to the coast until after Darlan was shot, in fact."

"It must make life simpler to be a mercenary," I said, "no politics, no complicated decisions."

The lieutenant shrugged and looked off into the dark. We shook hands and I pressed some more cigarettes on him which he, the Frenchman, accepted understandingly.

The campaign ended with two days of fighting beyond Colmar, a night attack to the south and a wild march bypassing clumps of Germans; tanks and infantry met Moroccans marching up from the other side of the Pocket to close the trap at Rouffach and begin taking prisoners and chasing some last Germans across the Rhine. France was finally completely freed.

After the battle we set up our command post in an inn in a town south of Colmar. There was some mystery about the inn, for while the rest of the village thronged with relieved, renewed civilian activity, the inn remained deserted; we couldn't find the owner.

That evening the mystery cleared when a small peasant in ragged coat and cap approached our sentries and tried to talk to them in French and in German, to the frustration of all concerned. I walked over to translate and heard that the worst Nazi collaborator in all Oberelsass was hiding in town, in the house of a Jew he'd sent to a concentration camp. Didn't we want him?

The man had been, we gathered, pretty ferocious; the farmer was afraid to come along, even with two jeeploads of us armed with tommy guns, and we had to hoist him in by the arms.

As we swung through snowy streets, an odd concern was fluttering, a matter of police etiquette. I was going to be interpreting, and what the hell do you say to someone when you arrest him as a traitor?

"Good day, sir; police here! Care to join us?"

"You're under indictment as a possible traitor; anything you may have to say ..."

"*American Sicherheitsdienst! Spreng auf marsch!*"

Nothing sounded reasonable; I was like some sod at a banquet wondering what fork to use, even while we swung past a manure pile into an icy courtyard, and at the very moment *Emil und der Detektiv* came to the rescue. Of course I knew Emil; everybody who studied German in the thirties got to know Emil at stupefying length. The book was a funny detective story for second-year students, and a whole generation had numbed their minds on its thronging clichés, but I fingered them now like a rosary as I led my squad up the stairs to the wooden double door. At my knock, the door opened on a Hollywood Prussian; there he was, just escaped from a 1926 movie, a man of maybe sixty, grizzle-haired, slack-jowled, stiff-collared, dark-suited, pig-eyed, looking at me as if I were trying to peddle something he didn't want to buy.

I asked if he were Herr Ekhof. He nodded. Silence; embarrassed shifting of weight from one foot to the other, and then, unbidden, came the lovely, singing cliché of Emil's Detektiv.

"*Bitte, komen Sie mit uns; wir möchten ein paar Fragen stellen.*" The sound of this standard, frightfully menacing invitation of the German police and Gestapo rolled ahead of me like an explosion; in the living room the man's wife and two handsome grown daughters went into agonies of screaming and crying and hand-wringing and entreaties from around my neck about not taking Papa out in the snow because he was an old man; the snow would kill him. Herr Ekhof gave a heartrending two minutes about how he, the *Bürgermeister*, had stood between his village and the Nazis, how he was really some kind of hero.

Embarrassing; I tried some civilized soothing. I told them that if Papa had done nothing wrong, there wouldn't be any trouble and he'd be right home. I couldn't have said anything worse; the roof really fell in to a room full of Wagnerian shrieks.

(Sense of ultimate divorcement from reality: It occurred to me that what I was supposed to be doing was wandering around a hospital in a white suit, prescribing pills and giving shots and comforting people, and here I was standing in an Alsatian living room, all menace and tommy gun, while three women flung themselves at me in rotation, screaming about not killing their old father. Where was I? Who was I?)

There was an irrational exchange when Ekhof spotted the farmer and screamed at him about being an informer, a traitor; and the farmer bent in apologies about how we had all made him do it, how he had been forced into it, about how God knows he didn't want to; reversal of roles into fantasy for a few paradoxical seconds until we all came back to where we were and whose house we were really in, and stopped the farce and marched Ekhof out while his crying wife tucked in his scarf and pushed his flying white hair under a fedora.

In our culture we go to irrational lengths to stretch a film of civilization over terrifying proceedings, and we were straining to be polite policemen doing the ordinary, the okay legal, the come-to-the-station-house-and-everything-will-turn-out-civilized all the way down the steps. That charade ended in the courtyard where we ran into a squad of infantrymen halfway through a bottle of schnapps; I can repeat the next conversation verbatim after teems of time.

"Who's the old guy, Doc?"

"Supposed to be a big Nazi collaborator; biggest Nazi collaborator around here. The French want him; we're just picking him up."

The elder daughter, who unfortunately spoke fair English, was trailing behind her father, Niobe all tears, reaching with bird-wing clutches for him, and she turned to the soldier who spoke, looking, it seemed, for any desperate hope of intervention, holding her arms out, crying, "Please, oh God, please...."

"Hell, lady, don't worry none," bottle up, bottle down; "all they're gonna do is shoot the old son of a bitch!"

Even the jeep tires squealed on the snow as we tore away, and I looked back, much as I didn't want to, to see the daughter collapsed on her knees in the snow, her head on the ground, screaming. . . .

Ekhof was locked in a room upstairs under guard, but that evening we were curious enough to invite him down to talk to us — the colonel, the S-3, and me. I suppose we all wanted to meet a real Hollywood top-drawer Nazi villain ; between the colonel's West Point French and my German we spoke easily.

Ekhof explained that he had been *Bürgermeister* for some time before the war, a successful businessman — the inn, other properties — and in 1940 he had had to make a decision. The people trusted him, the Germans agreed to let him stay on as *Bürgermeister,* and he had made the decision to stay on to do the best he could for the people. Oh, the Nazis were so easy to fool ! Head shaking, chuckling, ''All they wanted was someone to agree with them.'' Anyone with a German background who simply made certain gestures could get round them any time they wanted. He had wangled food and fuel for his people in all kinds of involved deals — the Nazis were easy to bribe — he'd saved young men from being hauled off to the camps.

Everybody couldn't run around the woods with Sten guns ; someone had to face the Nazis and work for the people, and that, gentlemen, had taken real courage. He hoped we understood it — real courage. He was a businessman, and he had fought for his people and his country the only way a businessman could.

The bad elements in the Resistance, the Communists (we knew they were in the Resistance ?) : well, first in 1940 they had been against the war on orders from Stalin ; and then when Germany invaded Russia they were all patriotic Frenchmen and firebrands. What could one think of people like that ? Weather vanes ? People for sale ? He thought they staged incidents of resistance just so the Germans would punish a lot of innocent people.

He, Ekhof, loved this land and this village. His family had lived here for generations. He had done his duty the only way he knew how to do it. He understood we were only doing our duty, too, and he was sure everything would be cleared up. Quiet good-night. The room was still, thoughtful.

Our command post came back to fascinated life half an hour

later when Pinckley and his colonel dropped by; we offered him
a drink, and Pinckley said he needed it. He'd seen the firing
squads in action and his delicately strung nerves were gone all
quivery. It seemed there was an apparel problem; all the people
being shot were wearing awfully decent clothes — suits, collars,
clean shirts — and the people helping drag them up to the wall
were positive draggle-tails, in old sweaters and workmen's caps.
One man, supremest horror, despite the cold had worn a sleeveless
sweater with his bare arms showing! Hoodlums! The hoodlums
were shooting the propertied people; that's what it looked like
to Pinckley.

"Senegalese hoodlums," my thought from around brandy.

"Huh?" from Pinckley; his surprise was genuine.

"Senegalese hoodlums are doing the shooting" — back to me —
"anybody can tell a Senegalese First Family, the terribly attractive Senegalese, not at all like Senegalese hoodlums. You're
dead right, Pinckley."

Pinckley sniffed at dangerous frivolity. He was serious. Were
we turning Europe over to the Communists? The great unwashed? There were lots of Communists among the French, we
must know that. How, for example, did we know that this man
we had picked up, this man Ekhof, wasn't some solid citizen being
persecuted by a lot of goddamn Reds? We told him about the
Jew's house, where we had found him, and what had happened
to that Jew — along, we had heard, with lots of others — but
Pinckley refused to let the comment reach him. "Jews! Kikes!..."

Bill Cooper was sitting with me listening to all this. As our
intelligence officer, he had been deep in the affair of Ekhof; he'd
been along when we picked the man up, and he had been the one
in communication with French First Army headquarters. Now,
listening to Pinckley, Bill suffered a sea-change all in his face.
He was normally ruddy, and the flush of anger, rising over the
vasodilating effects of two hours of schnapps, produced a skin
tone that I decided should be called Southwestern Sunset pre-
stroke crimson. I really felt concern for his middle cerebral
artery. Emotions reached a flash point beyond military courtesy and Bill clapped a hand on his .45, telling Pinckley to get

his fucking fascist ass out before he, Bill, shot it full of holes.

Next afternoon an Opel decelerated from highway speed through fifty feet of yaws and skids to a halt outside our door; a young French lieutenant in old horizon-blue overcoat and beret marched in with written authorization to pick up Ekhof.

He was very correct: he conveyed the respects of the French First Army. They appreciated our promptness in picking up Ekhof. They earnestly required his presence at headquarters, in Colmar. For questioning and disposition.

While we waited for sentries to bring Ekhof down, the colonel asked the French officer what it was, precisely, that he had done. The colonel explained that he had been informed that Ekhof was a collaborator, but he was curious about details. What had the man actually committed, so to speak?

As the French officer replied, it was obvious he was trying to restrain himself, to appear unemotional and convincing to a foreign audience. The usual run of crimes, we heard, turning Jews over to the SS and the Gestapo for deportation, providing aid and comfort for the Milice, the fascist thugs, helping organize informers to prey on the Resistance. Here the lieutenant paused, took a breath, and then abruptly, surprisingly jumped to his feet: he flung an arm wide and began declaiming, rather than speaking, in tones that let us know he was furious, sick with anger, and that he clearly didn't give a damn who knew it. Pose and words were theatrical but totally convincing.

There were two hundred families weeping in Colmar tonight, we heard. The lieutenant waved his hand to the north. They were weeping for fathers and brothers and sons, all dead, innocent men, guilty of no crime and accused of none, picked out as hostages by Ekhof to atone for some attack of the Resistance, and turned over to the SS. They had been marched out into a valley high in the Vosges, ringed with machine guns, and forced to freeze slowly to death. That was his last act, the last of a whole history. At this point the sentries brought Ekhof into the room. The last official act, said the lieutenant, pointing, of that ordure.

Ekhof made an impressive attempt at sincerity, even face to face with the French officer. We heard again how someone had to stay and face the Germans on behalf of the townspeople. Someone had to be responsible.

The Frenchman had resumed his military mask and he listened, unmoving, head bowed. When Ekhof paused, the lieutenant pulled a paper out of his pocket and asked Ekhof if he'd ever seen it before. The question was rhetorical: the paper was one of the death proclamations we used to see on the walls stating that So-and-so were to be done to death as enemies of the Third Reich, and at the bottom, right above where it said "Heil Hitler," was Ekhof's signature.

"Your signature?" The lieutenant bent to whisper a few inches from Ekhof's face. "They didn't forge it, did they? Did somebody hold the pen in your hand while you signed?"

Watching Ekhof collapse was like watching the air hiss out of an inflated figure: he left in the lieutenant's grasp, a mass of sudden wrinkles.

A little while later a nun came to my aid station in the headquarters building asking for help for the wounded; there had been heavy fighting when our infantry stormed the town, and as the nun put it, a lot of the people still bled.

The nun was a gentle, determined woman called "*die Schwester*" or "Schwester Rosa" by the villagers.

I made rounds with her and an aid man; we bandaged minor wounds and burns and sprinkled sulfa powder on outraged, infected tissues (a procedure much in vogue at that time, subsequently shown to be completely useless, but part of an immensely satisfying ritual for all).

At the end of each house call the peasants always asked what it cost. I gave everyone the same answer. "*Gar nichts*, Christmas present from Roosevelt." This was always followed by relieved laughter and a trip to the cellar to bring up a bottle of the superb Alsatian wine, which they insisted we take despite our protests. This was again followed by two glasses of schnapps. One could not drink one glass, they explained. A man stood on two legs, he had to have two drinks. House call rounds in an Alsatian village took a fair amount of hepatic stamina.

The last and worse of the wounded was a tiny old lady the neighbors called "Grossmutti." Grandmother had been pinned under a heavy beam when the house was shelled; her femur was shattered and the bone ends were pressing so hard against the skin that it was stretched white; it was a miracle it hadn't torn. For forty-eight hours the old lady had lain in bed with her leg bent at a forty-five-degree angle in the middle of her thigh, with some brandy and aspirin for relief of pain. We used a whiff of chloroform to put her to sleep and quickly straightened the leg and pulled the bone fragments in line, holding them that way with a traction splint. Between the dramatic relief of traction and the effects of a shot of morphine, the old lady in a half-hour was alert, chattering, out of her nightmare, and substantially free of symptoms. She became a little manic and kept up a delightful chatter while we carried her litter down the stairs of the farmhouse. Alsace, she giggled, was like a very attractive, well-endowed young woman with a couple of overattentive suitors. They both wanted to crawl in bed with her and they were killing each other and tearing her up in the disagreements. The pity, she decided comically, was that the mythical young lady had plenty to go around if they would all take turns or maybe share her favors on alternate nights. With the right equipment and attitude, Grossmutti giggled, a young lady could wear out any number of enthusiasts. She used an Alsatian colloquialism better translated as "screw them to death," and I laughed so hard I almost dropped my end of the litter.

Witty, she said, it's not smart to be witty. Witty means the handsome major might have dropped me. Now I'll be dull.

Something in a turn of phrase struck my ear as we slung her litter in the ambulance. I could have sworn I heard a Yiddish word — I think it was "gonif."

"How the hell are you so cheerful after all you've been through? If I didn't know I was in Alsace I'd think I was in the Bronx. Only a Jewish grandmother could be that funny after everything you've been through."

The old lady's face twisted into terror; she clutched my sleeve.

"Jewish." She hissed the terminal sibilants. "What made you think? How could you know? How did you find out?" She was swiftly collapsing, babbling.

"Easy, easy, Mutti; nobody said you're Jewish. I just said you sounded like some Jewish grandmothers I know, and besides, what if you are? The Nazis are gone forever; we're the Americans, for God's sakes. Jewish is good, Jewish gets you a medal; calm yourself, calm yourself."

The old lady's panic was quite out of control. It took minutes of soothing to make her let go of my sleeve and lie back on her litter, and even then she was perspiring.

"I don't believe they're gone; I don't believe they'll ever go."

While Jack drove us into Colmar I sat in the back talking to her quietly and discovered that she was in fact Jewish, mostly Jewish anyway, and that she had been semiconcealed by the farmers in the house where we found her. The little Jewish community of twenty-some people in Herrlisheim-pre-Colmar, she told me, had all been destroyed, rounded up, shipped off, dead, burned . . .

"Only an old witch like me lives, and for what? *'ne alte Hexe.*" She was starting to doze from the morphine. I asked her about Ekhof and the house in which we'd found him.

"My nephew," she whispered. "My nephew he sent to the damned camp, the pig. That was his house." We had taken Ekhof, I told her, we'd turned him over to the French.

"We know," she said, "we all know. Tell them to kill him quickly before he gets out. He'll get out, you know."

The old lady seemed to think of Ekhof as a caged beast, only waiting for a break in the bars to resume killing.

All the way into Colmar the old lady clutched my hand, babbling requests for reassurance. Did the Americans have lots of tanks? Tanks were important. Were the Americans going to stay? They couldn't leave and let the Germans come back. Did the Americans understand that among the French there were people who hated Jews, people who helped the Nazis find Jews and kill them?

"Don't let the outsides fool you," she was whispering in my ear now, drawing up close. "The people with the dignified out-

sides were the Germans' whores, their pimps. They were the ones
the Germans bought, they'd go back to selling the Jews to the
SS in a minute." Exhaustion and morphine finally took hold and
she fell back half asleep, not losing her clutch on my hand.

In the big Stadt Krankenhaus, now the Hôpital de Cité Colmar,
we delivered the old lady to the civilian physicians and nurses.

"Keep it secret," she was hissing in my ear. "Don't tell. Secret." I promised her.

"You still can't trust them. Tell them I'm French, Alsatian
French. Keep our secret."

I talked to the physicians in the receiving room of the hospital.
"A big beam fell from overhead on her leg," I said; "she has a
complicated fracture." The old lady sank her nails in my wrist.
"She's French, she's Alsatian," I informed the surprised faces.

"Well of course she's French," a nurse said. "We're all French,
thank God."

The old lady was wheeled away on a cart and as she disappeared
down a corridor she tipped her face to me and winked, finger to
lips; I winked back, repeating the gesture. A young French physician looked at us both and asked, "You two got some kind of
secret? What's going on?"

"Yes, you bet we have a secret," I told him. "A big state
secret. I'd be the last to tell you."

Die Schwester came to invite me to a party. Her invitation was
sprinkled with hesitations and delicacies. The party was rather
a private affair, she explained; there were some people — delicacy, pause — not wanted. Would I mind being invited?

Mind? Why wouldn't I be honored to be invited?

Well, the Resistance was various, it included various types.
There might be people there of a type I wasn't accustomed to.

I told *die Schwester* that nothing would make me happier than
spending an evening with people of a type I wasn't accustomed
to. She giggled.

The party was in a hall/*Gasthaus*/auditorium somewhere in the
middle of town. *Die Schwester* was meticulous about directions
but she needn't have been, for the singing came clear through

walls across starry snow: the building was luminous with sound. Inside through blackout curtains, lantern light flicked gold on starched peasant dresses and threadbare suits: it twinkled on bottles and glasses; it glowed on tricolors.

The village band was really *verschieden;* astonishing variety, splendid effect. As I walked in, everybody was shouting and stamping to a kind of military cadenza rendered on a fiddle, a bass drum, and a tuba. Pause, applause, a breath, and then a folk song rose and swelled in four-part harmony: the room chimed with resonant basses and high clear sopranoes. "*Oh Strasbourg, du wunderschöne Stadt,*" they sang, "you wondrous city, therein lie buried so many soldiers, so many, so gallant, so young" ... American hair stood up and skin chilled to hear the poor people, the peasants, singing the beauty of the centuries of their tragic earth.

Drinking was rapid and happy; the lantern light turned more golden and misty around its points; women in Alsatian dress twirled their wide red skirts, fluttering to clapping. People mounted chairs and tables to start toasts, but ended singing. Speeches died aborning; whenever someone started to make gestures with a red, serious face, they were stopped. "Wait for Alfoss," people said, "no speeches until Alfoss and the men come."

Alfoss? What men? Where is *die Schwester?* Not here yet, I was told. Wait.

I drank more, pumped hands, and was slapped on the shoulder by patients' families; I gathered that one reason I was the only American invited was that I had taken care of some relative of almost everybody in the village. It was also pleasant that I spoke one of their languages and appeared, as they put it, sympathetic.

After an hour a boy ran in, dancing in the middle of the room, waving his arms, twirling to catch everyone's eye.

"They're coming, they're coming"; the child stopped his waving with a finger pointed dramatically at the door.

The whole room turned to face the night, the band crashed into the "Marseillaise," and seven men marched in the door, one leading, six behind, two by two, rifles and Sten guns slung over shoulders, caps tilted, marching in step to the middle of the room, halting smartly in the middle of a volcano of cheering, a sound free, happy, thunderous.

"Resistance," someone was yelling it in my ear. "The Resistance fighters of the village, the real heroes."

The "Marseillaise" is one hell of a song any time, but that night, in that setting, it swept us all right out of control; everybody in the room was crying, linking arms, lifting voices over the brasses and drumbeats of the band. There was something very close to ecstasy in the room, a delirium of happiness not yet quite believable, the sound of people singing of victory incredibly won over legions of demons.

The men stacked guns in a formal ceremony, threw their caps in a corner, and began drinking, as one of them said, seriously. Alfoss, the leader, shook hands with me and thanked me for caring for some of his family; he semiapologized for the economic and social levels of the room. Poor people were the Resistance, he said, mostly the rich were for sale. I was an American, a physician, probably well-to-do, I might not understand.

I was indignant; I interrupted; "New Deal Democrat, dammit, and from New Deal Democrat to Norman Thomas socialist..."

Alfoss interrupted me and repeated the phrase with a bright, quick grin.

"From New Deal Democrat to Norman Thomas socialist is okay. I understand, see? I know American politics. It's a logical progression for good Americans. I withdraw my comment about reactionary rich; that was all *merde.*"

"*Salud, camarad.*" This came from the tallest of the Resistance men, a dark man, Gary Cooper creases vertically down each cheek around whiteness of grin. We gave each other the clenched fist; Alfoss and the rest of the squad beamed.

"This is Sepp," I was told; "he's our world traveler. He was in the International Brigade. He's been fighting the longest. He has no right to be alive."

The rest of the squad began shouting slogans from the Spanish Civil War. "*El frente popular del mundo!*"

"Better to die on your feet than live on your knees."

"Madrid is the graveyard of fascism. No, wait — *we* are the graveyard of fascism."

"Sepp taught us all that. In the woods he used to tell us stories about Spain...."

More drinking, dancing, linked arms, interruptions of singing sometimes so pure and so tightly melodic the room had to stop to listen, as if the music held us all in shimmering coils.

In the quiet intervals, while the musicians drank and rested, I could sense another level of conversation emerging, hard and bitter: it involved certain citizens of Nexheim who were at that moment cowering in their homes, lamenting the Wehrmacht.

A Resistance man argued with two middle-aged women.

"We can't be like the Nazis, of course, no, but we can't let criminals run around. With traitors, we give them possibly a little slap, ho ho, you naughty boys?"

One of the women put a hand across her mouth, shaking her head.

"It's just that it's hard to think about now: we're so happy, so relieved. Revenge, killing, my God."

"One must differentiate," the other woman waved a finger, "the passive ones, the cows. Forget them even if they raised their caps to the Germans."

By now a large group was gathering: everyone shrugged and looked expressive about the cows. Jo jo, the voices agreed, forget the cows. You don't expect a rabbit to act like a staghound; a sheep eats grass, it doesn't bite; give a pig a warm soft place and he doesn't ask your name.

"*Sprichwörter*, sayings, we've got thousands." Sepp was grinning behind my ear.

"On the other hand," I looked up to see Alfoss standing on the little platform where the band sat: he had the attention of the room; "*on* the other hand," he emphasized, "you can't blame a poison snake for who it's father is, but you still kill it."

The word *Schlange* — snake — slithered through the crowd: everybody lifted faces to the platform as Alfoss held up a hand and ticked off categories on his fingers. Informers, he listed,

Milice, profiteers, working for the Germans, out-and-out Nazis:
with each word people nodded, inserting names. Alfoss paused
and seemed to speak with difficulty.

"Father Schneider?" he asked. "What kind of animal is he?"

At once the room was still, divided: I had a sense that half the
people were looking at their neighbors with kindly sorrow, with
pity.

"We know what kind of animal he is," someone called. "Question
is, what do we do with him?"

Someone else observed that they hadn't cut a priest's head off
since the terror: he hoped they hadn't forgotten how.

"Baptism, first communion, confirmation, all my kids. I'll have
to do it over: none of it could count, not from him."

The crowd dispersed into knots and clumps: voices were low.
Alfoss walked me to one side and explained.

"Half the people in this town, in this room, are Catholic. I
am — I was. Father Schneider was the absolute ass end of the
collaborators. He used to preach sermons about how it was okay
to kill Jews because they were the murderers of Christ, so please
help the authorities. We used to see him eating, happy as a pig,
with the SS and Gestapo bigshots. He claimed it was official
Church policy to cooperate with the marshal — the emissary of
God, he called him — to betray all us subversives in the Resistance.
We think he informed: we know he got one of our boys
killed because he wouldn't hide him."

None of us had noticed Schwester Rose come in the door: she
was standing with a French officer, listening, twisting her fingers.

Alfoss walked to her, holding out his hands.

"But it's all right! Here's our Jeanne d'Arc. Sister, you redeemed
the Church in Niederelsass! I hear they're going to canonize
you."

"Please," *die Schwester* grinned, "I'm supposed to die first."

"Look out, *Schwester*, someone else called, "it was a bishop
that burned Jeanne!"

The air began to clear: *die Schwester* talked to me, apologetic:
she hoped I understood. I told her the situation had been made
very clear.

The French officer was introduced. He had been liaison with the underground : a Resistance man assured me he was *ein tapfere Mensch,* a brave man. "He used to cross our lines to get to us," I heard. "They would have burned him slowly."

"Pierre Stein," the officer explained his name. "Imagine, a Jewish Resistance officer spying. I was everything the Nazis had wet dreams about. I still have nightmares thinking about what they would have done if they'd ever caught me."

I followed Stein and *die Schwester* as they wandered through the room, shaking hands and bowing in toasts, and it became obvious that everyone was shaken, even shamed. The evening threatened to dwindle until Sepp lurched against a wall, threw up an unsteady hand, and yelled : "Clean! Attention!"

Surprise was welcome : everybody listened.

"You always knew the dirt was there! Don't be embarrassed! In the world, people cover up with paint and fancy clothes and titles and money, but these last four years, at least, by God, they showed the dirt! You just saw it!"

He bowed.

"Congratulations, ladies and gentlemen! Congratulations, you are clean," he corrected himself, "you are *the* Clean!"

People began to laugh ; Sepp grinned.

"Clean, and patriots and heroes and we won! Why are we standing around feeling guilty about some shit we washed off the floor?"

He raised his glass and shouted.

"*Dreck aus! Hurrah!*"

A few people shouted "hurrah" back, but Sepp shook his head.

"All voices! *Dreck aus!*"

This time most of the room shouted back. Sepp waved to the band. " 'Sambre et Meuse,' " he called, and as they crashed into that wonderful march, Sepp and the room kept up verse and response until the "hurrahs" made the glasses tremble.

The air cleared wonderfully : the band struck up a polka, the evening took wings, and from then on there was no such thing as silence. Whenever the musicians paused to breathe or drink, the conversation rose to an amiable roar as people shouted, laughed, gestured, and postured. Two men made mock political speeches announcing their candidacy for the premiership, promising hanging and dragging behind wild horses for some local figures (cheers) and gold and land for everyone in the room (pandemonium).

In one circle a gray-haired woman began a finger-wagging no-nonsense monologue with "*Ich will euch sag'n,*" — "let me tell you" — about the many years she had told the whole village that Such-and-such and So-and-so were scoundrels they shouldn't trust their daughters or their money with, but would they listen, oh no, and then the Nazis came and you saw what they were and now maybe you'll listen to an old lady. When she threatened to become shrill, an old drunken peasant turned her off by whacking her on the rear and shouting, "*Jo Mutti! Stimmt!*" which everyone found very funny.

The noise rolled on, happier and happier : I had never heard such intensity of speech. People were rolling and gamboling in words, savoring them, intoxicated. When Alfoss tried to talk to me I put my hands over my ears and winced : he dragged me off to a quieter corner, shouting "*Selbstverstandlich!*"

"How not ? " he went on. "They've only had seventy-two hours."

I looked a question.

"They've had the privilege of talking for exactly seventy-two hours. Since you chased out the Germans. They're not used to it yet. It makes you drunk. Imagine if the Inquisition had your balls in a vise for four years and then, *auf einmal,* the Inquisition was dead and your balls were still okay and somebody said, Go make love. For the first few days you'd screw yourself silly. It's more than Rothschild, being able to talk out loud. Listen to them : it's worthwhile."

I did listen, and Alfoss was right. It was almost impossible to believe these were poor people talking. Poor or not, Europeans know their history; for comparison one would have to imagine Nebraska farmers talking easily about the Long Parliament, the Conway Cabal, the Gadsden purchase, and Maximilian's fate in Mexico.

A wind-reddened peasant slammed a fist into a hand and shouted, "Since Dreyfus! Before Dreyfus! Who puts their careers on altars and lights candles to them? Who hates the Jews and says fuck the Republic, and prays for a king back at Versailles? The French regulars, the marshals, the generals, the little shits, the colonels, that's who." He struck a pose and saluted. "Certainly, General. Let me keep my rank and my pension and I'll sell my own mother. Naturally I'll sell my countrymen: anything else? A few Jews? Some patriots? Dangerous types, republicans? Name your price."

In another circle, a stocky man was posed with a raised hand. "One year we had a Republic, Napoleon was First Consul. Next year we had an emperor and the goddamn émigrés were back and the Revolution was lost. We never got it back. The émigrés screwed in a hurry and produced great-grandchildren, important ones, and they got in line to kiss the Nazi's ass. Nobles, bishops, millionaires, all back like poison. You see any of them hiding in cellars with Sten guns? Any of them shipped off? To camps?"

A young woman grinned with an idea. "Ideals are for the poor, Jean. The rich can't afford them!"

Everybody clapped and shouted the mot across the room.

"Be fair." The speaker was the schoolteacher, a balding thin man who swam in oversized clothes. "General le Clerc, for instance, he's from a noble family. Changed his name to protect them. De Lattre de Tassigny, the same. One of the top Maquis, they say he's a count or something, they still won't give his name. There are some, creditable."

"Sure. One percent. Vive the creditable one percent!"

That appealed to everyone too: "Ninety-nine percent to the guillotine," they shouted, "vive the one!"

I heard those peasants and workmen reaching into French history as easily as a roomful of Americans would recall last year's county election: they went searching through centuries for the powers and faces that had shaped their world, and at the end they all had to confront Ekhof. I heard the name everywhere: I saw incredulous headshakings. The man who gave candy to kids, the usher at church, part of their own lives: they had seen a man who was a piece of themselves turn into a happy, frenetic, fulfilled monster. It was like watching your father turn into a werewolf, they said.

Only slowly, after the fall of years, have I come to know what that room held, and who those men and women in poor clothes really were. They were the sparks that make humanity possible, the cells in the organism immune to challenges of fear or greed or pain or even extinction, the happy, happy few who had found motivation, belief, ideals to surmount anything the world could hurl at them, and, most moving of all, now, in the aftermath of terror, what they wanted to talk about was how ordinary they were. They had all, they told me, been frightened out of their minds and they paraded their terrors like medals, laughing half-sheepishly.

"That day I drove right past the Germans with the guns under the turnips, my God, I knew what it felt like to lose control; I almost pissed right there."

Die Schwester: "Under my habit I had all that old French army ammunition and the Gestapo stared and stared at me while I walked along the street. I was sure they could see right through me. I was saying rosaries in my head faster than a machine gun shoots. I hope God forgives me."

"God forgive you, *Schwester?* You have to forgive God for what he let happen to the people in the last five years."

The air in that room that night vibrated with the happiness and closeness of people who have faced ultimate fright and watched each other succeed as humans; the air was warm with regard and with intimacy, and later with a sudden sense of nostalgia as the night wore on and everyone realized it was going to have to end.

Before dawn, while it was still dark, Alfoss made a pronouncement from a table top:

"This is one party that isn't going to end gradually with everyone shaking hands good-night and wandering off. Not tonight; outside, everybody!"

In coats, scarves, and mittens, the crowd gathered in the snow while Alfoss and the Resistance men formed up, pointed their guns at the sky, and let go with a magnificent volley, the Sten guns emptying their magazines, the carbines barking as the men worked the bolts, the muzzle blasts gorgeous, orange, streaks and sparks against the black and white and blue of the night. American sentries, at first startled, grinned and waved and wished out loud they could join in the fun. Finally we all staged a triumphant, drunken march around the village, singing everybody home, and after many handshakes I wandered at last to the command post, sinking through frosty euphoria toward sleep, grasping with the last shreds of consciousness at some notion of a world of heroes and saints, and accepting the knowledge, suddenly and finally, that a nation without a leaven of people willing to die for an ideal, for some abstract imperative concept beyond any earthly utility, is a nation vulnerable, corruptible, already conquered.

We left Nexheim-bas-Colmar late next afternoon on a rare day of gold and blue, of late winter sunlight that spoke of spring. The villagers, *die Schwester,* the Resistance men, all lined up in the square and cheered us as the column roared away. A French fighter plane did a victory roll over our column, a good omen, we all thought, and as a small dab of whipped cream on this particular cake, we had that night the minute but intense happiness of being back of the light line, out of the blackout zone, so that we were able to drive with lights on, outside and inside, sitting in a suddenly delightful world in the back of the ambulance, stewing rations and reading paperback books, threading the passages of the Vosges on a clear night that blazed with stars.

14

The Captain's Story

WHEN WE WEREN'T IN COMBAT, we functioned as an efficient small hospital for cuts, infections, mild flu, and gastroenteritis. Patients were comfortable on litters, the aid-station stove was warm, the conversation was endless and agreeable, and the food was no worse than anything that came out of a ten-in-one ration box. Soldiers begged to stay with us instead of facing the long plunge into the rearward jungle, where their watches would be stolen by hospital orderlies, and where they might end in replacement depots to face reassignment far from their combat families. We forgot paperwork and carried them around with us.

The captain from the Third Infantry was passing through our zone when he fell ill of something he ate. While expelling the *cuisine du pays*, he whanged his head on a bit of sharp metal projecting from his jeep. Our diagnosis: food poisoning, acute, source unknown; laceration, scalp, three inches. We stitched his head and quieted his inward raging, and he spent two days with us. By the second night he felt well enough to accept stimulants and chat around the stove.

He had maximum Third Division credentials — Africa, Sicily, Salerno, the Rapido, Anzio, Marseilles, the Vosges, Colmar. He also had a close working relationship with God and the Angel of

Death, because he had survived all this in an occupation with a life expectancy of one hour. (Forward observers had to work close enough to the enemy to adjust fire by direct vision. The enemy went to great lengths to eliminate them.)

It was the first time I heard the usage, common in the Third Infantry, of the word *Truscott* as an adjective with one specific set of connotations, and the name *Patton* as an adjectival noun, on the other side of meaning.

"That was a Truscott operation all the way," we'd hear, or, Manichaean-opposite, "That son of a bitch pulled a real Patton."

We were fascinated; we asked the captain for instance, and he started with Africa. Patton had run about Africa screaming to make people wear neckties and leggins and helmets. Doctors operating fifty miles behind the lines had to adjust glasses and masks under absurd steel helmets and men in combat, digging foxholes, had to keep neckties knotted tight in hundred-degree heat. Reason? No reason. Patton said so. German intelligence officers laughed themselves silly; it didn't help us and it didn't hurt them. Georgie's screechy little ego went wailing over Africa yammering about neckties when he should have been worrying about adequate antitank guns and decent armor. We didn't have either.

Truscott operation? "Well," he said, "it was like Truscott training the Third Division in Africa to move faster than any infantry in history. Five and a half miles the first hour, four and a half the next, three and a half miles an hour from then on. Run, trot, walk, run, thirty miles in eight hours, full combat pack. Think about that next time you walk somewhere. Truscott went to each battalion to explain why. 'You all know how long it takes to dig a foxhole,' he used to say. 'Half an hour, forty-five minutes. It takes the enemy a certain time to dig himself in, to lay wire, to get his guns registered and his machine guns and mortars sited, and to organize himself into a unit that can kill you. He can't kill well or hardly at all unless he's organized. That takes time and you're not going to give him that time. You're going to hit him when he's still a mob of scared, useless, separated individuals, running away or wandering around loose. You'll stay alive and you'll win the war.' The Truscott trot, we called it, and we moved until we dropped. We believed him, see.

"Truscott got his reputation as an unbelievably tough guy on the beach at Mehedia, with the Ninth Infantry, time of the invasion. Everything was fucked up and shot up and Truscott picked up an M-1 rifle and kicked asses right off that beach through the Vichy machine guns and just about won the battle alone. That's when they gave him the Third to command. Old Stone Face, we called him, Injun Joe. He came from Oklahoma and the story was that he was anyway part Indian. He certainly looked like it: hawk nose, long jaw, face that was carved solid. He could move thousands of men around and send people galloping to bust their ass without changing his face any more than you would if you coughed a little.

"In Sicily, Patton commanded Third Army and Truscott commanded us; they had to meet a lot and we always heard what happened. Patton'd come assing his way into a headquarters with his hands on those bullshit pistols, and he'd glare and stare and yell and pull his mouth down while he watched all the little pimps shiver. (That's what we called his staff, Patton's Pimps; he picked them on account of how they could say yes and kiss his behind.) Georgie had lots of fun until Truscott walked into the room; he'd try all this tantrum stuff on Truscott, because it was the only way he knew how to communicate, and it would bounce off that hard face and those eyes that saw three feet through you, and Georgie used to run down like an old-fashioned Victrola that needed winding. Uhhhhhhh, he'd go, slower and slower, and then he'd turn away to a map or something. Truscott was always real polite, formal, and three miles ahead of Georgie. Everything Georgie screamed about, Truscott had already done, only better.

"Going north across Sicily, we went flat out for Palermo a hundred miles in four days, fighting. Nobody in the history of armies ever moved that fast, but by God, we did. It was like hiking through chemical smoke, chalk dust, and horseshit, and heat that dropped a lot of guys right over. There was almost no water, and there were Krauts and Italians fighting rearguard and we kicked their butts one hundred miles. Forty-fifth on our right, Second on our left, they did okay but we led all the way. Stuff I still can't believe; Second Battalion of our Thirtieth Infantry covered over fifty miles in twenty-four hours, carrying everything to attack a place called San Stefano, and they took it even with the guys so tired they were falling asleep over their machine guns.

"We were all excited, exhausted crazy, and the big word we yelled was Palermo. Palermo! We yelled it through the choke and the heat and the explosions. Truscott made sure we all knew how famous it was. We had a lot of Sicilian-Americans, and they told us about Garibaldi and the Redshirts, and the palaces, and the ocean, and the booze, and the broads. Palermo became a kind of a mania: it was like some kind of a dream out there on the other side of the machine guns and the dead men.

"After four days of fighting and moving like nobody ever fought or moved before, there we were standing on this big rim of hills, that the Sicilians called the shell of gold, and there was Palermo, and we were a real conquering army that just took one of the most beautiful cities in the world, like the old Romans or somebody.

"Everyone was kind of hysterical, yelling: we were forming up, to march in to be safe for a while and eat and drink — we hardly had any water — and be cheered and get drunk and screwed.

"Then Patton pulled a Patton. Radio message to Third Division. Troops will hold in place in the hills. General Patton will make the formal entry with his tanks to accept the surrender. On no account will anyone enter Palermo before Patton. Off limits to Third Division; camp in the nice dry hot hills.

"Well, we were ready to mutiny, but people at division said Truscott didn't even look surprised. He acted like he expected it. A couple of orders came out of Injun Joe, and two weapons carriers full of GIs took off down a side road into town. Couple of hours we sat there, thirsty, dirty, hot, ready to kill Patton, and then we heard a lot of shooting and yelling down in the town, and pretty soon we could see smoke from some buildings that were burning. Another hour and here came the weapons carriers back all over white flags and Italians, the mayor and the boss of this, and the chief of the other. All the big shots. MPs whipped them on to division, just like they were expected. The Italians begged good kind greatly distinguished General Truscott to, for chrissakes, march into Palermo. Looting everywhere, they said, burning, mobs. Italian cops and soldiers busy running away and *anarchismo* was going wild. Please, good kind general, protect our beautiful city ; also our stores.

"Truscott fired off a message about the looting and the burning and the danger to valuable property and military installations, and a lot of routine crap that nobody could argue with, and in another hour the Third Infantry was marching into Palermo, right into about a million screaming happy Italians, and booze, and broads, and all the wine we could drink, and a place to clean up and sleep.

"By the time old Georgie got there with his fucking tanks, the next day, there were Third Division signs all over the place, and Third Division GIs, all shined and beautiful, and Injun Joe met Georgie at the square down by the cathedral, with a real formal salute, and he said he was sorry to spoil the occasion but General Patton certainly understood about private property and law and order, and the Third Division was delighted to have been helpful. Sir.

"Guys who were there said Patton's lower lip stuck out like he was going to cry. Most poisonous thing you could do to Georgie was to put a cork in him so he couldn't yell and stamp, and Truscott was a genius at it. Georgie was so pissed he went off and beat up those sick soldiers.

"What made that operation a real Truscott we found out later. Guys in those weapons carriers were Italian-American GIs. All Sicilian background, most of them with connections in Palermo. Truscott's intelligence had them all picked out. They drove to city hall, carrying guns and looking tough, and in an hour they had a line on who were the anti-Fascist good-guy Italians that had been kicked around a lot, and who were the big local pricks that worked with the Krauts and turned people over to the Gestapo and the SS.

"In another half-hour, the good Italians were in the streets busting windows and helping themselves to stuff in stores. It was a very precise operation when you consider how fast it was; all the stores that got looted belonged to the worst Fascists and Jew-killers and Kraut-helpers in town. Then they let the mayor and his buddies come out to ask for help from the nice *soldati* of Third Infantry. So what happened, the good guys got to kick the shit out of the bad guys, and justice got done, and we marched in to enjoy our very own city, and Injun Joe as usual had been thinking ahead around six corners, even anticipating how Georgie would act and what he would do to head him off, which he never found very difficult.

"In Third Infantry we never had to be long-winded; we could use one word to describe that kind of an operation or that kind of a guy.

"Only sad thing about Injun Joe was he was too good; we lost him when they promoted him to take over VI Corps. Good for the whole army, though; he could run anything better than most people."

(Official histories verify practically all of the captain's story. Patton did order the Third Division to halt as it was about to enter Palermo, rioting did break out in the streets, and the Third Division did, in fact, march in at the request of the Italian authorities, thereby frustrating Patton. Did Truscott manipulate the situation? Third Division folklore insists he did, and the story is too good and too typical not to be true.)

We had to turn the other face of the coin to see Mark Clark. He was the Fifth Army commander who threw away the greatest victory of the Italian campaign just to get his photograph taken liberating Rome. The hell of Anzio, the freezing horror and piled corpses along the Rapido, were about to pay off in a trap that would catch the whole German Tenth Army and all its equipment and leave northern Italy defenseless, but Mark Clark had a rush of publicity to the head. (It was a recurring disease with him.) He deliberately disobeyed the orders of Marshal Alexander, the too-gentle British commander in the Mediterranean, and swung Fifth Army in a mad race for Rome, with correspondents hanging on fenders and photographers snapping Clark's handsome profile, every time he could put himself in front of a camera. He tried to push the great soldiers of the special service forces to get themselves killed at a roadblock so that he could enter Rome while there was still light for pictures; he posed his embarrassed division commanders on various historic steps, holding out maps they didn't need to look at. All the time Mark Clark was dancing before cameras, the German Tenth Army was retreating through the gap generously provided for it, taking all its tanks and guns and trucks safely north of Rome to settle in for another ghastly, unnecessary winter of shelling and freezing and mangling. Irrational behavior, cold, verified history. That's how a guy pulls a Patton, said the Third Division captain, see? We saw.

Publicity; the essence dissected further brings up Truscott's absolute exclusion of his name from dispatches. Such-and-such battalion captured this, or a particular regiment stormed that, or Private Somebody heroically did the other. Any attempt to use Truscott's name or names of Third Division headquarters officers in dispatches was chopped off with reproof.

The Patton complex, on the contrary, meant a shameless sniffing for newsprint and adulation with the commanding general's name leading every dispatch.

The abstract, as always, derives from the well-chiseled concrete. Essence of Patton: one who finds himself planetary, galactic. He is his own universe; he cannot conceive that any other exists. He has a frightening freedom to inflict his grotesqueries or cruelties on others; his gratification is everybody else's good. If egotistical satiety demands it, he'll destroy a battalion or a nation or the world. He is his own totality, and from angels through aardvarks to moldwarps, everything must dance to sustain his boundaries and projections.

And now, we said more happily, consider the Truscott. We did so for a long time, past the end of the brandy. Down on the same peninsula I named some warriors: Belisarius, Germanicus, Marcus Aurelius. Men like this are stamped, early in life, and the outlines of the mold spell honesty. They fill the mold without effort; it fits them and they have no question about who they are and what they can do. They're free of the need to grimace and prance; they're free to spend themselves on a cause, for an ideal, scorning advantage and chaining the ego in some remote corner to babble and shriek and rattle its shackles. Having won, they're satisfied with the achievement; they're not driven to seek their value in the gaze and the wonder of others, and they walk off into the quiet corners of history where the truth lives, grinning to watch imposters scribbling their worthless names across the walls of the public baths.

My colleagues thought this pretty highfalutin; they settled on the concepts of competence, justified confidence, honest modesty, total dedication.

Not bad.

Thank you, Captain, thank you, superb Third Infantry Division. I now have a calipers to apply to the rest of this war, and possibly a good way beyond.

(Note: Bill Mauldin described Truscott as a man "so tough he could chew up a ham like Patton without bothering to pick his teeth." He also described the time Truscott gave the address on Memorial Day, 1943, in the military cemetery at Salerno. He turned his back on the assembled windbags and sparklers and talked to the crosses in the cemetery, quietly, apologizing, and then walked away without looking around.)

☀ 15

Pictures on an Expedition

F OR TWO WEEKS we rested, in reserve, scattered through some hills west of Metz. In my diary I wrote: "Suspended in time: *sanglots longues de l'hiver mourant,* music of mist and fading snow on Lorraine hills where we sat, happy in mud, savoring with new and deep delight the squelching walk to the mess, the chunk of axes on firewood, the warmth of liquor on tongues, sacred sensations because we were still alive to enjoy them, talking sometimes of friends burned and gone, sometimes of the war that rumbled on in another planet."

Idylls are off limits for combat troops: ours lasted only until the gaps left by the winter fighting had been filled with new tanks and riflemen. Then, as is perpetually ordained in armies, we moved out in the dark, depressing, smallest hours, rumbling north through fog and speculation. The maddest of the rumors that had been circulating was correct: we were off to Third Army on some kind of cavalry raid into the rear of a whole German army group.

Consolation of geography. Look at the sign, someone yelled, for chrissakes we're in Luxembourg; and indeed we did cross the corner of Luxembourg, winding through cities of unknown names, spending a night crawling in blackout beside the wide sheen of the Moselle, here on its last northward plunge toward the Rhine, and toward dawn we recognized fires ahead of us as the city of Trier, newly fallen. Motion through geography is consoling; association with place names gave one an odd sense of importance, of accomplishment, infinitely better than the depressing, deadly shuttling from one forgotten mudhole to another of the winter past. Here was the big world and we were moving through it to great events; by now we could tell where we were and we had some idea of what was going to happen.

Tactics and strategy: The Saar Palatinate is a trapezoid, bounded on its east and on its northeast by the Rhine as that river flows north past the French border and then, after fifty or sixty miles, makes a bend northwestward heading for Holland. The Moselle runs into the Rhine a good deal west of that kink, thus forming the west boundary of the trapezoid; the southern boundary, running roughly east and west, faces France along the Siegfried and Maginot line positions.

All winter we had been facing Germans in the Siegfried line; Third Army's attack to the Rhine north along the west bank of the Moselle had uncovered the right flank of those armies, and when Trier fell the Americans solved the problem of the south-facing Germans by sending four armored divisions across the Moselle into the naked flank of the Germans in the Saar. Instead of glowering to the south from their cement pillboxes, they now had to look over their shoulders at a great mass of tanks cutting arcs from northwest to southeast, steel teeth closing in on them from above and behind. We were doing something intelligent.

We kept hearing from geography: from dark, gurgling throats, the Moselle called up to the pontoon bridge. You've lost your lovely French river of Épinal and Remiremont, the water was muttering. That was the river that was far up the current, far behind us in place and in time, and now under these pontoons, said the gurgles, is the German Mosel. Behind you is the world of familiar and charted danger, where one town predictably meant terror and burning and dismemberment, but another as predictably meant safe sleep and wine, where you could always feel behind your back the warmth of an Allied country. No more liberating: you're conquerors, you're advancing into fear and hatred all around three hundred sixty degrees.

A machine-gunner echoed the river: "It feels really like the end of something, you know, when you cross a big river like this into enemy country. Real tough trying to swim back. Guess we just keep on goin' from here to the end. . . ."

Dawn, and the classic rosy fingers glanced on earthen walls, astonishing us as they soared up from the roadside, turning into hills at impossible angles, festooned with stakes and vines. Waking, we realized we were marching through the fabled vineyards of the Moselle, the country of the great wines of Bernkastel and Trittenheim. The thing that made the vineyard infinitely more interesting, as someone pointed out, was that we weren't liberating this country, we were conquering it.

A whole squad of infantrymen listened fascinated while I explained about the vineyards and their products.

"What you're saying, Doc, is that there ought to be quite a lot to drink around here."

"Yes," I was happy to reply, "quite a magnificent lot of the best drinking in the world. We're about to conquer the goddamn stuff."

"Well, sir," the corporal's fingers were twiddling the catch on his tommy gun, "this war's beginning to make some kind of sense." Some of the tenseness on faces was giving way to savage grins, to anticipation; the lessons of the Vikings were about to get learned all over again. Conquering places and countries sometimes had a certain logic, especially if you were thirsty.

In the dragon's living room: The column ground its length through a village like any other village, over cobblestones, past half-timbered houses, manure piles, narrow, winding streets, and then someone in the half-track wakened.

"This is a *German* village, you guys! For chrissakes, we're inside Germany!"

All winter the German radio had been yowling about what we'd find if we ever poked our Bolshevistic American Jewish plutocratic noses across the sacred boundaries of the Fatherland.

The menu was impressive; it was supposed to include martyrs hurling themselves under tank treads with Molotov cocktails, death-defying home guards with Panzerfauste and fanaticism, Werewolves tossing grenades, a nation of heroes laughing at death.

Well, here we were. The streets were still. A couple of oddly dressed children, legs in long black stockings treadling under dark suits, darted from one house to another, the only life we saw. Faces were furtive behind curtains, telling us we were indeed conquerors, feared. As we advanced farther through the village, we found something that was truly Germanic, something unique, something the Deutsche Bevölkerung produced all the time, everywhere. The streets were alive; everywhere there was fluttering, waving, twinkling, always white; bedsheets, pillowcases, towels, handkerchiefs on sticks, anything white protruded out of every possible civic orifice, flapping, conveying surrender. We give up fast, said the pillowcases; don't shoot.

"*Frontgau Westmark tapfer und treu,*" the black scrawl screamed on whitewash. Along walls and houses other huge scribbles tried to convey defiance. "*Kapitulieren? Nie!*" "*Sieg oder Siberien.*" "*Wir kämpfen bis zum Endsieg.*"

Quite an *Endsieg,* I mused, quite a victory of peasant will to survive and final human concern with self and one's own epidermis over miles and years and libraries of bullshit.

Flutter, said the sheets not heroically, don't shoot. The handkerchiefs whimpered peace.

Metaphor of conquest: We are a skillful serpent, fanged and winged, as the advance guard flicks out its tanks at the defended town, searching the roadblocks. The prey lashes back with brilliant fans, whips, and flails, traversing machine guns. Around the tanks the ground erupts in flashes; unharmed, the advance guard sinks into folds of earth and messages ripple along the monster's length; steel joints and sinews coil.

The killing starts with a chant; artillery observers, tank commanders, squadron leaders lounging through clouds, call commands and responses through compressing air; the voices coming out of radios are eerie, toneless, implausibly calm, a ritual of schizophrenics.

Shellbursts tighten over German heads; over, short, left, right, on, fire for effect, the electric muttering plays checkers with explosions until whole hedgerows and garden beds of flaming blossoms twinkle over the targets. Tank commanders define the anatomy of resistance through binoculars and periscopes; a flanking column writhes away, reaching around, safe behind earth.

Design for eruption: Messages oscillate back and forth along the column from air-strike officer in the half-track ahead of me to the battalion CO somewhere on a flank, back to air-strike officer, out to artillery, who will mark the target, back to air-strike officer again, and finally vertically, up some thousands of feet to the P-47 squadron droning, roaring, tilting circles in and out of vision through clouds.

The air strike is directed in the voices of tired derelicts slumped against Bowery walls.

The groan from the clouds says okay; uuuhhh, the noise comes; somebody up there is scrabbling at boredom; uuuhhh, he guesses he'll go downstairs first; orange two will cover, okay? Sequence will be thus-and-such, uuuhhh, well, now. No emphasis, dying fall . . .

Tone and event flee to opposite ends of comprehension as the speck tips its wings and becomes a fury, snarling toward earth, toward the red smoke the artillery puts on the target, screaming in that plunge to death I never quite believed before the flattening behind trees and houses and the soaring up and away, leaving behind a tower of black smoke and parts of those same trees and houses floating, turning, turning, crashing. Four times the specks drop, scream, thunder, and disappear, swift verticals up through sparkles of fire into fleece.

(Those voices; by now we know they're the voices of men hiding in tonal entropy from chronic closeness to dismemberment. Any emotion would rip the edges of clenched control.)

Smoke clears and the artillery snorts again, covering the defense with layering explosions; everything under there, living and earth, must be shredded with steel shards. Tank guns begin their slam-boom, slam-boom from front and flank, the muzzles winking only a little ahead of the burst of the shells. Last, the black, swift dots, infantry, jump from tanks and move in sprints. Tracers are a storm of orange-red sleet from tanks, machine guns, infantry weapons, and the radios for the first time begin to sound slightly human as tank commanders begin kiyiying like Indians, and the infantry, swift, roiling ants, disappear into the smoking streets. Defending fire dwindles abruptly to pops.

Through streets of burning houses and crashing timbers, past prisoners and wounded, we thread the quivering, torn prize; we are refreshed by the flap of tablecloths.

Waiting in column while the advance guards searched out the next strongpoint a few kilometers away, I had a just-over-the-edge-of-consciousness feeling that what I had seen was significant beyond the conquest of some roadblocks.

Western civilization had almost collapsed for the want of the simple skills I'd been watching. It wasn't until 1944, in France, that the lordlings of the air force allowed control of the air strikes to be placed up front, on the ground, in the hands of the men doing the fighting. The desperate years since 1940 had been littered with catastrophes: the men facing the enemy had groaned and cursed as air commanders hundreds of miles away tried to respond to the fluid uproar of a battlefield through layers of paper and hours of delay, sending our planes to attack the wrong targets, or no targets at all. Tragically, often they attacked our own troops. American air force generals were bad but the RAF was worse by several exponents: air vice-marshals found their careers and their mustaches threatened if any groundling presumed to tell them what to do with their very own private air force. I talked to officers who had fought in the invasion of Sicily in 1943: requests for air cover had to be relayed through a maze of command because the RAF's awfully decent chaps were having an attack of autonomy and couldn't stand to "lose control." Five hours of radios and message-stamping interposed between requests for help and the appearance of the Allied planes, a generous interval that gave the German planes time to bomb, strafe, and return safely home, wondering, no doubt, what kind of damned fools were running the Allied war.

The murderous effect of egos went further than air strikes.

The Russian disaster at Kursk in 1942, the slaughter at Dieppe, the floundering defeats in the Western Desert at Rommel's hands, were all consequences of an epidemic disorder. Stalin and his sycophants in Stavka, the Russian general staff, suffered a tertiary or advanced form of the disease, and as a result, millions of Russians died who shouldn't have, but no command was immune. Wherever fulfillment of self was the god on the altar, whenever the power of decision was taken from the men who were locked with the enemy and vested in pomposities a thousand secure miles away, weapons were splintered and brave men died for nothing.

The truth's a mad sea-creature that waves a tail and dives: the honest chronicler will persist for years, across thousands of miles, just for an occasional sighting. History isn't the alphabet scholars would like it to be, where A proceeds through B to X, rather it's a succession of images flashed on human perception. Collecting a family of them and putting them in train may take most of a lifetime. Ghosts are helpful.

Conversation with some wraiths: A Chicago bar, 1950, and across from me I see a round, pink cherub, Bart Bartholomew, brave commander of D Troop of our reconnaissance squadron. We used to call Bart the *pear-shaped* commando because all winter he went around with three coats, giving the appearance of an ovoid with little feet sticking out the bottom. To complete his soldierly exterior, he wore a fur hat on top of which his helmet teetered casually, and he blinked around gold-rimmed glasses.

During the Saar Basin raid his troop was awarded a Presidential Citation and a carload of individual medals. Five years later I heard the specifics.

"We got so far out we didn't know where the hell anything or anybody was; we only picked you guys up now and then on the radio; you were the hell and gone back over the hills, and we weren't at all sure where we were, really. First thing we knew, we came over this rise and there was this whole damn German column on the road in front of us, guns, trucks full of infantry, half-tracks as far as we could see, so I says on the radio, What the hell, we may as well die young, and we zoomed right beside those pricks with our sirens and horns going like hell like we belonged there. What I remember when I think about it is just whole rows of funny white faces, kind of ovals, like faces on funny-paper characters, looking at us from three feet away, and then a lot of backsides and legs moving like hell while they ran away, and we traversed guns on them all across some fields. Christ, they had enough stuff to blow us off the road if they ever got set, but we never let them. That's the trick, you see: don't let the other guy get set. We just kept on driving and shooting and screaming like crazy men; some guys jumped out of our scout cars and tossed thermite grenades down their eighty-eights and into their vehicles, and *wham!* the gasoline went up and everything burned, and there was so much smoke and flame hundreds of feet in the air, we must have looked like ten armies instead of just two hundred guys. Important thing, see, is what we looked like, not what we were.

"A couple of kilometers on we came to a town; we got some fire from one side of it, and we screened it with one platoon and the rest of us just tore into the town. Well, the town was filled with Kraut vehicles, all kinds of them, and all the drivers and their crews were sitting around saloons — you know, those *Gasthaus* things — not even knowing the war was anywhere near them, so that German-American sergeant of ours, the guy that spoke German, you remember him, he jumps off and kicks open the door of the nearest saloon and yells at all the Krauts there.

" 'Get your fuckin' vehicles off the goddamn street,' he yells it at them. 'You're blocking traffic. You'll all be arrested. You've only got a couple of minutes.' And they did, by God. Like good Krauts they all marched out and moved their goddamn vehicles off the streets and stood there, calm, all at attention, while we went floating right on through, hoping we looked like a lot more than we were.

"Got near Kaiserslautern; didn't know what or where the hell next; we sure didn't know where the rest of the United States Army was, so we had a council of war. Always made us feel good to have a council of war, sounded official, you know, as if we knew what the hell we were doing.

''Somebody found a railway yard full of locomotives with fire in the boilers, ready for all the retreating Germans, and when we pumped fifty-caliber slugs and thirty-seven-millimeter shells through them they went up like a whole skyful of big white clouds, all billowing and beautiful, blowing up steam. End of any retreat for a lot of Krauts.

''We kept on like that, tearing around like a bunch of insane bees who've lost their hive and can't do anything but sting and move on. Moving and raising a lot of hell was our only way to stay alive; any time we stopped we were dead.

''Finally we had about a thousand prisoners; the question was what the hell did we do with them? Full colonel there, so I put him in charge. 'We're going to march you back,' I says, 'and the whole American army is coming up right behind us, so no shit.'

''I put a light tank at the head of the column with the turret turned around so the thirty-seven-millimeter cannon was pointed right square at the middle of the colonel's tunic, and you'd better believe he was one obedient Kraut. The other thousand of them got in line; after all, they were following a colonel, so they figured everything was legal. A lot of times now when I think of the word *legal*, I see that whole thousand stupid Krauts following that one goddamn colonel with a gun pointing at the middle of his chest.''

The wraith begins to fade, and from remnants of gold-rimmed spectacles, over a ghostly highball glass, the voice drops a note.

''Don't know if anything I learned in all that crap really does me any good nowadays, like maybe in my business, except that the way to bust up a very superior opponent is to keep kicking him in the balls so much and so fast he thinks the whole world is doing it to him and he better give up easy. I'm in a very competitive business, you know.

''I also became permanently aware that impressions, not reality, are what count most of the time, most places. Sometimes when I can't sleep I see our little column out in the middle of all the Krauts and danger in the world, staying alive by attacking everything in sight, with this nutty kind of conviction that we had, that it was official that we were supposed to win and they were supposed to give up — and by God, mostly they did.

"Then I think of myself charging into offices and cutting the competition's throat, and I think about my wife and kids I'm really doing all this for, and I wonder where the hell I'm really going and where the big army is back behind us, coming up to pick up the pieces and make sure everything's all right, then tap me on the back and give me a medal; except that isn't how it is now. Reality is lonely, just me and the family, and everybody's depending on me, see, and what if I got sick, or what if I don't make it, or what if I'm not good enough? No Combat Command B filling up the roads back there, no Twelfth Armored Division, no corps headquarters, no great, big network that you're going to fall back into. It's lonely where we live, you know?" The wraith fades.

Wraith the second:

Through smoke and flame the figure of Chuck Willis lounges in natty paratroop outfit, crisscrossed with bandoliers, hung with grenades. He juggles a carbine by the handle as he chatters.

" 'Jingle, jingle, I am all atinkle.' I think I recited something like that when I was a fairy or a twinkle-elf in some country day school. You know, we have skins like snakes, or maybe like birds: we molt when we go into battle. We shed this layer of crap the rear echelon thinks we need like extra shoes and prophylactics, and we grow this other skin of assorted kinds and species of shit that we really need. Well, not shit, because that implies superfluity, but a lot of stuff that we really need or we wouldn't carry it, like lots of ammunition. Sweet Christ, though, it does make a chap tinkle; I sound like a Seventh Avenue whore with three sets of earrings. Lieutenant Chuck Willis will now do the dance of the merry sleighbells." He bounces up and down, clinking.

An unshaven infantryman appears beside Chuck, talking at us, staring at us, not seeing the lieutenant. "What one brave son of a bitch can do is win a whole battle. One guy, for chrissakes. Here was our platoon pinned flat-assed down with more tracers going over us that I ever thought there was in Germany, knowing it was a question of time till the Krauts would start dropping mortars on us and kill us, and then this Lieutenant Willis — he's our guy from the paratroops that got stuck in the dog-faced infantry and he talks funny — he bellies along the ditch to where one of the guys has a radio and he calls down a fire mission with white smoke on the woods where all the Krauts are. In three shots he's on them and he yells, 'Fire for effect,' and then there's white smoke and big clouds with the tracers comin' out of it, only now they're wilder because they couldn't see us, and this Willis he stands right up and starts blammin' with his carbine at the smoke and all the time he keeps yellin' at us funny. 'If they can't see you, they can't hit you; those guns are to shoot with, you know. You shouldn't be lyin' on them; you can't fuck them,' and he walks along the platoon kickin' asses and pretty soon we're all standin' up banging away and he says, 'Hey, you fellas, let's go calling. Let's send them some calling cards and let 'em know we're coming.' And he has some guys start firing rifle grenades and he gets the bazooka team shooting rockets, and you know that all adds up to a hell of a lot of explosions. Then he runs ahead of us and we all follow, and we do fire and cover, taking turns firing and covering, just like we're supposed to, just like in basic training, belting hell out of them woods all the time, and then when we were less than fifty yards from the trees Willis calls off the artillery and gives a scream like a wild fuckin' Indian and we all start yelling like maniacs and runnin' after him, and for just a little while we weren't really scared, any of us, we were so busy screamin' and yellin' and bangin'. I mean, we were different inside. Them Krauts must have thought they was up against some kind of murderin' lunatics, 'cause I never saw so many white faces under them big helmets and handkerchiefs wavin' and there was Willis kickin' asses to get them lined up and still talkin' funny...."

The infantryman fades; Willis is talking, sometimes laughing. "There are certain things you're supposed to do; well, I don't mean to use the phrase 'supposed to do' because that implies a lot of slightly insane crap like dinner parties, but I mean things you ought to do, things that are right to do, and the thing is to actually do them no matter what the hell, or how scared everybody is, or how wild the situation becomes, because if you do you'll win most of the time. When the sky falls, most people do everything except the right thing, and if you just go right on doing the routine, ordinary, reasonable right thing, you'll be the exception. You'll be in a remarkably small minority.

"Philosophy, sociology, and selected short subjects; now how will all this come across at some cocktail and tail-chasing party on Lake Shore Drive?"

Chuck's face moves closer; the grin becomes defined as a set of hard creases around bared teeth, and the eyes become what they really are, not really humorous, eyes looking for danger, for death, eyes that are windows into the cleanly functioning primordial killing machine behind the pleasing, pleased mask.

"If I ever stopped talking? I'm ass deep in something I never thought of being in, and it's certainly an interesting world; not that I'd like to stay here, only a nut would, but I guess I'm different than I thought I was, and I have to keep on making the same noises outside because they're the only ones I know how to make and I don't know what kind of noises would go with who I really am."

The light drops; figure and face dissolve into dark, leaving eyes glowing with the green of a hunting leopard, teeth white, snarling, a brave snarl against terror and dismemberment....

Eine kleine Nachtmusik. Performers include the lead company of the infantry battalion, Jack and me in our ambulance (present by mistake), and a battery of German artillery we all blundered into by turning down a wrong road at two A.M. The selection opens with roaring and slamming of an intensity that bursts heads and splits eardrums; white-hot streamers explode twenty feet above our inadequate ditch.

I have a secret! I'm shaking so hard in this ditch I remind myself of an epileptic, but it's so dark nobody can see me in my shameful twitching, while Jack, on the other hand, lying just ahead of me, can't keep *his* secret because his heels on either side of my helmet are bonging a convulsive tattoo.

From behind, on our port quarter, an 88 flames from possibly five hundred yards away and I'm looking right down its muzzle while it fires; almost instantly the road fifty feet ahead erupts in white and silver plumes. Silly bastard is hitting right between our vehicles; he is rich only in the explosion of dirt, whereas if he had the sense to traverse one mil left or right, something would go up in flames and we'd all be ducks for shooting, but thank God Teutonic habit prevails and he goes on hitting the empty crossroads just ahead and just behind a lot of gasoline and ammunition all ready to go *WHAM*.

To define is to reassure: from the truck behind a calm voice floats out in words, small clouds in the night: "Just an eighty-eight zeroed on that crossroads," say the reasonable clouds. Well, we know it, but the definition reduces all that thundering and impending death to a couple of guys squinting through a gunsight. Great irrational comfort.

The small blue jewels of the blackout lights are guiding the German gunners; calls come down the ditch to turn them off, and I run for the ambulance to lick the switch. Instead of diving back to the partial security of the ditch, I succumb to a delicious hallucination. The warmth of the leather seat penetrates the shaking chills in my back and I begin to feel brave. Fear is just being cold, I decide, and now that those shaking muscles in my back are still and warm, everything is perfectly all right, and since I'm not afraid there's nothing to be afraid of, and I lounge and stretch in the dark accustomed front seat in a velvety security and sweeping happiness, and then the night roars and flames and showers of dirt and rocks dump all over my abode of ridiculous bliss, and I come out of my reassured trance and run for the ditch.

High, arching, gold against black, a trail of fire touches the top of a parabola and drops near the muzzle flashes of the 88. Sudden stillness and welcome unpierced dark, and as the German battery ahead lifted its time fire to the crossroads half a mile behind us, we stood, many relieved shadows, moving around luxuriously in our suddenly defined safety under the high hissing of the shells crashing back down the road at the edge of town. A military mystery, or whom do we thank for our necks?

The mystery cleared years later in a bar in Casper, Wyoming, where I was yarning about the war with an attorney friend of mine, one Dick Bostwick. He'd been in the Ninety-fourth Infantry. Hell he had. That was the division that followed us across part of the Saar. Had he been at a place called Winnweiler one night when there was a lot of shooting and shelling? Sure had; he was sitting in this traffic jam at the edge of town, see, and he could see this Kraut antitank gun shooting up an armored column down the road about half a mile ahead and nobody was getting on it, so he got the 4.2 mortar platoon and they did the best shooting in the dark he'd ever seen. About a half-dozen rounds and the Krauts were either dead or running away. He guessed he'd saved those guys' necks.

My neck, Dick; my personal, unique, highly prized neck was one of the ones you and your mortars saved that night. That was the end of the mystery of the fiery trails, and Dick understands the drinks are on me for a lifetime, with a perpetual toast to the Ninety-fourth Division, the 4.2-inch mortar platoon, and my friend and subsequent fellow citizen, Dick Bostwick.

I filled the ambulance with lightly wounded men and we threaded and pushed and cajoled our way through a tangle of guns and tanks back into town, recognizing the patches of another division, the Ninety-fourth Infantry, with a warm, neighborly, reassured feeling. Behind the village there were hills, darkness, confusion, no sign of a rear to move to; we created our own small secure enclave by breaking open the door of a house and disposing our wounded on beds and couches. By lamp and flashlight I checked the dozen men and found none seriously wounded. Then I had to do something extraordinarily difficult: I had to tell them that they were to wait there for assistance from the rear. I would put a Red Cross flag on the side of the house; they had their guns, they were really okay, and I had to go on to catch the column and keep up with the fighting. They nodded with each statement, white and stained faces agreeing over an underpinning of uncertainty. This was our first experience in the handling of wounded men in breakthrough fighting. The ones who weren't critical, we left with wounds dressed, Red Cross flags flying, guns ready, waiting for ambulances from the rear to catch up. All very logical, but the sense of loneliness was wrenching as I closed the door on the pool of yellow light and the roomful of faces, some bloody, some bandaged, all struggling to plaster reassurance over a sense of fear and desertion.

Lines written in dejection:
I'm wondering about a lot of people who are supposed to get off the battlefield and into a hospital: I'm the guy that's supposed to get them there and I don't know how the fuck I'm going to do it.

Here we are in these complicated, burning mountains away in the rear of a whole German army, and our last ambulance just drove bravely off into some uncountable miles of exploding towns and wandering furious Germans and marching Americans. If it gets anywhere useful, it will be because God loves us.

We've finally knocked out all the twenty-millimeter flak guns guarding the autobahn: there was a very pyrotechnical afternoon with the P-47s playing through the flak and the artillery firing red smoke and white smoke and the German guns sparkling, and now we're ready to roll to the Rhine. Couple of problems, though: We've had an awful lot of wounded today, and anything that can carry them back is gone, used, shipped off loaded, and with five days of marching and fighting through woods and around blown bridges and along incidental byways, we've lost a lot of our little helpers. Like the medics.

I'm hearing a voice in Scots about the best-laid plans and what happens to them. Pete, the medical company commander, and I agreed that he'd attach three ambulances to each battalion with a good liaison noncom to read maps and send them back, and the medical company would keep advancing behind us to Karlsruhe, on the Rhine. Keep coming on this road-net, we said, you can't lose us.

Well, you take a couple of ambushes and night excursions, and a complete change of objective that swings us to the south to Mainz and beyond, to meet Seventh Army, and all the neat plans went down the military drain. We're out in a fiery limbo, and from here on to the Rhine we'll carry our wounded with us in trucks and half-tracks, and they'll die before our eyes, a lot of them, because we can't operate on serious wounds this far forward. TIME! It's our four-letter word; head wounds, belly wounds, chest wounds; with every half hour that passes survival falls on an exponential curve. By the square. Bad night coming.

In between calls for ammo and gas, our radio's calling for the medics. How the hell's that ridiculous peeping going to traverse those miles and mountains?

Long after agonized time the sergeant calls roger. We got a roger from the medics. Map coordinates are tapped out; get the hell down here, in code. Roger again.

Now, if they'll get here before we have more casualties, or before we disappear from this hilltop into another night of uproar and explosions and wandering. Please God.

Later, the Archangel Gabriel and first assistant wandered up the hill, grinning, Pete, the medical company commander, and Alex, the exec. Guess where they'd been? Nobody told them we turned to the other side of Germany and they went marching on to our original objective, right past the advance guard of the Eleventh Armored Division, ignoring shouted warnings. They were so convinced we were ahead of them they were about to storm a city full of angry Germans with their ambulances and trucks and red crosses.

The chirping of the radio stopped them a little way short of dedicated suicide. The message was garbled (of course), but the map coordinates told them something had astonishingly shifted, and they came streaming south through the snarls of three or four other divisions, and by the luck that's kind to hurt soldiers, they found us.

The ambulances are out, nailed into the combat units, the treatment sections are set up a little way back, and the network's intact. Nobody's going to have to bleed to death in an all-night ordeal in a half-track.

We keep pulling everything together by the last thread and the ultimate minute. S.O.P.

Technology, theirs: One afternoon, as we drove down the hills to the Rhine plain, a monster came howling along our column so fast we couldn't believe it was anything terrestrial. The ME-262, the German jet plane, went by so fast that we felt as if the twenty-millimeter slugs were still tearing up our column while the damn thing was whistling out of sight.

Being strafed by jet planes in 1945, when the Germans had them and we didn't, was like being sprayed with death rays by little green chaps in flying saucers; it was a science-fiction nightmare, real and deadly in broad daylight. All through the war we had known the Germans had better tanks and antitank guns, but everyone had thought of the air as being our very own, our unassailable, superior dimension, and here, for God's sake, we were back to being the dunces with the bows and arrows; American fighters puttered after the German jets like arthritic old ladies chasing swallows. The jets were slightly vulnerable; our gunners learned to fill the air ahead of them with flak, leading them by half a skylength, and sometimes they disintegrated in a flash of kerosene, but much more often they streaked far past our trajectories and velocities, sputtering twenty-millimeter shells along our columns every day until the end of the war, instructing us in helpless fury that underarmed races must have felt for centuries facing the Western world, their courage and skill made ridiculous by assorted lethal machines. (Savage gratification came later when we saw the rows of jet fighters on Bavarian airfields with their middles shot clean away by strafing American planes, caught on the ground, the only place we could reach them.)

We're the forefront of the spear-point of the *Schwerpunkt:* our combat command was attacking along the Rhine plain to meet Seventh Army coming up for the Siegfried line; we didn't realize it then, but we were the leading element of the whole Third Army attack in the Saar Basin; we were in headlines in every newspaper in the United States as Patton's Mystery Division. We were leading the dash to the Rhine; we were the ultimate fang in the jaw closing on a whole German army group. We were the subject of a lot of purple news prose and newsreel film; we were carrying history on our tanks, but all we could tell was that we were fighting very hard against desperate German rearguards, the best of their men and machines, dying in place to hold some kind of escape corridor while their comrades ran for the Rhine.

All that historic significance was baffled for a whole day by one machine, a King Tiger tank, a monster with a hundred-and-twenty-millimeter gun and armor like a battleship, backed into concrete overpass, where it was almost beyond the reach of anything we owned. Even after direct hits by artillery and an air strike by a squadron of P-47s, it was still there when the smoke cleared, sending six of our tanks up in flames and shreds when they attacked. That massive gun swept every possible road and approach in our attack zone.

There was a reasonable pause while our reconnaissance flanked around Tyrannosaurus: we then suffered an unreasonable descent by Fatty, our corps commander, who swept down in a cloud of aides.

Our headquarters was in a farmhouse and it shared a wall with a barn; Fatty had just tuned up his standard first aria about taking our losses and advancing and for chrissakes weren't we soldiers, when a cow stuck her head through a foot-wide aperture in the wall and let go a hundred-decibel ''moo'' to tell everyone she was hungry. Fatty spun hard left; the trouble was he was short, and his quarter-whirl put him nose to nose with *die Milch-kuh,* staring through twelve inches of sounding air at enormous brown eyes and a drooling red cave all tongue and roaring. Fatty was at the other side of the room before anyone could figure out how he got there. Panic cleared, his reflexes as a corps commander took over, and he reached for fury.

We heard that this was some goddamn fucked-up headquarters with a zoo in it. What the hell was that thing doing in here? What the hell!

Right then Corporal Refus achieved immortality; he was a

farm boy from Oklahoma who was really stupid and we kept him busy picking things up, but he knew all about animals, that they were supposed to be loved and tended and fed and soothed, and he had been agonizing to a lot of us for two hours about the farmer who was begging to be let into the headquarters to feed his cows, and he had twitched with visible hurt when the guards told the farmer to fuck off because there was a war going on and he was lucky we didn't shoot his cows and eat them. That had all been hard on Refus; Fatty was more than he could stand. He snapped to attention and said, ''Sir,'' — there was real patience over outrage — ''she lives here. This here's a farmhouse. That's a barn. She's a cow, see, and she b'longs in that barn . . . it's her'n. Sir.''

Refus saluted; the only part of Fatty that could respond was his hand, which saluted too, reflexly. There was a short but memorable silence : then came ten minutes of antiphonies, with Fatty trying to snarl and back himself into significance and the cow mooing thunderous counterpoint, drenching every emphasis, all this over the staccato of six soldiers trying to drag Madame out of the stall which she damned well wasn't going to leave unfed, and, floating musically, the even singing line of our colonel's responses, deprecating the interruptions, apologizing for these rude field conditions, assuring Fatty that he was dying to hear whatever had been so rudely drowned out.

Finally *die Milchkuh* emptied her voluminous nether parts and the room was earthy nitrogenous; Fatty had his forty-five half out of his holster, near hysteria, and had to be talked out of shooting the cow by an aide who hissed a warning about awful publicity and asked him to remember the time that General Patton shot the mule in Sicily and how awkward the press had been about it.

Fatty and aides diminished into sunlight, waved off with an intensity of soldierly salutes and courtesies. We were so grateful. Thank you, General. We'd attend to everything. Consider it done.

He was gone and we got on with the attack, flanking, shelling, not throwing any lives away. Our colonel never commented beyond referring to Fatty as "that kindly old gentleman who dropped by our command post this morning."

Zimmerman, the infantry battalion surgeon, grins as he finishes a dressing.

"We're not Johns Hopkins, but by God we're adequate. Efficient, even, when you think of where we are, what we've got to work with."

I agree. "Johns Hopkins bunch have a base hospital somewhere. Up here, they'd throw up."

A shell explodes fifty feet away, at a crossroads, and the room shakes. "Scream, more like," Zimmerman turns to the next casualty, "maybe cry a lot."

A twenty-millimeter flak battalion is strung across our path, part of a frantic wedge pried into the jaws of the trap we're closing. The Germans in the Saar are fighting to let the last scrambling bits run for the Rhine. Flak guns are made to shoot at planes, high and fast, and when they're turned down flat against infantry, the air fills with sizzling, killing streaks, a thousand lightning storms flashing horizontally, thirty inches off the ground. All the space where anything could live is dissected by white-hot metal shards. Our infantry battalion is knocking the guns out one by one, but the price is flooding our aid station.

Zimmerman and I have become pretty efficient flood-managers; we've learned to concentrate our skills as physicians where they do the most good, and let our aid men do the rest. Wounds in bellies, heads, and chest are beyond definite help here: we can only support life with plasma, adrenaline, caffeine, and morphine, and ship them off for surgery. We pray for speed. Our aid men can give them all the care that's available as we call directions over shoulders; they also handle the routine bandaging and splinting. We concentrate on bleeding from the extremities, the neck, and the face; by stopping this bleeding we can stop dying, and to do it we have to find blood vessels and suture them. There's no relation to what happens in a clean bright operating room where the anatomy is well sliced and plain. In the aid station, blood comes spurting through a mass of torn clothes;

muscles, bones, and subcutaneous tissues that have been ripped by white-hot, toothed fragments are a red, fronded, twisted, matted jungle. The word *anatomy* is irrelevant.

We cut clothing away; we apply a tourniquet if one's not in place already to stop bleeding. So far, well, but we can't send men off on three-hour ambulance rides wearing tourniquets. As we sponge with an aid packet, a helper gently loosens the tourniquet to let the bleeding start just enough for recognition. Arteries, carrying the highest pressure, start spurting, but the vessel itself can almost never be recognized. We simply have to put a suture around an area of bleeding tissue and hope for occlusion. With more release of pressure the veins flow, and we tie off the larger ones, hoping that pressure dressings will be enough for the small veins and the capillaries. We have no sterile gloves and no time to boil instruments, but we do pretty well with instruments carried in jars of sterilizing solution, and we tie sutures using two hemostats while a helper holds a third. It's efficient, live-saving, gratifying, but in the course of nature there's a snarl with higher headquarters. Suturing without anesthesia would be painful and sometimes agonizing; it's inevitable that we'll catch nerve-ends and, of course, we have no way to put these men to sleep. We learn to inject a local anesthetic, quickly, all through the wound; it works fine. Then our novocaine supply was cut off. Division medical supply officers went sniffy; tables of equipment for battalion aid didn't call for all that novocaine; we were far over our quotas, and what the hell were we doing? I heard that the division dental officer was short of novocaine for some fillings in staff officers' teeth and there was hell to pay.

We tried reason briefly, but without much hope. Then I erupted all over the radio and sent as much fury as I could concentrate on a message pad. The division surgeon was still recognizably human, and our novocaine was delivered along with a reproof telling me to control my temper and have more regard for the sensibilities of those who guarded our rear.

A sergeant I knew from the Sixty-sixth Infantry was sitting, without groan or comment, looking at what was left of his right arm. It was dangling by the triceps; the bone and the rest of the arm had been blown away. Thank God for the heat of high-velocity missiles: the main artery in the upper arm, the brachial artery, had been cauterized automatically; otherwise, the man would have bled to death on the field.

As I looked at the wound, the sergeant took the cigarette from his mouth and said with great calm: ''Cut the son of a bitch away, Doc; ain't gonna do me no good anyways.''

Simplest amputation I ever did, there was so little left to cut. A few cc's of local anesthetic was all that was needed.

After I dressed the stump, I looked to the man to try to say something gentle, but he was back in his role as sergeant, talking to the other wounded, telling them what a great job they had done knocking out those flak guns, and to stay calm because they all had million-dollar wounds and they were now a bunch of fucking heroes. He might have had a tooth pulled or a boil opened. I hoped the army would let him go on being a sergeant for a long time; it was clearly the only way he could live with that throbbing empty air where his arm used to be.

By dark, the American wounded were gone, but German casualties trickled in all night. With the enemy in the aid station, perception changed. We were in the world of cloak and dagger, and anything the German wounded said might be important.

Our prisoner-of-war interrogation officer was a native German, a refugee from Cologne. He had profound reasons to hate the Nazis; squeezing them for information was a job he approached with love and much cunning.

In the aid station we could forget cunning; when enemy wounded came out of shock to find themselves alive and kindly tended, they became babblers; we couldn't shut them up. By the time they rode off in ambulances, we could name their regiments and battalions; we could recite litanies about captains who were shits and stole from their men, and colonels who were hard-nosed Nazis, and where the latest rumor said they were going, together with assorted and often accurate observations about tanks, guns, mine-fields, and intact bridges.

A friend of mine who was captured twice by the Germans said

that being taken alive and unhurt by people you thought were going to kill you was the damnedest relief you could imagine, a thousand times more profound than peeing after one's bladder had quivered near to bursting. Reactions, he commented, were not controllable.

At midnight, the last three Germans came through the aid station. One was a captain, a Nazi missionary. (They always referred to themselves, with total sincerity, as idealists. They'd been to an idealist school, one of many organized by Rosenberg. They mentioned it as an extra qualification, like a postgraduate degree.) Even with compound fractures of both bones in the left leg, the captain was a chatterbox. He was so grateful for our care that he invited me, as a fellow Aryan, to join him in the great crusade. This wasn't a privilege he'd extend to everybody — just me. Crusade? *Bestimmt!* His explanation was kindly, patient. I must understand about the dark *Untermenschen* who swarmed hatefully over so much of the planet. There were waves of swarthy rodents, vermin; there was also Northern European civilization. Our duty was clear and mutual.

I brought the POW officer in to listen as lunatic history went galloping on a pale blond horse. It wasn't too late if all us idealists would just listen to the *Führer;* even at this next-to-last hour we could pull it off like the Greeks at Marathon, and the Visigoths against the Mongols. All us Aryans, see.

As interested Aryans, we asked how.

Well, two batteries of his flak battalion had escaped across the Rhine and they were supposed to be digging in right now, right north of Mannheim, ready to blast away, and there were lots more like them, we'd better believe!

Oho! How impressive!

Ja, and the whole Seventeenth SS Panzer Grenadiers, right now, spreading out to man roadblocks in the Odenwald.

Aha! Fearsome!

We encouraged specifics and they came bubbling, details of troop movements and locations that we could use if we only had the good sense to march together, brother Nordics, to keep the

Aryan blood, the hope of the world, washing pure through heroic veins, free of black, brown, red, or, above all, Jewish contamination.

I didn't tell the captain he was a practicing, professing idiot; he'd been much too helpful.

Very little of the corporal was still visible; he consisted mostly of scarlet and white wrappings. His condition and station spoke in the rare spikes of graying hair, hands crusted with a lifetime of labor, and a voice that dragged deeply over rocks.

Ja, he heard the captain. Did he agree? What a question! All that education and you ask a poor man, a peasant! How could a man argue against all those names? *Gelernt ist gelernt!*

Politics? Ask him of turnips and potatoes, not politics. Just the same, it was a shame those Polacks and Communists and kikes forced the *Führer* to go to war.

Now look! What a mess, and whose fault was it!

He'd been hauled up to combat from a labor unit, and *ach!* The things he'd seen, marching! Look out, we shouldn't write the Germans too much down! All those big guns in the woods outside Freistatt! And the tanks and the soldiers, camped in that big field, all *so gut organiziert,* right by Kehl; by God they'd hold the Rhine bank! The Germans weren't dead yet! We put tremolos in our questions. Gosh, that made a fellow think twice. Was all that deadly stuff really out there where he said it was? Pop went right on dribbling; we gave him an extra slug of morphine for his trouble.

As soon as the Austrian private opened his mouth, the air became simple. Hot watches on Times Square, pimping on Piccadilly Circus, Schweik, the Good Soldier, and who's going to flog Grandma's gold teeth?

A shameless con man is a cheery sight in a pack of gloomy fanatics; he resurrects the human condition, even if it's smudged. The Austrian used the slang filler *"gel"* the way modern illiterates use "like."

Like, Herr Officers, he was grateful and he knew that under the civilized Americans, a man got good treatment, like maybe special rations? A guy got awfully tired of Old Dead Man. (German soldiers had even more penetrating names for their rations than we did for ours. Old Dead Man was what the Germans called the meat rations they had chewed with loathing from Tunis to Moscow.) With some good food and maybe a little pocket money if a guy was protected from all those *saupreussen* fanatics, he could be really, like, helpful. He had always opposed Hitler in principle, but what could one little man do?

All those nuts! Too bad about the Jews, but a fellow had his family, and his home, and his business to think of. Was there anything in particular he could help us with?

As soon as his scalp laceration had been sutured, and his concussion had cleared, we turned him over to the POW officer. He was received with chocolate, cigarettes, and enthusiasm. Cowards were helpful, said the officer, but to save democracy, give him a happy crook every time.

After the last ambulance whined off, the POW officer and I walked past patrols and parked tanks, along a silent street.

What had I been seeing? Those wounded I talked to, did they equal something? Is that what's there, now? Is that all of it?

The POW officer told me I was looking right into all that was left of Germany, the part that stayed behind and cheered Hitler, the part that giggled when they murdered Jews. Sounds dramatic (he said), but you're looking at the heart of Germany.

Heart of darkness.

What's that?

A novel, an English novel. Written by a Pole, actually.

The POW officer was fascinated. "A Pole wrote a book with a name like that? Somebody must have told him about nineteen forty-five."

Technology, finally ours! The rockets' red glare; Speyer was the last city between us and the approaching Seventh Army, the last narrow crack for escaping Germans to squeeze through, and the last resistance in the Saar Basin came from a group of misguided enthusiasts, all SS troops, holding out in a shoe factory. After some annoying casualties we brought up the Chicago pianos, sixty-barreled rocket launchers mounted on tanks, issued to us during our hiatus in Lorraine, and they let go what was incongruously called a "ripple," an irregularly timed blast from all sixty barrels, the flame of one rocket lost in the smoke of the next. White handkerchiefs filled the windows, and crying, hysterical former bullies stumbled out to face our guns; the jaws closed when our tankers met some yelling, waving infantrymen from the Seventh Army, and the battle of the Saar Basin was over, there on the cobbled streets under old cathedrals.

Sixty four-inch rockets mounted on one tank were the equivalent of five full battalions of ordinary artillery, and thoughts came unbidden about the exponential concentration of power in surprisingly small sources. In warfare, from Hittite raids to the beginning of the twentieth century, lines of men visited death on other lines, pretty much one for one, with stones or swords or arrows or bullets, but in our time the source of killing power has focused down into ever-smaller tubes and orifices while its range spreads exponentially until one day almost nothing will be able to kill practically everything and that will be the end of the drama.

On the streets of Speyer: The day was ours, the victory won, there were no more Germans west of the Rhine, and I stood in sunshine watching files of our infantrymen coming along the street; and in these men, many of whom I had known for years, I was suddenly seeing strangers, strangeness, a quality that needed identifying. They were unshaven, filthy from the morning's fighting, slung with ammunition, many shirtless, blinking through red eyes, looming a great deal larger than life, formidable, plausibly murderous. The difference was that they had become parts of their weapons. The hardness of these veterans, these survivors, was the hardness of fighting men, steel hammered out of many bathings in fire, an almost graceful ease with danger and killing, the unself-conscious reflex competence that Xenophon's infantry must have carried through Kurdistan, the quality that loped with the cataphracts through the marches of the Byzantine Empire, the aura of men of legality and civilization who have just renewed the Pleistocene gift for the redeeming savagery that can keep their world whole. In the Second World War our men didn't torture or ravish; they were still decent human beings, but they were taking the measure of the worst, most perverted gang of murderers in history. These men had won their armor....

Loot, loot, beautiful loot, looting from bastards, virtuous loot!

For some reason Speyer was the center of the pink champagne importing business for Germany. The town was awash in the stuff; so, in a very few hours, were we. Under our headquarters we found three cellars, one above the other, nurtured by a departed Luftwaffe general, lined with the superb vintages of the late twenties.

We handed it out by canteen-cupfuls, we washed down K rations with it, we gargled with it, we rinsed our teeth with it, we sloshed it around like soda pop. By nightfall the whole combat command was euphorically sodden. Someone commented the Germans could have come back across the Rhine with twenty boy scouts and a canoe; well, maybe it wasn't that bad, but everyone was pretty drunk. There was so much priceless pink champagne around it began to pall, and therein lay the germ of the medical horror story I shall relate.

I found a bottle of what was labeled as scotch and shared some with a staff light colonel just to clear our palates. It was ersatz, it was really disgusting, it was about the worst stuff I ever tasted with alcohol in it. It tasted as I imagined pig bile would taste, or maybe the dissolved droppings of a queasy vulture. I was at the paranoid-fanciful stage of drunkenness, and I remembered a lot of warnings about booby-trapped liquor, poisoned liquor that the Germans would leave behind for the thirsty Americans; obedient soldier that I was, I went to the bathroom and threw up the scotch, together with a gallon-odd of pink champagne, and advised the colonel to do the same, but he was looking at me all pasty when I came back because he had never thrown up in his whole life and had no idea of how to go about it. He really believed my mumblings about poison, and he described with considerable emotion the seeping of the deadly symptoms through his extremities even then. We tried every trick known to medical science to stimulate his gag reflex, but nothing worked; by this time he was in a genuine panic, all drippy wet and white, begging me for an antidote or an emetic. Two standard emetics taught in every medical school are dissolved hot mustard and dirty dishwater. No mustard around, but right out the window was a thirty-gallon GI can filled with the disgusting green disinfectant soap we always used, and since the whole headquarters company had just sloshed their dirty mess kits in it, it was pretty emetic stuff just to look at. As I hope for salvation, the colonel was in such a dripping flap that he actually consented to drink a canteen cup of the hideous, greasy mixture, and I stood back waiting for eruption. Worst of all possible worlds, nothing happened; there was more panic, more clutching at gut, more sense of terminal dissolution while the green loathsome settled into his stomach, where I presume it gnawed off a good deal of the lining. Most fascinating color scheme of the campaign was the splendor that crossed the colonel's face as he realized that the stuff was there to stay. The whiskey wasn't poisoned, as it turned out, but the colonel almost was.

Farewell to picturesque Speyer. A green infantry division marched up to relieve us as we pulled back to get ready for the crossing of the Rhine. They thought they were taking the town from the Germans, since American intelligence was keeping right up to its usual dismal performance, several days behind events. Our vehicles were off on the other side of town forming into columns, and the approaching boy scouts saw only empty streets all filled with menace. We watched, enthralled, as patrols tinkling with shiny junk ran toward us, waving the kind of hand signals nobody ever used in combat, looking all tense and dedicated, swinging to point weapons tensely down various side streets. They were going through a lot of gymnastics out of training manuals and in a real battle they would all have been dead in about ten minutes. The whispered critique from the experts all around me was a glorious mixture of scatology and Clausewitz, but the soldiers below us were so lost in their battle with the ghosts of the German southeast army group that none of them thought to look up until the air over their heads filled with yells and jeers and the streets around them crashed with thrown bottles. Jaws and weapons dropped; slack, stunned faces looked to the second-story windows. Soldiers called to their officers, pointing up to us as if we were interlopers, villains to be dealt with. The streets ran with cynical applause, solicitous hand-clapping, renditions of "The Stars and Stripes Forever," and assorted commands.

"Go get them nasty Krauts, fellas."

"Shoot all the bad Germans."

"Hut, two, three, four cadence. Count!"

Self-conscious straightening of shiny uniforms, mutters of "Aw, shiiit," hoots of laughter from the shaggy drunkards above. Baptism of ridicule.

Our column winding out of town was fired on by some snipers in a tall building. Bullets lacerated the top of the mess truck, and while most people dived for cover one of our adopted Russians piled out with a tommy gun. We had acquired more Russians since the youngsters on the Lorraine front; at Colmar we picked up a whole platoon, who by now were pretty well equipped with American uniforms and guns. The man who jumped out was named Mikail; he was a large, Mongoloid, dark man who had been the top-kick of a Siberian rifle regiment, and as I watched from behind a half-track I found out exactly what being top-kick of a Siberian rifle regiment meant. Mikail loaded extra clips of ammunition in his pockets, shot open the door of the building, and ran up the stairs where the snipers crouched, lashing ahead of him with forty-five-caliber slugs until he kicked in the door and bellowed some German monosyllables through the muzzle blast of his gun. Four terrified Germans marched down the stairs with their hands up; knowing Mikail, it was a miracle they were still alive to march. Lesson learned over and over in this war: One genuinely savage man can move mountains, or mounds of enemy, or almost anything; there really aren't many of that kind around.

In a rest area before we crossed the Rhine I was talking to the division psychiatrist who dropped in to chat one day. I was feeling exhilarated, and as far as I could tell simply splendid, until I tried to light a cigarette and my hand shook so hard the match went out. Concerned stare from the division psychiatrist; an offer next day to rotate to a safe job at division headquarters. I declined with thanks (pure vanity).

✳ 16

Over the River
and through the Woods:
Hoka-Hey!*

NOTES ON THE BANK OF THE RHINE, Seventh Army bridge
near Mannheim, late at night. Smoke pots fill the valley with
a chemical fog that's dense, white, pulsing and flickering with
gunflashes on the far bank. Within the fog it's impossible to see
more than ten feet: the steel shapes are startling when they loom,
tilting, squealing, and snarling onto the treadway. In half-tracks
and tank turrets faces flash into brief sight: they're surprising.
It's normal to wear a mask on the way into battle, to cover emotion
with a dead stare directed at shoes or gun butts, but tonight the
men are excited, they even seem to anticipate. A certain enthusiasm seems reasonable; after all, these men aren't fighting for
anonymous dirt this time. They're crossing the Rhine, the great
military moat of Europe: they're marching with the ghosts of
Charlemagne and Gustavus Adolphus and Napoleon, they're going
in for the kill, right into the monster's smoking den.

Then the lead half-track coughs and stops, just short of the
east bank, and everything on the bridge is still. Like well-trained
acrobats, on cue, the soldiers leap from their vehicles and form
a single line along the bridge: even above the swift gurgling of

*Hoka-hey was the Sioux war cry shouted as the warriors tore in for the kill with short
bows and lances; it was probably the last sound Custer heard on earth.

the Rhine another sound becomes audible, a plashing and tinkling, and a soldier comments that he's been waiting to do this
all the way from Cheyenne, Wyoming, and the man next to him
adds, Rhinelander, Wisconsin, and the names of homes roll on,
proudly announced into the fog, the wellsprings of the offerings
now entering the German water.

At the lead half-track the driver holds out a hand to an in-
coherent MP lieutenant. "Flooded," he says, "son of a bitch
floods. Take a few seconds." The MP officer screams between
maddened teeth that this is the tenth time tonight some wiseass
has done this and he'll have their balls, but the half-track driver
whirs the engine, fruitless, and grins as he asks the lieutenant if
he's going to send them back. After a minute, no more, the engine
coughs, and the column moves, a few tardy soldiers sprinting
after half-tracks while still buttoning flies. Now the faces trapped
in gunflashes are smiling, beatific, and an observer with a spiritual
ear might hear an angel chorus: "Hallelujah," the voices are
rising, fluting, "hallelujah, first, second, and third Walküres, Faf-
ner and Rhinemaidens and Logi, guttural hallelujah to Ariovistus
and Barbarossa, to Friedrich der Grosse and Heinrich Himmler,
hallelujah, all you dark Prussian bastards, the United States
Army is pissing in your upturned faces, fuck YOU!'"*

Dawn. White. Thick. Remarkable. You'd have to say remarkable, looking out the window after wandering around lost on the
German side of the Rhine all night through artillery flashes and
seeing in the first luminosity of gray a zebra, looking at me,
curious and quiet from a foot away, and then watching the light
pick up other shapes, glistening, beaded silver in fog, giving them
horns and snouts and turning them into wildebeest and eland,
and it occurred to me that if I had gone insane this wasn't such
a bad way to do it.

Then everybody else saw them and we convinced each other
we weren't really hallucinating, and the African animals mounched
and stared at our wheels and tracks and guns and helmets parked

*The urge to defile the Rhine reached Olympus. There's a well-preserved photograph of
Churchill and Eisenhower pissing in the Rhine while Montgomery watches with an in-
dulgent smile.

in some nobleman's private zoo, all of us swimming together in dawn mist. With strangeness, gentleness, soldiers tiptoed on grass trying to pet the animals, and they wouldn't listen to the heartless few who wanted to kill them for meat. Even to relieve the semi-starvation of K rations they wouldn't break this spell of childhood visits to zoos and loving animals.

Coiled blue, lines of knots of coiled blue floating five feet in fog, bobbing toward us; closer, they were turbans; under them, Indian troops, just liberated, marching soldierly and erect with British army pride in dress and kit and drill and manhood still intact after years of degrading imprisonment. They glowed with a lot of history, clear back to North Africa and El Alamein, and it was great to see them marching out the other side into sunlight and victory, making noises like Atcha' and Ek! Do! Tum! Back to the adventure movies; they made us feel what we were doing was important, reaching across continents and cultures.

The madman had whiskers; through them we heard croaking phrases from some song about *die blauen Hussarn* and how they were guarding Alsace. He seemed to think we were the German army of 1914 as he teetered on the edge of the road, haranguing us. " '*Ran an den Feind, Kameraden! Schlag nach schlag! Für Kaiser und Vaterland!*' "

He was having such a hell of a good time with his imaginary army we broke all the rules and gave him cigarettes; he trailed zigzag down the road singing "*Ich hatt 'ne Kamerade.*"

Some cynics tried to spoil the scene by insisting the old man was a well-trained actor simply bumming for cigarettes, but I preferred to think he was lost in the delights of cerebral syphilis. The old medical school doggerel describing the stages of the disease floated to memory:

> *He now has paresis,*
> *Converses with Jesus,*
> *And thinks he's the queen of the May.*

It's a world singing with delight where the paretic syphilitic lives, he's rich, he's universally beloved, he's easy with fame, and of course a German paretic would be swimming in military euphoria, seeing an enemy army as his own victorious host.

Madmen, exotic beasts, Asian warriors, miasms, esoterica, *alles ganz in Ordnung,* everything weird, everything consistent, for this was the land of the fantastic savages, the world of rare and dangerous beasts where men fled into medieval dark under archaic banners, murderous, where Ovid winked and looked knowing while humans sprouted manes and fangs and pranced below bestiality.

Them Fucking Mountains. That was the effective name of the mountain ranges east of the Rhine plain. Veterans of the Seventh Army named them; ever since November they'd been squinting across the Rhine at the blue-black, fir-dark peaks, remote in mist, mountains all coiled and wrinkled into defiles in walls, mountains, the veterans pointed out, where one 88 and a few machine guns could hold up a battalion. Like the Other Fucking Mountains, the Italian ones, like Monte Trocchio and Monte Longo, and most of all like Monte Cassino, and reaching farther back like the Apennine walls along the Volturno and the Rapido, and like those especially fucking goddamn Alban Hill mountains right over Anzio where the German gunners could see to drop a shell right in your mess kit or up your ass when you went out to take a crap. The Seventh Army hated mountains that held enemy with a professional and reasonable hatred: they knew that you started a battalion out to take a mountain, and a company came out the other side after you took it. They'd been hating and conquering mountains ever since Salerno in July 1943, and here it was spring of 1945 and after they had chased the last goddamn Krauts across the Rhine they still had to go through the Last Fucking Mountains.

"Well, crap," the veterans said; "here we go," and Seventh Army charged out of the Rhine plain into the passes of the Odenwald ready to make a final furious effort with experienced, skillful savagery. Up through twisting green the tracers of the advance guard sparkled in the fir forest like giant Christmas-tree lights; Germans ran and trees burned. Heavy log roadblocks were suddenly masses of matchstick wood and charred Germans as the guns hit them; men who had been fighting up and down mountains forever were leading recruits up sheer forest walls, clutching roots and branches, grunting excited encouragement to come on up here and flank those pricks, goddammit, we're gonna flank 'em this time....

Nightfall. We sat on a divide looking east across a tumble of mountains and forests, a night landscape intricate with roads and villages, twisting along stream bottoms. Our two combat commands were swarming out there in task forces, small units of a company of tanks, a company of armored infantry, some guns, some engineers, all fused and sulfurous, prowling every goat-path that they hoped might support wheels and tracks. The night was like a great room filled with explosive fumes; whenever any careless Germans struck up tracers or antitank fire, he and his locality went up in a brilliant sudden galaxy of starred explosions of tank guns, artillery, mortars, and assault guns, all interlineated with machine guns and small arms. There was no place out there that wasn't a potential Vesuvius; violence went winking and booming across the horizon, and seconds after it struck, towns bloomed, first with dull glows, and then swiftly, with titanic blossoms tossing fire-petals hundreds of feet, hysterical redness splintering the night. In two hours of watching, every town we could see across miles of darkness was burning; we stood in a vast glowing room with a ceiling of low red reflecting clouds and walls of glinting fir forest....

"One town burning, you know, that isn't all that remarkable by now," philosophy from around a machine gun somewhere. "But to stand here and see every town there is as far as you can see, all the way to the horizon, burning, that's kind of wild, know what I mean? It's like it's a long time ago and the Huns or Mongols or something were burning the whole Roman Empire, or whatever it was they burned."

Whoomboom; in giant mouths of pain, the towns were mumbling. *Whoomboom,* muttering, turning red ...

Back on the breakfast tables we were the point of a black arrow transfixing the middle of Germany; over scrambled eggs in Scarsdale we were bypassing this and crashing through the other when we weren't overrunning everything else. To the civilian world it must have seemed an exhilarating hunt, and we the exhilarated hunters.

Actually being the very point on the end of the tip of the spear wasn't pure exhilaration; sometimes it was excessively lonely, like the morning when we heard on the BBC that the Twelfth Armored Division now stood farther east in Europe than any other Allied unit; since we were leading the Twelfth Armored Division, it was borne in on us with sobering force that our combat command was really the hell and gone out in a world of resentful Germans with no neighbors on our flanks and very few immediately behind us. At night especially our lone universe asserted itself, when we were coiled along roads far behind what the Germans thought were their front lines, our nearest infantry stepping along three or four days behind us, a single column of half-tracks and tanks and jeeps with darkness and forest for flanks and confusion a real protection. We kept smashing ahead, all right, not to belie the newspapers, but we were leaving peopled dark behind us, and the last trucks of our columns pointed machine guns into a closing night full of neglected enemy.

Turnabout: In France and along the border the attached army ambulances that hauled our casualties to the rear from our medical companies had really had a pleasure outing; a child could have driven where they went. Now we had to force the drivers, stare-eyed, at the edge of panic, to head back through forests and mountains ready to erupt with fire, back out of our island of shot and safety. Poor bastards. We knew it was dangerous to send our wounded back that way, but we had no choice; there was nothing else to do with them. We never heard of some of them again.

The logistics of sanity, or, "The Army Makes Men!" Orly Stover, bow gunner in a tank, was a raconteur and minstrel of renown in the Carolina Smokies. It was fortunate that he was present at one of the great moments in the history of our combat command, and I was lucky enough to hear him describe it to some replacements a few days later. I have reproduced it as near verbatim as memory permits, but nothing could really do justice to Orly's nasal splendors. ''Foggy Mountain Breakdown'' would be appropriate incidental music.

''Old sarge, when he was kickin' our ass through them obstacle courses, he used to say, 'Some day you're gonna thank me, you bastards, you're gonna thank me and the U.S. Army we made sojers outta you, not no fuck-assed civilians; you're gonna know what to do when you face all them foreign foes across all them oceans and seas! Pick up your packs and move your asses; this trainin' is to get you ready for any eventuality, so here comes some more goddamn eventualities, all you sonsa bitches.' That's what old sarge used to yell at us, and by God you know he turned out to be dead right, 'cause here we was standin' in this big cave with lights in it way the hell in the piny woods the other side of the Rhine, and one side of that cave was piled high with Kraut munitions like them egg grenades and Schmeisser-guns but the other side, floor to ceilin', as far as a man could see, was solid booze, and I mean it was the kinda booze none of us country boys could of bought if we would of robbed twenty banks; and that was the kind of eventuality the army prepared us for, I want you to know! I mean, if we'd been some fat-assed old civilians, you woulda heard us hoo-hawin' about property and rightful owners and pieces a' paper, see, but by God we was sojers, we was army through and through, and we knew exakly what to do with that eventuality of all them shiny bottles! The one thing all us army-trained sojers, we never had no doubt in our minds was that between the crooks behind us, livin' off us, and the crooks in front of us we was busy killin', there wasn't only the color of their uniforms was any different, and if we had one patriotic duty it was to grab first, because if we turned our backs more'n a minute or two that solid wave of bullshit comin' behind was gonna wash up and leave Off Limits signs all over everything.

''Ol' Doc, he was there and he told his boys they was practicin' preventive medicine. Guess ol' Doc had a couple of shots of that forty-rod, 'cause he talked pretty good; he said they was preventin' the Krauts from gettin' cirrhosis of the liver or pickling their dumb Kraut brains any worse than they already was, and

they was preventin' the rear echelon from another outbreak of
sociopathic behavior, and most of all they was preventin' the men
that was winnin' the war from dyin' of frustration and anger
and excessive so-briety, and that chain of ol' boys kept them cases
comin' till the half-tracks and the tanks and the trucks and the
jeeps was damn near bent right over their axles. Them battalions
drove away gurglin', you could hear 'em splash a mile.''

The floor of my ambulance was lined solidly with cases of
French West African rum negre, five-star brandy, benedictine,
and champagne; we gave the wounded all they could drink on
top of their morphine shots, and it did them no end of good. We
didn't draw a needlessly sober breath until the end of the war.

The charge of the enlightened brigade. Sometimes you have a
feeling that a day or a time is going to be memorable; I wasn't
sure at first — it was only a sensation hanging off the rim of
recognition while I drove along in the ambulance following Chuck
Willis and a half-track full of infantrymen, all of us headed back
for replenishment to our cave during a day's halt in the fighting,
and it was only when we swung around the last turn and saw the
division MPs with their Off Limits signs all around our own
personal fought-for cave that I realized that significance was
about to burst out all over the landscape.

If the MP sergeant had had a snail's brains he would have seen
the meaning of those red holes of anger under helmets that were
the squad's eyes, and he would have vibrated to the deadly rage
whitening under Chuck's party manners, but the MP was having
too much fun being an archetype to be aware of anything. He
was lost in the role of smug-cop-from-on-high, the bully surrounded by unassailable security, the smirker you want to evis-
cerate even as he hands you a ticket or a summons, and to make
things worse, this procurer had his feet planted in the injustice
of a military hierarchy where the Bill of Rights and the U.S.
Constitution were thought of as subversive if they were thought
of at all. He had two stars floating somewhere behind him and
he had autarchic authority, and he rocked on his heels and shook
his head, eyes closed, while I tried to tell him who had really

liberated this cave — the very squad in the half-track, as it happened — and who had been killed and wounded coming up that valley, and who really needed this booze and who had earned it and bled and died for it.

I was still arguing when I heard Chuck's voice behind me making the barking noises he used in his battle drill.

"Dis-MOUNT!"

I swung around to the clanking and tinkling of heavily armed men leaping to the ground.

"Extended order!"

The men spaced themselves out a few yards apart, the way they always did when they advanced as skirmishers; faces under helmets were beginning to crease with the beginnings of grins.

Chuck walked over to the machine-gunner leaning on his thirty-caliber water-cooled weapon in front of the half-track and asked him if it was working all right. The machine-gunner looked hard at Chuck, then nodded in sudden happy comprehension and let a string of tracers churn the dirt all around the MPs and then do some fancy hemstitching in the branches over their heads and said yes, he guessed it was working okay.

Then Chuck talked with his men, ignoring the frightened shouts from the MPs, standing the way he always did when he explained a mission, in an odd, almost formal pose, thumb in the sling of his carbine, one knee cocked, his other hand on his hip.

We were on orders from battalion and combat command to pick up this booze from this cave that we had personally liberated, this very squad — Chuck paused while the men nodded and looked at each other — and for all we knew these MPs were really a bunch of goddamn German spies all dressed up in American uniforms, understand?

The squad was delighted to understand, smiles turned to grins, teeth white, savage in dirty faces.

"Okay, fix BAYONETS!"

I never realized the beauty of that archaic command before, and as I watched the men I could see them relishing the clicking and clanging of steel on steel, and then with sudden swift emergence came Chuck's yell of CHARGE! and the faces under helmets were wolfish, howling, inhuman, as that squad fulfilled every honest man's dream of running a fat, corrupt cop ahead of his lunging bayonet.

The MPs weren't at all brave; they chose life, and for the next thirty minutes they were a collection of whimpers behind trees up the hill while the infantrymen lugged cases of booze and the machine-gunner checked a few bursts from his weapon every now and then to see if it was still working.

Oh, God loved us on that day, us honest working stiffs, and out of the whole screwed-up universe he sent Lieutenant Wendling Pinckley III rolling up in his jeep to make sure his boss, General Beaky, got his booze, at the very instant that same booze was being hustled on its way to inferior gullets.

Pinckley did a progress of slow comprehension; he swam from complete disbelief into a misty groping for words, thence to a falsetto rage, hands on hips with head wagging, and finally into something almost like a tantrum, very near to foot-stamping.

The MPs stood from behind trees and rocks, all relief and potential malevolence; their own species of sanity was being restored, they were in the presence of their champion, their tamer of beasts, and they waited for cringing. Nobody cringed. For all the effect Pinckley produced he might as well have been going through a set of ritual dances before a frozen stone. Chuck faced him, lounging, unmoving, thumbs in cartridge belt, staring through him at some invisible but fascinating sight about three feet the other side of his chest; it was the first time I realized one could chew gum contemptuously.

Silence, and then Pinckley did another progress to stunned recognition and relief, almost to happiness.

"Willis," he breathed the word, a man waking from a nightmare. "You're Chuck Willis, for chrissakes. Choate 'thirty-six. My God, we were at Choate together. Remember me, Chuck? Pinckley? Wendling? This is all some joke, right? God, you know, a Choate man; uh, it's all right, isn't it? I mean, we don't steal. We're not outlaws. Well, glad I recognized you. Everything's okay."

Briskness returned. Wendling drew himself to a caricature of gravity: "Pretty heavy situation you've got here, Willis; you know, division headquarters involved, lots of important property, enemy assets, uh; I know how you guys feel, see, but, uh, division headquarters, uh, General Beaky ..."

He ran down. An angel passed: the little glen was still. Chuck and Pinckley held everyone's attention.

Then Chuck turned to me and his voice had a finicking, precise quality. He needed my medical opinion, something interesting about old Pinckley, here. He was an officer, Chuck observed, and he looked pretty normal — wouldn't you say normal? You know he must have gotten through Officer Candidate School, so he is capable of some kind of functioning, right? Well, the interesting thing to Chuck was that back at Choate one night a bunch of them had sneaked up on old Pinckley's bed because they'd never liked him much anyway, and they whipped the blankets off and by God there was Pinckley *jacking off!* They called him Jack-Off Pinckley ever after; most of them used the initials J.O., and the poor bastard had to leave school. Well, by God, here he was an officer and he looked pretty normal! How did the medical profession feel about that? Did masturbation really dry up people's brains? I mean, could a guy get over with it and go on and be normal and even be a general's aide?

Pinckley stared as he would at a creature from another planet; he was catatonic, frozen. Chuck waved a thumb and the unloading of cases of liquid gold flowed right around Pinckley's pinned and helpless form while the infantrymen, to do them credit, did no more than grin, saving guffaws for decent privacy, and the MPs shrank around their exseminated hero.

Last glorious touch: As we left, the infantry staff sergeant put the point of his bayonet against the MP sergeant's chest and spoke out of his throat with words that I recorded as we drove away: "We hate you pricks enough to kill you; we hate you worse than the goddamn Germans; you ever give any of my boys trouble, I'll find you and spill your fuckin' guts right out on the pavement wherever you are," and the MP knew he was hearing this from an experienced gut-spiller and didn't even move his eyes from the point of that bayonet.

Retribution? Not in our military world; Chuck had calculated his odds precisely, and he and his men knew that the general's reputation and promotion and postwar career and pension and financial security all depended on how fast the combat troops under his command advanced, and the rate of advance of the combat troops depended on a few combat geniuses like Chuck Willis. Short of possibly matricide, there was nothing Chuck could do that would cause the general to stop Chuck from exercising that genius on the Germans.

Some while later the colonel of the infantry battalion asked Chuck about rumors at division headquarters about disorderly conduct on salvaging missions. He explained to Chuck just how delicate relations often were between combat battalions and division headquarters, and asked Chuck if he didn't feel reproved, and Chuck said, "Yes, sir," standing at attention, he felt mightily reproved, and the colonel saluted and Chuck saluted, both keeping straight faces, and Chuck took his platoon off as usual, on the point.

That was no lonely eruption; you who read these words in the second half of the century be instructed now in some history, verbatim true, that you'll never read anywhere else.

In 1943 the men of the First Infantry Division marched back from beating the Afrika Korps; these first Americans to face the Wehrmacht so impressed Rommel that he commented to his diary that they had learned in one battle — Kasserine-Faïd — what the British still hadn't figured out in two years, and they used that learning to beat him in a bloody trap in the mountains. The First Infantry took on the Tenth SS Panzer a few months later at El Guettar, and even using their obsolescent American weapons, with no air support, they sent the Germans scuttling back east through the mountains, leaving a valley floor smoking with burning tanks and littered with German dead. The Big Red One was a hell of a division; its commander, Terry Allen, was one of the truly gifted commanders of the Second World War.

Some correspondents reported the speculations of the First Infantry Division as they rode to the rear for a rest that was months overdue. Booze, they talked about, women, safety, real beds, and maybe some appreciation like even a parade with a speech from a general or a congressman; after all, they — with a little help from the Ranger Battalion and the Ninth and Thirty-fourth Infantry Divisions — had just won the first American campaign of the Second World War against Germany. Pretty damn big deal. Nice to get some credit. Going to look great in the headlines.

Then they found out about rewards and appreciation and heroism: the trucks dumped them in a sandy, hot cactus patch in the desert. Put up your shelter tents, people told them; it gets real hot here. Dig latrines. Look out for those Tunisian flies. Those crates over there, they're K rations. Have a nice rest....

Bad enough; worse followed. The First Infantry found out that the city just over the hill was swarming with redundant thousands of fat, well-rested, rear-echelon idlers from quartermaster and port-operating and headquarters units who already had all those beds and broads and booze, and whose commanding officers were indignant when anyone suggested their men should make room for the soldiers who had held the Wehrmacht off their necks all winter. *Furor indignatio:* the First Infantry swarmed into town like Tamerlane's Mongols and they chased anyone not wearing combat olive-drab uniforms down cellars and through alleys, tossing them off roofs and into manure piles, clearing the bars and the brothels, beating MPs over the heads with Off Limits signs, and in general making Oran a reasonable city, fit for the delectation of the warriors who had saved it. It didn't last long, but it was a marvelous ventilation.

In Italy, General Lee of the Peninsular Base Section harassed and exploited fighting troops beyond any reasonable belief. One must conclude that General Lee actually nurtured some pathologic hatred for combat troops, possibly out of a sense of his own subhuman role in the war. Infantrymen back from the flaming, towering hell of Anzio for a three-day pass were thrown in jail by MPs who had never heard a shot fired in anger, because their passes weren't typewritten. Typewritten? Who the hell on the line ever had a typewriter? The MPs didn't know; every office they hung around had a typewriter, so get the hell in jail, soldier.

Bill Mauldin drew one of his greatest cartoons showing a bearded, weary infantry captain with jeep driver staring at a city square bristling with signs stating that all the bars, brothels, and places of amusement were off limits to everybody except Base Section troops or possibly Base Section officers. The driver is turning to the captain and saying, "To hell with it, sir. Let's go back to the front." Mauldin, as usual, caught hell for the cartoon, but he didn't withdraw it; it was an accurate statement of the criminal behavior of the rear echelon in Italy. Not only criminal, schizophrenic. When someone commented to General Mark Clark, the commander in Italy, that the American troops that awful winter of 1943/44 didn't have adequate clothing and often didn't have adequate equipment or food while they shivered, starved, and froze in snow, mud, sleet, and rain, past the point of human endurance, Mark Clark, never having been close enough to the front to have any idea of what went on there, fumed, "That's all nonsense; they're up there killing Krauts and they love it." See what I mean by schizophrenic?

Finally and with great justice the men of the Third Infantry Division descended on Rome and cleared the scum from the temples of pleasure before they embarked for the invasion of France. Very cleansing.

Saving indignation, that charge in the Odenwald, holy indignation, the desperate statement of humanity. When fools and peasants bow their heads and with sincerity bless the hand that takes their crops and rifles their daughters' virginity, why then they are gelded and spayed, steers and pigs, and humanity is fled.

Up the rebels!

Die Deutsche Bevölkerung, sociodemographic, 1945.

Violence on the roads, violence of dunces; the German corporal's head was a red wig, all clotted with blood. He sat stoic in the aid station while I sutured a six-inch slash in his scalp.

Despite my adequate German, he wanted to parade his slender English, and he said that he had had "*spek.*"

Spek? I hadn't heard the word.

It was, how you say in English, bad luck.

Bad luck? Most of his fellows were enchanted to be captured, only wounded a little, and by Americans, not Russians.

No, he hadn't wanted to be captured, and some soldiers lounging in the aid station told us that he sure as hell hadn't, that he had refused to surrender, giving everyone a big argument because a German soldier couldn't surrender with honor unless he was wounded, and finally a tired combat MP said, ''Okay, you dumb shit,'' and slammed him over the head with the barrel of a forty-five. As the blood ran the MP pointed out that he was really wounded, and with honor in his pocket the German surrendered, and here I was stitching him up while he was explaining that it was all bad luck.

Why hadn't he wanted to be captured?

He had wanted to go on fighting!

What the hell for?

Pause, erect stance, defiant glare under bandages: TO VIN THE VAR!!

Well, that was a refreshing flight into lunacy, and the aid men and soldiers ranged around the aid station bayed at him like delighted hounds around prey.

What the hell was he going to win the war *with?* No heavy German artillery since we crossed the Rhine, very few tanks, the Luftwaffe shot out of the sky. What the hell with?

To each question the corporal faced around the circle of tormentors and kept pulling himself more tightly erect.

The Russians were halfway across Germany and knocking on the edge of Berlin. How the hell was he going to win the war? With girl scouts? By poisoning the Allies? By giving them all clap? All the German girls had clap, didn't they? They certainly were interested in spreading around whatever they had.

Every question pulled the gray face into tighter lines until it exploded, hysterical.

''Hitler knows how! Hitler knows how!'' The determined yelling went on over gales of American belly laughter, everyone slapping thighs and whooping while a pathetic madman kept bellowing at the aid-station ceiling, ignoring comments from all around him about Hitler's perverted sexual habits and canine ancestry and coprophilia, and the poor lunatic filled his ears with his own voice, screaming that Hitler knew how, that he would win the war, that he would show us all, screaming finally through tears of rage and hysteria until someone kicked his ass out the front door into an ambulance. . . .

That poor bastard was one of a horde. They hunkered in fox-holes with Panzerfauste* at the roadside, ready to die for the chance of knocking out just one tank, and they often succeeded because the Panzerfaust was a superb weapon until our infantry learned to handle them. I watched from the top of a mountain, looking down a series of switchbacks as our infantry rode on tanks, the tanks spraying the roads with machine-gun fire, keeping the Germans in their holes, and the infantry tossing grenades with a looping trajectory very carefully into the holes from where they sat on top of the tanks, so that the fanatics ended with a squashy *whump*, and those who lived were really hell to take care of, all bloody scrambled.

They crouched between pine-tree roadblocks until our tank guns blew them away in white flashes and splinters; they dug lines of fortification that were target practice for our artillery observers, and all their frantic bravery did was to let the cold, calculating criminals of the Nazi high command organize their escape routes, and send orders about their Swiss gold, and slip into disguises to vanish with the help of that German bishop in the Vatican to places like Chile and Argentina, where they live in ease and wealth to this day, while those poor, dumb oxen paraded their lunatic heroism and ended torn or dead, kept at it by even worse lunatics and criminals, their officers, who hung anybody who didn't look enthusiastic about dying to help some swindlers escape.

Be brave! Have faith! Ah, what hellish jugglers they are, the hucksters of attitudes without thought; they send us wandering through time and mankind looking for something to be brave about, something to have faith in, that we may assert greatness.

---

*The Panzerfaust was a German antitank weapon that held a charge six inches in diameter on the end of a stick. It had a range of about seventy-five yards and could blow apart any armor in the world. We had nothing nearly as good.

We wander, responses looking for a stimulus, until, desperate, we decide to be brave defending the vices of Caligula, or to have faith in the delusional screamings of the current madman, or in the droit du seigneur of monster organizations, or possibly in Adolf Hitler. Please, good Pastor Kierkegaard, kindly Professor Wittgenstein; tell us again that the ultimate evil is a separation of words from the human reality they should define; tell us that the cloud of abstract imperatives gives blessing to the capering of fiends.

Case Study: The German masses conquered.

Ever think how you'd act if our country were conquered? How would you think and look and feel if enemy tanks and guns and infantry marched down your streets? Defiant? Stern? Grief-stricken? Angry? Conspiratorial?

Well, the resplendent German population, the most polished-up collection of Aryan genes in the world, didn't project any of those praiseworthy or at least understandable attitudes.

The first fear for limb and entrails lasted about as long as it took our advance guard to clear a town. By the time the main body arrived, relief had fertilized the atmosphere; faces were sprouting like ingratiating crocuses out of every dooryard and window. When we halted, they swarmed over and around us, gabbling through rebuffs, poking into our vehicles, frantic to tell us about Uncle Max in Milwaukee and what they had read about Clark Gable in the movie magazines.

They were shameless and indefatigable; you had to push them to get them the hell out of the way when you wanted to move a vehicle or load a casualty. We couldn't keep their heads out of our vehicle windows, especially ours, with its red crosses on it. They all seemed to take great comfort in the picture of Penny and the children pasted on the ceiling.

"*Guk' mal! Madame und Kinder!*" They clucked and wagged their heads and opened eyes to convey astonishment because we had wives and children; apparently someone had been telling them we reproduced by budding.

They were a swarm; they made you want to brush them off like flies or fleas, and they went into gales of nervous laughter at the suggestion that any of them had been Nazis. Nazis, we simply must believe, had been a tiny handful of fanatics who had been bullying the good-natured, endlessly patient, fun-loving, decent Germans — them — who were just so damn glad to see us all they did everything but kiss the collective ass of the United States Army, and they'd have been happy to oblige if anyone had suggested that.

Them pricks don't have no fuckin' dignity, said the soldiers, and when you considered how they transformed themselves without shame or guilt, from the mobs that howled for Jewish blood and heiled German victories with stamping boots and raised arms and torches, to the whiners that capered and fawned around us, they certainly had no fucking dignity whatsoever.

Hypocrisy was also popular. Often we advanced so fast that we liberated our own men who had been taken prisoner. They were always half-starved and they were usually sent back to us to carry them in the ambulance if we could. There were two of our newly freed soldiers riding with us one day as we drove through a German town to the usual hurrahs and massed gemütlichkeit.

"Let us out, Doc," one of them asked; "the Krauts marched us through here the other day. Let us walk along here and we'll show you."

I walked with them along the lines of faces as they pointed and accused.

"That son of a bitch here hit me with a rock."

"That broad there threw a bucket of horseshit on us and the guards thought it was funny."

"That one came at us with a pitchfork."

On the German faces, jubilation melted into sick, incredulous recognition and terror: they all knew perfectly well that if we had been Germans they would have been hung. I whipped out a pocket of emergency medical tags as if it were a notebook and asked them their names, but they could only gasp incoherencies.

It's degrading to inflict terror, even when it's pretense: I gave up and we climbed back in the ambulance. The rest of our drive through the town was remarkably quiet.

Speaking of Americans: I always knew there was something I liked about America, some reason to be grateful for Mark Twain and Ring Lardner and Thomas Jefferson, a Landgeist that gives us our fairest hope of survival, and I for one had taken it so much for granted that I didn't even know what it was until I hitched a ride in an infantry half-track one afternoon and watched it spring to sight and hearing. That afternoon was swift; we dropped out of evergreen gloom into an immense plain, a blaze of space and spiculed light, dotted all across its horizon with fleeing Germans: our column tore and screeched and rocked along at highway speed, racing for a broad river with an unblown bridge.

At the entrance to a village, we rode into an abrupt human sea. The Germans must have had thousands upon thousands of slave workers in the area, living in villages and farms around one of the dispersed factories set up to escape the Allied bombers, and the road was enclosed with living hedges of screaming, crying, laughing faces from every country of Europe. French officers were standing rigid, all cleaned up and starchy in their old uniforms, saluting every half-track; a Russian prisoner, wide, tall, and drunk, staggered against the stream, hugging and picking up everyone he could find, disappearing through files of grinning, surprised American riflemen. Jews with Stars of David on their coats were waving and trying from unfathomable depths to reach up for the forgotten emotion of happiness; they didn't seem to succeed; most of them stood there with hands clasped and a baffled half-smile, half-grimace, like people who knew the time had come to look joyful but had lost the skill.

Most of the workers had saved some scraps of national costumes: Yugoslavs sported lamb's-wool hats and embroidered vests; Ukrainian girls twirled in ribboned skirts and boots; people kept yelling up to us what they were — Czechs and Poles and Dutch and French — and then yelling, "Thank you, thank you" in their own language and in English.

Hell of an afternoon; brightest part was the epiphany that came as I watched a garage mechanic from Chillicothe and a farm worker from near Peoria and assorted entrepreneurs from lower New York grapple with the aesthetics of being heroes.

Reflexes of a lifetime spoke for understatement, for the half-formed, self-deprecating words of schoolboys, "Well, okay." "Awright, awrightawright," emphasized with putative gestures, mere flippings of fingers from helmets, but there was a distinct awkwardness in the half-track, like a painful silence at a party, a sense that something much more was called for. There was ice to be broken and Corp finally broke it.

The squad corporal was a wide New Yorker, and I watched him bend suddenly over a bundle and unstrap something. When he straightened he held an American flag about two feet long in his hand, and then I remembered that this squad was famous in the battalion for hoisting their flag whenever they took a tough objective, or liberated some prisoners, or captured a particularly well-stocked warehouse.

Suddenly the squad had something they could talk about comfortably: American portmanteau constructions bloomed.

"Watchedoon, Corp?"

"Gettinagoddamnflagout, canchus see?"

A really deep-dyed New York accent is one of the delights of American speech, and Corp was right down there with the deepest.

"Hey we're on'y s'posed to runna flag up when it's important."

"We're supposed to vote on when we do it."

"Well look out there, ya dumb shits, ya got eyes? What's important, a lotta booze or a lotta people, for chrissakes?"

The men started to let themselves feel and see what surrounded them while Corp lashed the flag to the mounting of the fifty-caliber machine gun unhindered, and with the breeze and the speed we were making the flag fluttered quickly, excitingly, to trebled cheers and shrieks.

People were reaching bottles of schnapps and wine, newly liberated from the Germans, into the half-track, and as they passed around, drunk like pure water, inhibition washed away. We all began to rise on the wings of an aural intoxication compounded of screaming euphoria and the fast growling of the tracks behind us and under us and ahead of us, and the swift fluttering of our flag; somebody started to whistle "Over There," and it struck me that the tune could not have been improved on — the notes fitted precisely into our slots of space and time — and pretty soon everybody was whistling or singing while we all stamped a rhythm.

An Italian New York private closed the communication gap; when some Italian workers screamed, "*Grazie, grazie,*" he leaned across the armor and flipped a hand to indicate ease of performance.

"T'ink nuttin' of it," he smiled, a duke tossing largess, "it was nuttin'. T'ink nuttin' of it!"

There it was, perfect and easy. Everybody knew what fork to pick up; they put their roles on and found a perfect fit; they leaned out over the sides of the half-track talking the way Americans ought to talk:

"*Any* time, any time!"

"No problems, you guys, see? Glad to do it. No sweat."

"You got a problem, you call the U.S. Army..."

"Twenty-four-hour-a-day soivice!"

"Reasonable rates!"

Now the men were splendid in easy eloquence; they swept helmets off with sweeping bows and they made deprecating hand gestures to show how easy everything had been. No big deal, fellas, no fuckin' big deal.

The column halted and a light tank came by, going the other way, with four high-ranking German officers, prisoners, on the deck. They clutched their inevitable briefcases, scowling, looking in their ridiculous getups like badly costumed Hollywood villains. They were leaning on their dignity, using it for armor: a German general's dignity was ferocious stuff, really impressive until you stopped to think what he was being dignified *about*. For the slave workers the Germans were still frightening; the crowd drew back and grew quiet before the recent tormentors; sensing the chill, the Italian private jumped out of the half-track, pulled a general's high-visored cap familiarly down over his eyes, and turned and spoke to the crowd in Italian and English: swift translations rippled through hundreds of watchers.

He, the American private, wanted to assure everybody that they were looking at a bunch of real incompetents; these dumb bastards couldn't punch their way out of wet paper sacks. The American army had just licked them, and we could lick them any day of the week, with matinees on Saturday.

They come up against a real army, they run like a bunch of fuckin' rabbits. All they can do is kill women and little kids. We beat their ass. No big deal. No sweat.

The German general made some attempt at sternness but it didn't last long. The American made the fuck-you sign, arm over flexed elbow, and then held his hand out, thumb and index finger less than two inches apart, pointed to the general, and then slapped his hand over his forehead in mock despair. Italian obscene sign-language is magnificent: the meaning was crystal, and girls hooted and covered their faces while men roared and the general wrinkled his face into real horror. The slaves plucked new courage and the German generals were lucky their tank started off again before they had their clothes torn off or worse happened to them.

Our column went on south, with more bowing and witty sayings:

"We will not be undersold!"

"Soivice wit' a smile."

"You name it, we liberate it ..."

"Ass, booze, countries, try our soivice ..."

Corp, by now inebriate but not voiceless, was hanging at a forty-five-degree angle from the flagpost, wagging a finger at the performance.

"Fuckin' wise guys, Doc, buncha wise-asses; they ain't happy unless they're bein' a bunch of goddamn wise-asses; it's the only way they know how to act."

He shook a finger; "You dumb shits ain't got no sense of approp —" pause, search for syllable — "appropriate, goddammit!"

The squad was delighted; Corp was gonna make a speech: shut up, you guys. Yay, Corp.

Corp swung from forty-five degrees left to forty-five degrees right, then clenched himself into vertical: great effort.

"Awright. This is a historical fuckin' occasion, so listen and you can tell your kids you seen one. Historical occasion."

"Historical *fuckin'* occasion you said, Corp."

"Leddim talk, for chrissakes: I wanna hear a historical."

Corp reached for his drill-field decibels: Stentor sounded from around the flag.

"LADIES AND GENTLEMEN AND ALL YOUSE FOR-EIGNERS: IT GIVES ME GREAT PLEASURE TO AN-NOUNCE THAT THE SECOND PLATOON B COMPANY EIGHTY-SIXTH ARMORED INFANTRY BATTALION HAS JUST LIBERATED" — uh, pause — "IT LOOKS FROM UP HERE LIKE THE *NATIONAL GEOGRAPHIC* MAGAZINE IN MY DENTIST'S OFFICE, SO I GUESS WE JUST LIB-ERATED THE WHOLE FUCKIN' WOILD!"

Cheers and applause from the squad, sustained delirium from the roadside, gracious swing of helmet by Corp to rght and to left, bowing; "YER WELCOME! YER WELCOME!"

The squad decided the glass had run out; whether he knew it or not, Corp's speech was over: he descended when two men pulled his feet from under him, dumping him on a pile of bedrolls, where two soldiers sat on him. Mendacious modesty was the *virtu* of that half-track, and the squad wouldn't let Corp forget it. As I jumped over the side to join our command half-track, I could hear one of the soldiers telling Corp he was a regular John Fuckin' Barrymore, he was.

The column moved on south, but through a tossing thicket of arms and bodies I could still hear the squad, easy in character.

"We're your friendly neighborhood extoiminators. Krauts and other pests..."

"We're Goiman extoiminators!"

"Accept no substitutes! Look for the patented trademark U.S. Army!"

"Satisfaction guaranteed or you get your country back!"

Ah, thank you, thank you, dwindling shapes of helmets and guns, thank you second platoon and Ambrose Bierce and W. C. Fields, thank you Groucho Marx and S. J. Perelman; especially thank you Misther Dooley: fervent thanks for the Bronx cheer and the leveling cry of horseshit that snatch us out of swampy heroics to foot us hard in sanity. Stay with us, friends and ghosts: we might just make it!

Hoka-hey!

✳ 17

An Easy Leap

W HEN I REMEMBER MANFRED, I'm grateful to the keepers
of documents and official histories. They keep assuring
me that he really existed. Left to my own memory, I might decide
that I dreamed the whole thing.

We were a day's march behind the German lines waiting for
the rest of the army to catch up, surrounded but composed. At
that stage of the war we were usually surrounded: it was how
the armor fought. A column of tanks and guns and armored
infantry would go banging and flanking its way twenty or thirty
miles into German territory until supplies ran thin or somebody
in higher headquarters started to worry; called to a halt, the
column would coil its tail into a steel covered-wagon ring around
a half-dozen or so villages and wait for the infantry to catch up,
which might take three or four days. The Germans immediately
around us were no special concern; they might be fanatics but
they weren't such complete fools as to throw themselves at an
armored combat command. Getting supplies up and wounded
back, on the other hand, was often hair-raising; scattered through
the woods and fields behind us were thousands of enemy, all
alarmed and despondent because they were *really* surrounded,
and nothing seemed to raise their spirits more than getting the

sights of their machine guns on a supply vehicle that couldn't shoot back, and they didn't seem to care much whether it was a ton-and-a-half truck or an ambulance.*

Injun country, we called it; we learned to travel through it in armored convoys.

Odd time, lacunar time, out on the far side of danger; the surprising thing was that there really wasn't much to do. We used to sit around on our vehicles drinking, listening to the BBC to find out how the war was going, and watching our patrols bring in prisoners, and that, come to think of it, is exactly how I was occupied when I met Manfred. He was a young, straw-haired noncom marching with his hands on his head with a couple of hundred other prisoners, and, as he came abreast of us, he stepped briskly from the ranks, took two steps toward the nearest officer — a young second lieutenant from the infantry battalion — and began talking quickly, before the guards could stop him, with an intensity that told us he knew his life depended on being understood and believed.

"Sir, I am American agent. It is important I get to G-Two Seventh Army. I have information; I am American agent."

He repeated the words "American agent" and "G-Two Seventh Army," leaning forward with the effort, standing almost on tiptoe, as if he were trying to catapult the truth and meaning of his words with his whole tensed body.

All the figures in the little square were suddenly pillars of salt, arrested in motion. The guards' hands were stopped on their guns, the lieutenant's mandible drooped, remote from his upper lip, the other prisoners were caught in faces of astonishment, short of comprehension, while alone in the stillness the boy's voice rose to something like desperation, repeating his message.

None of us, we all admitted later, believed what we were hearing; cloaks and daggers weren't worn in our war. If we had thought about it at all, I'm sure we all expected a spy to look dangerous and different, possibly like Peter Lorre, but here was

---

*The Germans abused the Red Cross as a matter of official policy, carrying troops and munitions under its cover on every front. They were such liars and cheaters themselves they couldn't believe anyone else was honest.

this lump carved out of the word *ordinary,* a small, shabby, tired prisoner, claiming to be a character from a paperback novel. Nobody's mind could stretch that far.

A guard resumed motion and speech. ''Get the hell back with them other Krauts.'' He began pushing. The youngster went sweaty white. The upper part of his body gave with the guard's shoving, but his feet didn't move on the cobblestones.

''I am American agent. American.''

''American what?''

''A spy. One of your people. I am an American soldier. *I am an American spy.*''

By now the other guards were struggling back to thought and action.

''Sure, you're an American spy, and I'm Santy Claus. Get the fuck back there.''

The German shook his head in a no that almost swung a hundred and eighty degrees.

''You put me back there, they'll kill me. I must get to G-Two. G-Two Seventh Army, you hear?''

Murderous comprehension was beginning to darken the other prisoners' faces, and there was no doubt about what they'd do to the young noncom if they got their hands on him. I felt it was time to interrupt.

''Hold it, you guys, I speak German. Let me talk to him.''

When he saw my rank and heard me speak German, the tension started hissing out of the youngster; he seemed to shrink several sizes inside his uniform with pure relief.

''I am really American agent, Major, truly — intelligence, you know. I parachuted in over a month ago. In my pockets here I have minefields, bridges, tank parks; I've been carrying this stuff; they would have burned me over a slow fire.''

He was pulling squares of paper covered with penciled diagrams out of his pockets while he talked; his hands were shaking so much the papers fluttered.

''*Sei ruhig,* take it easy. We'll get you to intelligence.''

The lieutenant was starting to stir, apparently feeling called on to assert his status as a line officer.

"Boolshit, Doc." (Cynical, soldier-of-the-world grin, low-Texas nasal register, reassuring hand on shoulder.) "You don't wanna go believin' these Krauts. They all pull some kind of crap. This ain't no spy."

(Condescension; superior knowledge of how spies were supposed to look; I instantly identified with the youngster.)

Perfectly possible, I agreed. He might be a smart Kraut pulling something, but IF he was what he said, and IF the lieutenant put him back with the other prisoners and he got killed, *then* whose ass would be in a sling? It was the ultimate military appeal, as old as soldiers: Don't get flogged, don't get decimated, don't get skewered; run from your own murderous hierarchy; survive.

The argument died aborning, and the guards, the lieutenant, the prisoner, and I marched to battalion headquarters; where the lieutenant and I went inside to tell our story to S-2 — the battalion intelligence officer — thereby putting the poor man spang on the prongs of a dilemma. On the one hand, the presence of a real, live spy for him to verify and interrogate promised to light up an otherwise compressed career; on the other hand, if the whole affair were a hoax, and if he were taken in, he was likely to find himself out on the line with a platoon, scraping in the dirt for his life.

The air in headquarters was dense with preoccupation; the commanding officer was trying to find a replacement for a company commander who had recently been killed, while the various staff sections were screaming over radios and telephones, trying to prepare for the attack that had been ordered for the next day. These harried men reacted to us and our improbable exhibit predictably: they had important paperwork to do, and they would have been happier if we hadn't turned up. They were irritated, they were skeptical, they were curt, but at least they permitted S-2 to bring the prisoner in and begin questioning him with the help of one of our native German speakers. They were only a few questions along when the steel roar of a half-track blotted out speech. Out the window I could see infantrymen piling out, and behind the half-track a medical detachment jeep with two wounded on litters. While I was checking their wounds, somebody told me the story. The men had been on patrol, scouting a bridge across the stream that lay a mile ahead. While they were stalking an antitank gun on the far side of the bridge, two machine guns had pinned them down. They had barely extricated themselves with the help of covering fire from the fifty-caliber machine gun on the half-track: one dead, two badly wounded, a number scuffed.

I went back into the headquarters; the lieutenant who had led the patrol was stabbing a bloody finger at a map.

"Eighty-eight, or something like it, here; didn't shoot at us, though. Two machine guns about here and here. No mines we could see. If we could get some time fire on that AT gun and smoke the bridge, we could rush it. Couldn't see any demolitions on the bridge."

Behind us, the young German, standing rigidly at attention in the corner, cleared his throat. He was listening intently, looking at the map, shaking his head.

"Who the hell is that?" The lieutenant snarled with understandable hostility; after all, a lot of people wearing the same uniform had just nearly killed him.

Somebody explained.

"That pak, that gun . . ." The young German was bursting with disciplined, polite eagerness. "May I speak?"

"What do you know about that gun?" The battalion commander was interested by now.

"I helped to put it there two nights ago; it isn't a real gun, it's a dummy, with a pipe we found."

"Dummy, shit!" It was clear the lieutenant felt his credibility was being challenged. "I could even see the muzzle brake."

"Yes, a bottle. We taped it on to make it look like a real pak. There's an eighty-eight up the road three hundred yards covering that S-curve in the bend. There are six machine guns, here, here, here." The German pointed to the map. "There are mines on the far side of the bridge, twenty-four, mostly schu mines. We sprinkled dirt and twigs, you can't see them. There are airplane bombs under the bridge. It's a trap, an ambush. They let some across, then they blow the bridge."

The lieutenant by now had had time to react, and he walked up to Manfred with a boy's grin wrinkling his nose.

"For chrissakes, you're one of our guys? You're an American?" The lieutenant had the artless enthusiasm of a small boy finding an ally in a strange street gang.

Manfred grinned back. "Yes. I am American soldier, Lieutenant. PFC. A real American soldier," and he weighted the last words happily.

I could see that the rest of the staff weren't caught up in the lieutenant's simple pleasure. Decisions are always wearing and worrisome, and it was clear that one was going to be forced upon them.

Manfred went on talking as though everybody in the room were his pleased superior officer. "There is a ford you can cross tanks a kilometer down here; we moved some across at night to get away from your planes. A small road goes behind past where the machine guns are."

"How the hell do we know you're not getting us into some trap? How do we know you're not an SS spy yourself?" S-3 was talking; he sounded resentful, almost savage.

The young man beamed.

"There are code words. You send them to G-Two at division. He will know," and he named a string of irrelevant, unconnected words — something about daisy sixteen football, as I remember.

S-2, appealed to, tried to look knowing. Yes, there were guys like this, agents, line-crossers; no, he personally didn't know anything about a code, but it sounded reasonable. No, it couldn't hurt to send it off to division G-2.

"Yes," Manfred spoke with happy confidence, "you will see."

An hour later all anybody saw was frustration. Radio contact with division was sputtering and fragmented; G-2 was off someplace in a meeting; the captain in charge didn't know anything about anything and absolutely refused to take any responsibility at all. No, he couldn't go bother Colonel So-and-so. It was typical and nobody was surprised, but the tension in the room began to mount and to coil around the young German.

The afternoon drew toward evening; the commanding officer and his staff had to organize an attack for the next morning. If Manfred was right, they were walking into a trap. On the other hand, if he was double-dealing...

Radio contact faded away, division headquarters left our ken, and the staff was alone with a judgment. How could anyone balance the wildly implausible affair of Manfred against the probabilities generated by their accumulated years of war? As it grew dark, the commanding officer made a decision, and what he decided was, to hell with it. The prisoner would be placed somewhere under guard; sooner or later we'd raise division. If Manfred wasn't what he said he was, the commanding officer promised to stick a forty-five up his ass and pull the trigger.

Manfred and a couple of guards marched off to a beer hall down the street while the staff began planning an attack across the bridge. They planned to send a combat patrol off to check for Manfred's ford, just in case. One could feel the staff settle in to the comfort of the workaday. Fifteen minutes of time fire from the 105 Battalion, covering fire with assault guns and mortar platoons, the engineers to rush the bridge in the wake of the infantry and check for demolitions. The staff officers were like businessmen who had just turned down a flight in a UFO in favor of the 7:45 from the commuters' platform.

After supper the combat command, intelligence officer, and I walked down to the beer hall. Manfred was chewing a C ration unhappily. (It was common to find that German prisoners didn't really believe that the American army lived on C rations. They often pointed out, correctly, that they weren't fit for human consumption and made a miserable contrast to the health-giving bratwurst and black bread the Germans regarded as essential. Bill Mauldin also noted this in the Italian theater, so I supposed it was a Wehrmacht-wide complaint.) He put the unfinished C ration down enthusiastically when he saw us.

Manfred spoke first.

"Have they heard?"

We shook our heads. He didn't seem disturbed.

"They will hear. It's okay. I hope they believe me about the bridge, that it's a real trap. They don't need to cross that bridge."

We invited him to sit down.

"We'd like to ask you about yourself if you don't mind."

"Certainly. I am now officially American soldier." He quoted his serial number. "PFC. Big pay," he laughed.

"You were in the German army."

"Yes. Three years. Wounded at Leningrad." He rolled up his sleeve to show us the end of a long, wriggling scar.

"And you were captured by the Americans?"

"Yes. In the Vosges. Near Bruyères. Your Thirty-sixth Division."

"And you volunteered after all that to be an American agent?"

The boy smiled with the grin of someone who's been waiting for you around the corner.

"And you're going to ask me why."

"Well, yes. It's surprising."

Manfred cocked his head and rolled his eyes slowly across the ceiling, the way a man does when he's looking for important words. Then he spoke slowly, leaning toward us with the force of his answer. "I am" — long pause — "anti-Nazi. Anti-Nazi, do I make myself clear?"

The term *anti-Nazi* was inflected with concern and intensity that made it clear that it defined a morality, a way of life, a cause worth all the hazards.

"Antibullshit! Anti-fuckin'-bullshit!" The Southern accent gushed from behind my shoulder, all wet with whiskey, and I knew without looking that Bob Randolph was standing there. Bob was a captain in the rear element of our combat headquarters, carrying out some vague liaison mission with division; he was a Southerner, a stockbroker in a large city in peacetime, a reactionary, a giggling racist, a lissome type who preened around the rear echelon delighting in the petty vendettas of the staff sections, a total opportunist and self-seeker, trapped up front at the moment by a simple error of logistics. He had bummed a ride on the wrong truck at the wrong time and to his horror ended behind the enemy lines with no immediate way back.

Manfred had sprung to attention, as he did whenever any of-

ficer walked in; for a few seconds he looked keenly at Bob, and
then he moved to parade rest with a quite deliberate motion, a
man poised and watchful. Bob was weaving on his feet; the sound
of gunfire always shattered his fine-spun nerves, and whenever
possible he took refuge in drink. Drink made him meaner and
less rational than usual, and at that moment he seemed ready to
do his worst.

(Christ, I thought, we march to a lunatic piper and the sun
will now rise in the west; I was watching a cowardly American
fascist baiting a German *Freitheitskämpfer.*)

Bob wagged his head with the infuriating, knowing, condescending smirk of the ignorant drunk; we heard that we were
buying the Brooklyn Bridge, believing that somebody was about
to leave three squares in a safe American prison camp and take
a chance of getting his balls pulled off with a pliers just because
he was *anti* something. We were advised to use our heads; the
Kraut was pulling a fast one. Wink. Smirk, with pity.

Bill, our intelligence officer, told him that it was quite possible
Manfred really was an American spy; he pointed out that we did
have agents, as Bob knew from a lot of briefings. Bill was a
Southerner, too, from Texas, which raised him a couple of points
in Bob's sodden esteem.

Silence of a moment while Bob leaned back in a chair and
gathered himself for another offensive. If Manfred really was a
spy, he wanted to know, what the hell was in it for him? Bob
didn't want to hear any of this Joan of Arc crap, either. What
made Manfred turn traitor on his own folks? He get paid a lot
of money?

Bob's hostility was seething; I was baffled by what I was seeing
and hearing, but it was clear that something about Manfred was
arousing the wildest emotions in Bob.

Manfred was quintessential politeness as he answered, pointing
out that he was a PFC in the American army. He gave his serial
number and named the ridiculous sum he was paid per month.

Bob fetched up short; personal gain was the only motive he
could comprehend, and the word *idealist,* in his lexicon, was the
ultimate snarling pejorative. I began to understand why Manfred

worried him. Manfred, on the other hand, seemed poised; he was almost grinning.

Bob was a tough campaigner; he came on again. Was Manfred a Communist, something like that? That seemed a consoling solution, and Bob worried it for a while. Manfred had to be some kind of a political fanatic, a Red, something like that.

Manfred explained that by the time he was old enough to be political there were only Nazis left in Germany. He commented that his father and mother were Social Democrats.

Bob pounced on the word *social*. He made it into "socialist." He began to gloat. He had known that Manfred was some kind of goddamn radical.

Bill put in another quiet clarification, explaining that the Social Democrats were like the Democratic party back home, like the New Deal Democrats only probably not so liberal.

Manfred said, "Yes, like your President Roosevelt."

The word *Roosevelt* was the final flutter of the red rag. Bob came in with his horns swinging. It's hard now to remember the utter vileness that the mere mention of Roosevelt's name evoked from American reactionaries in the thirties and forties, but it was an impressive phenomenon. He tapered off into mumbled obscenities about the fuckin' New Deal, nigger-lovin' WPA pinkos.

It was peculiarly humiliating to hear our national vileness aired before a foreigner, but I noticed that Manfred was nodding over a slow grin, like someone listening to familiar music.

When Bob ran out of pejoratives, Manfred, with exquisite courtesy, posed a rhetorical question. What would the captain do if the Communists conquered the U.S.? Wouldn't he oppose them? Wouldn't it be patriotic to join whoever was fighting them?

Ridiculous; no way the fuckin' Commies would ever take over the good old U.S.A., boy.

"Well, but. In America, for example, there are Nazis. People who sympathize with the Nazis."

"Like who?" Bob was ignorant and indignant.

"Like Gerald L. K. Smith and a man called Pelley, and that priest. Father..."

"Coughlin," I filled in.

"Others too, yes?" I nodded.

"If those people without any law took the country, shot who was against them, and killed Jews only because they were Jews..."

Bob was wagging his head, eyes closed, to indicate cynicism, disbelief. Manfred persisted.

"Anti-Semitics, yes. They are. They tell us on the German radio even. Anti-Semitic right in the United States...."

Bob had been pushed to some kind of a limit by Manfred's self-control; now he burst over an edge. Don't give him any of that Jew shit! He was sick of it! Fuckin' Jews... Bob stopped with a sick look on his face, because Sergeant Lebowitz, one of the guards, wide, tough, a veteran of every battle the battalion had fought, had put down his M-1, stood up, and was walking toward him.

Bob took a hard look at Sergeant Lebowitz and collapsed in whining folds, a deflated blimp. He certainly hadn't meant, he wouldn't want anyone to think, some of his best friends, see, that goddamn cocksure Kraut made him mad.... Dying fall, and silence.

"Captain," said the sergeant, "if that guy done what he says he done, he's a brave son of a bitch. Too bad there ain't more Germans like him."

Bob fumbled for words where there were none; one could almost feel sorry for him. He found an excuse to leave quickly, and Manfred sat down, a tired picador, his grin gone.

I talked to him in German: "You did it, goddammit, you goaded him into that on purpose. It was brilliant."

"It was easy, I knew him so well."

"Knew him?"

Manfred expanded his metaphor; Bob had a thousand twin brothers, shadows, doppelgängers. He was a guide in the *Pimpfen*, he was a *Gauleiter*, he was an *Obersturmbannführer* in the SS. Manfred had seen him all over Germany. He predicted that I would see him when I went home, too. Bob lived everywhere. He'd be making excuses for Hitler after the war back in America. (Manfred foresaw with astonishing accuracy the postwar capers of the *Chicago Daily Tribune* and the Milwaukee beer vulgarians.)

Then Manfred told me about Captain Jackson. He had been one of the Seventh Army G-2 officers who had trained Manfred and his fellow agents. He had pointed out that they must ask themselves why they were facing such incredible danger. No money, no medals, no cheers, no slaps on the back, going out in deadly opposition to their homes and their flag (Manfred shook his head sadly at the thought of the Nazi flag being his), all the symbols they had grown up with, assuming evil words like traitor and turncoat, knowing they couldn't go home after the war, knowing that lots of the Amis, themselves, would scorn them, and finally, the very toughest problem: facing people like the fascist captain. Captain Jackson seemed to have been a very perceptive man, because he explained that most people did things only for money or power or some kind of gain and couldn't comprehend that a man might do something out of unselfish belief, out of dedication to an ideal. Manfred had been told that what he was going to do would scare hell out of people like that because it was the one idea they couldn't handle, to see someone who isn't for sale or doesn't do something out of fear. It meant there were people they couldn't possibly control by any of the conventional whips or clubs, people who were infinitely dangerous. Manfred had to expect to be called a fanatic by the self-seekers, because it was the only way they could justify their own lives.

The more I thought about what Manfred relayed from the extraordinary captain at Seventh Army G-2, the more profound it all seemed. Bob had been baying around Manfred, looking for something to attack, wildly agitated, out of control, and the illuminating fact was that Bob's own motives were totally vile. The sight of someone out of reach of any of the impulses that moved him threatened his whole being.

We talked with Manfred about his adventures, but he explained he couldn't tell us much — he had been under strict orders to wait for official debriefing at division and army. From the little he told us about bluffing his way past identity checks and living in a constant state of alarm lest any of his old outfit appear, I felt sympathetic chills. He looked exhausted; we stopped talking and let him doze on the couch while we walked back to battalion headquarters.

The radio was still sputtering uselessly; the air in headquarters was growing frantic. It was getting on to midnight and C Company was dragging past headquarters down the road to get into attack positions. Artillerymen were in and out, contacting forward observers, firing registration rounds on checkpoints.

I started down the street looking for the medical section and ran into the usual snarl of traffic when the supporting platoon of tanks lurched across the path of the infantry company half-tracks. Poking along through the dark, listening to the tensions like fiddle-strings turned tight in men's throats, I heard one infantryman growl to another:

"Hear this is going to be a fuck-up. There's a Kraut spy in battalion and he says this is a trap. I mean this is a guy who was an American spy only he was disguised as a Kraut."

"Naturally he was disguised as a Kraut," the voice of rational analysis floated back through the night, "how the hell else could he of spied on them?"

"Well, you know what I mean, for chrissakes. Anyway, this guy says they're waiting for us and they're gonna blow the bridge when we're halfway across and we shouldn't try to take the bridge anyway 'cause there's a ford up the stream the Krauts ain't even watching where we could walk across...."

I should have been astonished, but I wasn't. One learned early in the game that there was no such thing as secrecy in the army; information spread like oil on water. Obviously some T-5 from headquarters had talked to someone in a line company, and from that point the news about Manfred and his information had spread swiftly to the loneliest outpost.

A blue-covered flashlight was moving over a map behind an assault gun where two platoon leaders were talking with a forward observer from the artillery.

I walked over. They asked me if I knew about the Kraut spy and about the bridge. I told them what I knew, but I didn't tell them my own hunch that Manfred was the real article, out of a somewhat cowardly fear of the consequences if I turned out to be wrong. The lieutenants, however, were drawing their own conclusions.

Attacking across the bridge was stupid, they agreed. The company commander loomed out of the dark bearing the same concerns. It was heartening to stand there among all those masses of weapons listening to the real fighting men make their own assessment of the situation and hear them calmly, professionally ignore the dithering going on at headquarters as they revised their attack to take Manfred's news into account.

The company commander pointed out that it was ridiculous to try to cross the bridge. Let them blow it, he said; he'd get a Bailey bridge up in a few hours anyway. Battalion always wanted to look good with a nice, intact bridge, but C Company was not going to get anyone killed just to get S-3 a goddamn commendation. They were going to wade the river; it didn't look all that deep.

In ten minutes the four officers had a sensible attack plotted; it would be a sham at the bridge, with lots of firing by the weapons platoon, smoke from the artillery to land just across the bridge and drift downwind a few hundred yards, and then, while the Germans were blasting away at imaginary attackers on the bridge, two platoons would wade or swim the stream under cover of the smoke and flank the position. Tanks and antitank weapons had good fields of fire across the stream to cover the infantrymen when they deployed on the far side.

There was some marking of maps and checking of watches, and the officers disappeared into the black. Thank God for irreverence and mutiny, I thought; no Light Brigades in the American army, no floundering in the mud of Passchendaele. During the next hour, while I talked with company aid men and looked for routes of evacuation, I was composing somewhere in the back corners of my mind an essay on military disobedience, possibly not so much an essay as a paean to those who confront and overcome reality, compared to those who live by its reflection as seen palely on bits of paper.

The last couple of hours wore toward dawn. At battalion and

combat command headquarters men were drawn fine with worry about Manfred and his warning, not realizing that the soldiers out in the forests and fields had already digested the news. The whole fighting machine had accommodated itself with no help from above. It couldn't accommodate itself completely, of course, because if Manfred's story was true, the men were still going to attack a dug-in German infantry battalion with predictable heavy casualties, when the whole position could be painlessly flanked. Men of the assault company told me later that nobody slept that night; machine-gunners, mortar crews, and riflemen argued through the dark about the truth of Manfred's story and the consequences to all of them if he was right. The battalion collectively chewed its nails and stared into the dark.

The first break came in a radio message from the platoon sent to check on Manfred's ford.

"Apple pie okay," the message said, which meant there was a ford. Twenty minutes later came another message: "Apple pie with cheese," which meant the patrol was across the ford, it was practicable.

"Apple pie okay for baking" came minutes later — there was a road suitable for tanks on the far side.

S-3 told the patrol to set up a perimeter defense on the far side of the river and wait for orders. He was really agonizing now; halt the other attack? Send tanks to the ford? Switch the artillery? Someone went to wake the CO, who made swift, sensible dispositions. A company of tanks was ordered to move down the road to the ford and B Company of the infantry battalion was sent along the same road after the tanks to "marry up" and be ready to attack. ("Marrying up" meant that infantrymen climbed on the backs of tanks and established communications with the tankers inside — not always an easy thing to do.)

At four A.M., when the faintest light was paling the east, the radio finally made contact. G-2 was back; communications worked; the codes were sent and the responses were electric. Someone went running to the tavern to get Manfred to bring him to the transmitter. A series of questions came from division intelligence; Manfred answered them with a set of apparently irrelevant responses. I remember hearing him say New York Yankees, Cleveland, Ohio, and so on through ten seemingly meaningless exchanges. The signal officers of combat command and battalion were hunched into earphones, and as the exchanges ended every face switched into brightness, grins all around. The message center clerk scribbled, ''Absolute verification; identity established; division will make special arrangements to pick up this individual your headquarters as soon as possible; this man completely accurate, reliable; provide maximum security.''

There was a flurry of enthusiasm; people shook Manfred's hand and thumped his back; runners went to wake both commanding officers.

Headquarters became an ordered bedlam; orders went out over the radio to hold the attack on the bridge; liaison officers were sent in case the messages went wrong, which would have been usual. The attack plan was altered to send the company of tanks and infantry across the ford while artillery officers scrambled to switch fire plans. A complete sham attack was ordered on the bridge with barrages by 105s and tank guns, mortars dropping on the far side of the bridge, smoke, firing by fifty-caliber machine guns and assault guns, and maximum possible hullaballoo to keep the Germans looking the wrong way.

In a green unit, confusion would have begot disaster, but in a veteran combat command like ours the tentacles withdrew and extended swiftly; responses anticipated orders.

The sounds of their engines drowned out by the racket on the other flank, the tank company rolled down to the river at the first light of dawn, across the ford, and into the thankful arms of the patrol on the far side. One of the tank officers described the battle scene later:

''I couldn't believe they didn't know we were there, but this road went right around the Krauts; they weren't even watching it. They were all looking at the bridge. I came around the bend and up a little rise and I felt as if I was looking at the back of the whole German army. There were these guys around an eighty-eight, and a lot of infantrymen around machine guns, and they didn't dream we were there until I got my platoon in line and started down the hill shootin' like hell — seventy-sixes, coax machine guns, fifty calibers, and the infantrymen on the backs of the tanks blazin' away, having a regular Fourth of July. It must be really demoralizing to get run over from behind like that; the Krauts just broke and ran. There must have been the biggest part of a battalion and they didn't get to fire hardly a shot. We put a couple of seventy-six rounds through that fuckin' eighty-eight first and then they had nothin' to fight us with.''

The battle was over in an hour. It was the cleanest, neatest victory of our campaign: no serious casualties on our side, and all the Germans who weren't killed or wounded marching in with their hands over their heads or running for Nuremberg. By mid-morning most of the combat elements were over the river, tally-hoing to the east under the protecting wings of a squadron of P-47s.

All through the battle Manfred had sat in a peculiar tense, half-crouched huddle near the message center following the voice radio descriptions of the actions. The feeling of everyone in headquarters, I sensed, was one of awe and unwilling alienation; what could someone say to a man who had switched the latitude and longitude of his existence and was helping us kill his countrymen? After it was all over he almost collapsed. The battalion commanding officer shook his hand and thanked him officially, but Manfred wavered on his feet. I made him lie down, and in minutes he was in a stuporous sleep. Messages kept coming from division G-2 about holding Manfred, keeping him safe, someone was coming for him — there was no question that division regarded him as a species of crown jewel. Late in the morning, four medium tanks from the reserve battalion rattled up the street and halted outside headquarters. The platoon leader came in, stating they were a special convoy from division G-2 to escort Manfred back. One of the noncoms shook him awake.

"Manfred," he said, "look what you got; talk about importance, you've got a whole fuckin' tank convoy to take you back."

Manfred was groggy and frightened at first. It was obvious that the simple fact of safety after a world of horror was taking some getting used to.

We found him a helmet and a field jacket from the aid station.

"You're an American soldier," someone told him, "you gotta look like one. Hell of a thing if some nut shot you now." Manfred grinned from under the helmet and shrugged in the oversized jacket.

While the tanks maneuvered around the narrow street, we passed some final words.

"How did you feel this morning?" I asked. "How much did it really bother you to watch us attack your people?" I used the German word for countrymen, *Landsmänner*. He grinned at the word and shook his head.

"I've been thinking. All of us thought, I suppose, about that more than anything, maybe even more than getting caught. It's what pounds on you in your sleep, and you have to answer. After a long time I answered."

"You answered?"

"Yes. I say, Who is a countryman of who? Someone drew a line on the ground after the Thirty Years' War." (He was talking with sudden animation, defending himself against an accusing world; he was making a speech he must have rehearsed to himself a thousand times.) "Why do I have to feel loyal to everyone on that side of the line? Do all Englishmen feel loyal to that Jack, that very bad man, that Jack who cut up ladies?"

"Jack the Ripper."

"Yes. Does an Englishman justify Jack the Ripper or feel sorry if he is caught and hung? Or suppose all the Englishman's friends went insane and helped Jack the Ripper find the people, the victims, and held them while he cut them. Wouldn't the decent Englishman who was left help anyone to stop them? Even if the policemen were French, or Polish?"

"Right, right." I was reassuring him; Manfred was getting pretty tense, and his hands were starting to shake as they had the day before when he held out the maps in the street. I decided it was going to take him a while to come out of the effect of chronic terror; maybe some medical care.

"A man's countrymen, the people he should feel loyal to, are the people who believe the way he does about what is a crime and what is not a crime. I'm sorry if Germans got killed this morning, but I've lived through a *Kristallnacht*. You know what a *Kristallnacht* was?" I nodded. "I watched those truckloads of lunatics smashing the storefronts of the Jewish stores. They beat up my friends in the streets, and I stood there. I was a kid. I couldn't do anything. It went on for years. You stand in the streets of a German town, you see vans going to death camps. Everyone knows what's in them, everyone pretends they don't. Even the clergymen look away like goddamn hypocrites. I heard them threaten my father, shouting in the hallway of our house while I sat upstairs in my room with my hands over my ears, when I was fifteen years old." Now the anger almost choked him. I put a hand on his shoulder.

"You're right," I told him. "There is no other kind of country. A country is ideas, not dirt and rocks."

The tanks had swung around; he put his helmet back on and held out his hand. *"Grüss dich Gott,"* he said. "Hope I meet you in America." As the platoon leader came in the door to meet him, Manfred stopped, turned, and said to me in German, very softly and thoughtfully and with an air of sudden surprise:

"My God, I may even get to sleep with a girl again. When you're busy thinking all the time about not getting killed, you forget things like that."

He ran down the stairs and up to the tanks.

Outside there was a small crowd of soldiers. From the vehicle markings I gathered that some of these men were from the company that had made the sham attack on the bridge that morning; they were the ones that Manfred had specifically saved from wandering into a trap and every man of them knew it. Their admiration was obvious, but they were strangely restrained as he climbed on the deck of the tank and slid into the turret. They were brave men themselves, survivors of a lot of terror, and as experts on bravery they had the quiet admiration professional athletes might show for one who had just broken all existing records. There was also, I suppose, the element of the ultraromantic, the adventure story embodied and smiling at them, the resource we didn't dream we possessed, the deus ex machina who had saved their lives and handed them a victory. They waved hands and tossed pretended salutes; Manfred grinned like a kid and waved and saluted back. It was a quiet, intensely happy moment.

As the tank motors started to roar, Bob Randolph came along the street, and he and Manfred spotted each other just as the column began to move. Manfred stood rigid, upright, froze his grin, and held a rigid salute, looking hard at Bob, until Bob, bound by military protocol, had to return his salute. Then the roar deafened, the column rolled off into the street, and I saw Manfred for the last time, leaning out of the turret on one elbow, so relaxed he seemed draped over the steel. The words *human* and *decent* kept floating in my mind, and I realized that he must be the happiest, most acutely alive being on the western front at that moment. He was, I thought, in a kind of happy hiatus, between the horrors he had just faced and the nameless terrors of loneliness and exile that must lie ahead of him, but at this beautiful gap in his life everything was shining and golden for Manfred as it might never be again. I devoutly hope he enjoyed it.

Historical footnote: I forgot Manfred in the years after the war, until one day I picked up a book called *Decision at Dawn*. To this day I can't imagine why I picked it up, but to my pleased wonder, it proved to be a semidocumentary novel about Manfred and the Seventh Army anti-Nazi Germans — I presume it must have been written by someone from Seventh Army intelligence; I've forgotten the author's name, but I am greatly in his debt. The book described in authoritative detail the recruitment and training of these men and followed some of them throughout their adventures. Seventh Army, in the dark of the winter of 1944, went into the prisoner-of-war cage at Chalons and recruited anti-Nazi Germans to act as American agents. These men were superbly trained, given minute cover stories and false identities, and parachuted behind the German lines with instructions to pick up certain specific items of information plus whatever serendipity put in their way. Later a movie with the same name was made, following the book almost verbatim. I think it was the best film to come out of the Second World War. The scene of the young

Germans climbing into the planes that were to take them off into the winter night for their drop into Germany is a masterpiece of almost sickening, heart-clenching suspense — God knows what it was like for the men who really did it.

In the course of an argument in the command post somebody said, "Oh, shit, let's be practical," and I looked over to see Manfred staring at the floor, shaking his head, muttering in German. When I listened, he was saying, "Oh, shit, practical again, here comes practical, marching. I'll never be free from practical." I asked him about his little chant, and he told me his definitions of "practical." The word *praktisch* had been a two-syllable club he'd been beaten with by fellow students and teachers and businessmen and clergy all through the nightmare years. "Stop being such a goddamned idealist! Be practical!"

"You know what practical is?

"Practical means I know right from wrong but I'm too fucking scared to do what's right so I commit crimes or permit crimes and I say I'm only being practical. Practical means coward.

"Practical frequently means stupid. Someone is too goddamn dumb to realize the consequences of what he's doing and he hides under practical.

"It also means corrupt: I know what I ought to do but I'm being paid to do something different so I call it practical.

"Practical is an umbrella for the everything lousy people do."

I handed Manfred a bottle of brandy. "A toast, Manfred. Here's to the destruction of the practical!"

"The cowardly, greedy, vicious, plausible practical!

"God send them instant destruction before they destroy us!"

"And the world!"

We drank.

The best way to tell if something is important in your life is to notice how often you think about it. Thoughts about the Manfred adventure have been frequent for years, and they've been fertile; they're still putting forth new twigs.

Consider Voltaire's definition of absolute, isolated moral good. The philosopher requested you to imagine that by pushing a button you could kill twenty million Chinese, and that as a result, you would receive every form of earthly wealth and happiness imaginable, with no punishment either in this world or the next, and to imagine finally that having pushed the button you would be guaranteed instant and complete forgetfulness of the act in two seconds.

Now, would you push the button?

Voltaire was isolating ''good'' in human moral terms, excluding completely any question of punishment or reward.

Manfred and his fellows were fingering the obverse of that coin. They had had a bedfellow acquaintance with death and terror; many of their friends were dead and more were mangled. Now they found themselves secure in an American prison camp, ready to spend the rest of the war in Texas eating three reasonable meals a day and marching home to a hero's welcome. They had done more than their duty for their country, as most people understood it; they were beyond criticism; in today's jargon, they had it made.

Instead, these extraordinary men made the cold-blooded choice to face weeks and months of suspense and terror, living with the probability of death by exquisite torture, with little or no praise from those they helped, with no thought of medals or fame, and certainly none of money, in the teeth of every sentimental attachment of their lives, to friends and hills and towns and great-uncles and third cousins, with the final chapter — if they lived — a life of exile in a strange continent.

Most of us are commanded to what courage we have by duty, by the need for approbation, by the fear of shame, by rewards of many and subtle kinds, and possibly, most of all, by the gallery of our peers and our countrymen, always just out of sight over our shoulders, but Manfred and his friends were free-floating objects, the quintessential *Ding an sich*, without rewards or whips to urge them. It was demonstrable by swift exclusion that they were acting purely and only because they believed in some abstract moral concept so deeply they were ready to risk torture and death for it. Mr. Thoreau, Mr. Emerson, you've been waiting in the wings. We must believe that everything we do is significant in some unimaginable titanic scheme; we must believe that the voices in our minds transcend advantage or survival, or we go clattering down the ladder of the phyla to land in a crawling heap somewhere below the annelid worms.

Another twig : Patriotic to what, to where, to whom ? Patriotic to the current politicians running a country ? To a particular stretch of soil and rocks and trees ? If all Americans were transplanted to the moon, wouldn't we still call ourselves Americans ? What on the moon would it be that made us Americans except for some abstract moral notions enshrined in the Bill of Rights of the U.S. Constitution ?

Ideals are the only reality ; they're all we have to define us.

The last twig : What did all that bravery accomplish ? The Allies would have won the war with or without Manfred's band, but it is almost certain that the intelligence they brought made the American advance swifter and saved lives and prevented destruction on both sides. The great victory, as usual, was not material. A man does have a soul, an ultimate lonely voice in his mind, hammered out of millions on millions of years of ions and cataclysms and protoplasmic scrabblings, and when he hears that voice and follows it beyond the limits of human fears or endurance, he truly saves his soul, and, if such a thing can be said to exist, the soul of his nation.

Finally, from me, a low bow ; gratitude : the Manfred-adventure was a clearing wind that blew a whole gaggle of fetishes squawking and twittering out the window and started me across the world on a hunt for polestars and azimuths. A man never knows when he'll need them.

✳ 18

The Chambered Nautilus

E VER SINCE HIS COURAGE AT HERRLISHEIM, the colonel could
do nothing seriously wrong in our combat command; down
to the last rifleman everybody knew that he had thrown his career
and his life into the balance for them, and they all sensed that
he had torn his way out of a straitjacket of class and calling.
They had some idea of what it had cost him to do it; reverent
recollections about "that time the Old Man told everybody to go
fuck themselves at Herrlisheim" expanded with soldierly logarithms until it appeared he had told everybody in the ETO up
to and almost including Eisenhower to go fuck themselves.

Back in England someone had commented that the colonel lived
in a strictly regulation olive-drab shell; I used to imagine that
his lopsided grin and tipped head were the cephalad extremity
of some creature peering out of an operculum, and I wondered
what was really crouched back in there. At Herrlisheim he had
stepped into wider and astonishing worlds; in the mess one night
I said something about building statelier mansions, but nobody
caught the simple reference. Trouble was, the German war kept
pushing horizons past everyone's personal infinity; while we rested
in Lorraine, after Colmar, the next impossible reach came at us

in the shape of a lot of black reinforcements for our infantry battalions.

The United States armed forces in the Second World War were racially segregated, both in geography and function. Black troops were not only isolated, they were dumped in rear-echelon, non-combat, lower-caste battalions like quartermaster, truck companies, and assorted housekeeping units, the dignity of combat being reserved for Anglos, Chicanos, Japanese-Americans, and Indians. The winter fighting left some dismal statistics strung along the rifle companies of the western front. As our British cousins would put it, we were damned thin on the ground, and the high command was jarred into the unthinkable obvious: they decided our black troops had earned the right to die in combat instead of in truck accidents.

The colonel brought the news from division to a meeting of staff and battalion commanders. We were tipping back in chairs in the Lorraine farmhouse that served as a command post, while I tried to decipher the colonel's odd expression. I finally decided he was trying to look cheery, but with enormous effort.

He spoke.

He had good news and, pause, difficult news.

The good news was that each infantry battalion was receiving an extra company, D Company, all volunteers from rear-echelon units. Polite cheers; smiles; comments that we could sure as hell use them. Very welcome.

Now the difficult news. Much longer pause. The reinforcements were all black.

I remember the faces I saw contorted in that late afternoon light, and the words that I heard, and I reach for understanding. These were all men from lower- and middle-class American homes; they had survived combat together and they were meshed, all unknowing, in an archaic force they didn't begin to comprehend, a force familiar and household to the Lydian cavalry and the Knights Templar and the Janizaries and the Bashi Bazouks, the terrifying union of men who rely on each other for survival, the cult of the brothers in arms. Mates, children, and siblings are remote one from another by comparison; the tensions of exclusion in a warrior cult are murderous, and telling these men to accept strangers of a race apart was like asking a Polish steelworker's family in Pittsburgh to organize a welcome party for their beloved eighteen-year-old daughter's black fiancé.

After shock, expostulation, with pacing about the room; after fifteen minutes, acceptance of the inevitability, and the men turned to sarcasm and denigration. They'd use those nigger bastards all right, for latrine orderlies and truck drivers and for handing out VD packets. They'd wish their worst officers on them for a cadre. If they couldn't defy, they'd circumvent.

The colonel spoke with some coldness when he told them that instructions from above and from himself were almost excessively clear. D Company would be used for combat like any other; the colonel gave them the names of the officers he had already picked as company commander and platoon leaders. The infantry colonel pounded hands when he heard it, for they were a collection of his best men.

The colonel went on that there would be promotion for the new jobs; he recognized there would be difficulties, but the army rewarded men who handled difficult jobs. That was *all*.

Silence; unmoving faces; the colonel swung his eyes around the half-circle, and then stood and talked like a teacher.

He explained that at the Point they had studied military history a good deal; some surprises in that history. Did everyone in the room know that there were thousands of black soldiers in the American Revolutionary Army before the families of most of the people in the room had left Europe? Fact. Whole Rhode Island regiment was black. Half the Continental regiments of the South were black, since gentlemen sent their slaves instead of themselves, an accepted practice. Black cavalry in the Indian wars; black soldiers tracking Geronimo. Black men had been fighting for the United States of America for almost two hundred years. We were part of a long tradition. That was really all.

I walked back through the room a little while after the meeting; the colonel was flicking a nail against a window. He turned, and forced a smile.

"Wish I was sure how much I meant all that, Doc."

I told him I thought he meant all of it, but then he knew my liberal notions. He walked off, moving his head in his own peculiar one-sided shake; "It's never easy." He turned to the door to face me and said it again: "They never make it easy...."

The colonel kept the edge of decency flaring around our black soldiers. D Company wasn't called on to do much serious fighting in the Saar campaign until we deployed out on the Rhine plain, attacking south to meet Seventh Army and close the giant pinchers. I was standing near the Old Man when the tank battalion commander called about an attack he was making on a heavily defended village. D Company was named to ride in on his tanks, and the tank commander was being difficult. Give 'em some real infantry, goddammit; the voice was floating clear for anyone listening on that channel all over our network; he wanted some real infantry riding his tanks.

The Old Man was reassuring for two exchanges, and then his voice took on the edge of Potsdam. The tank colonel had his real infantry. He'd get going and fight them and use them like real soldiers or the Old Man would find somebody else who would. Over and out.

The combat network and the listeners from division were left in no slightest doubt about the Old Man and the tactical deployment of D Company. The black soldiers rode into their first battle on the backs of tanks, and won it.

Challenge and response, unrelenting: Somewhere in the middle of Germany we were host to a black one-star general who was touring the front to see how black combat troops were doing. He joined us at our mess, sitting next to the colonel. Our colonel was courtly, with an effort that I could see if others couldn't. He certainly concealed the effort from our guest, but I noticed a lot of hard staring at the single star on our guest's collar, and I realized that our colonel was leaning against the habits of a lifetime, on structured discipline and authority. When somebody told a funny story, there were a couple of unaffected, healthy African guffaws. The staring at the star became more concentrated, but the colonel carried everything off magnificently and cowed the racists in our headquarters into smiling good manners.

(We listened to the black general talk to D Company about how fortunate they were to be front line fighters for freedom and democracy; he told them how much the United States was going to appreciate all this.

Coop made the noises of grim humor.

"Wait till they go back to Mississipi and Alabama and ask some goddamn civilian for permission to vote. They're gonna feel real appreciated.")

The psyche's only a collection of cells, after all, and growth in any biologic system has limits. The affair of the Basque major and the slaves imposed demands that outran the nutrient supply.

When we conquered towns or cities, the newly liberated slave workers often helped themselves to the food and wealth they had been creating, to the great and ridiculous indignation of their former masters. Even the West Pointers turned a deaf ear to guttural demands for law and order, for everyone felt we had a war to fight, and besides, what the hell had the Germans expected, anyway?

It wasn't disorder that bothered our colonel; rather, it was the sudden appearance of discipline and order that pulled him quite beyond his limits. In a town in Württemberg Province, the slave workers had organized themselves, gotten hold of some weapons, and run out the small German garrison. There had been a lot of purposeful activity on the day before our arrival, and a whole new civil authority consisting entirely of slave workers appeared to have been established. The German civilians had been kicked out of their mansions and were living in the slave workers' former pens, and everywhere the removal of German wealth was progressing in an efficiently coordinated operation carried on by the recently enslaved creators of that wealth. In the town square figures were capering around a bonfire; faces moving into firelight explained that the former slaves were hauling boxes of Nazi proclamations and propaganda out of the house of the local *Gauleiter* and burning them, along with some oddments of his ornate furniture. Enchanting fireworks; with every box of solemn lunacy dumped on the flames, clouds of sparks floated across the square to cheers and healthy laughing, humanity triumphant one more time.

All around us in the ruddy dark we could hear shouted commands and see purposeful responses; it was nice to see the forces of light getting themselves sorted out swiftly and efficiently, but we wondered to each other who had done the sorting. Then we heard the unmistakable sound of well-drilled boots thumping in step and a squad of men marched up through the flashes of red light to slam to a precise halt at the colonel's jeep. The leader swung a wide British salute and introduced himself: Major Santiago of the Spanish Republican Army, at our service.

Maybe we always think in pictures; as I walked up I was wishing Margaret Bourke-White could have been there with some kind of ultrasensitive color film to record the lifting and flaring of the firelight on the eight men in ragged clothes and workmen's caps, with their carbines and automatic weapons slung, standing at rigid, proud attention until the major gave a command and they all moved to a precise parade rest. American voices were saying, Hey, those guys are soldiers. They all recognized professionals.

The major went on addressing the colonel. (European speech in those days was madly eclectic; the major used a word salad of Spanish, French, and English, with some reluctant German when everything else failed.)

The colonel heard from the major that he and his men were our allies; they would help to maintain order and justice and secure our lines of communication until our military government and rear echelons could take over. They had prisoners locked up in the local jail and they would be delighted to hand them over to our MPs; the prisoners were in some danger, considering the feelings of the former slaves.

The major spoke out of a dark, quick face, and under his beret his eyes were searching the shape of our colonel's responses. From the American side there was an initial Well, uh, yes, thanks, glad to see you, and an inevitable offering of cigarettes. That led to further ease in conversation, and in answer to questions about origins, the major explained that he was a Basque, a veteran of the whole civil war in Spain, interned in France and enslaved in Germany. In his motions and in his speech the Basque gave an instant impression of toughness, of quickness, of dense fiber; it was clear he was still uncowed and unbroken, still very much an officer and a leader.

As initial surprise waned and deeper attitudes emerged, it was clear the colonel was profoundly uneasy. I could see him withdrawing into his odd, cold chamber, and finally he came out with it.

All that looting was going to have to stop.

Looting? The Basque was trying hard to look perplexed.

"Those people over there, taking things out of stores, those lines of people with boxes and bags of things."

The Basque spoke with force: Those people, he pointed out, were taking what they created themselves. A lot of them had been working there for four years and the goddamn Nazis had been living off their sweat. None of them knew where they'd be going or what homes they would have after this mess, but they all knew they had to eat and stay warm, and there was no reason why they should have to be the ones to go cold and hungry. He asked the colonel to remember that they were our allies, and he pointed out that if anybody went without things, it should be Germans.

By this time a dozen more slave workers had wandered up; tilted caps and slung carbines made a half-circle. They heard the colonel's words as they were picked up and translated; laughing and bitter sounds came out of the darkness in a half-dozen languages.

"Shit; the Americans are defending Nazi groceries."

"Law and order for the criminals."

"It's what the Communists said: The Americans are business first, business with anybody."

"We're hungry, goddammit. The Germans have been starving us. We're your starving allies."

I translated the German elements for the colonel, and he picked up the French comments himself. Meantime, the Basque major seemed to have been rummaging in his assorted languages for a metaphor; finally he produced it.

"Speaking of looting, the Germans looted these people's lives if you want to think of it like that; why the hell are you concerned about looting some groceries?"

The colonel reached for his ultimate vocabulary; he was embarrassed and fighting anger.

"It's not military, looting; that's not for soldiers. . . ."

The faces under caps passed laughter along like a chain; fingers pointed to American infantrymen wandering past with cameras and field glasses and German sporting weapons. The Basque nodded his head toward them:

"Looting, Colonel?"

The colonel hung in chains; how could he say what he really felt, that the men in old clothes and caps with their slung weapons rang the chimes of Red Square in 1917?

Because he couldn't say or even recognize what was seething in him, he began shouting, the same rage-coming-out-of-a-shell I'd seen in England and in Texas.

"If you were really an officer you'd understand —" Then he was interrupted.

When the Basque heard the phrase "really an officer," he took two quick strides to the colonel and began to deliver something between a denouncement and a classroom lecture, certainly one of the most memorable passages of speech I've ever heard; the curious inversion of his language made it the more penetrating.

He leaned on one elbow, easy, on the windshield of the jeep and wagged a finger as he spoke.

When the colonel was playing war-games in America, like Indians with cowboys, he, the Basque, kept fighting the Nazis, those same Nazis that had damn near conquered the whole world.

He and his men had been not mechanics, but by God soldiers; they had nothing to be mechanics with — wave of hand — so they had to be fighting men.

The Basque began to draw the colonel into a series of practical professional questions and answers.

"How would the colonel like to with rifles fight dive-bombers?

"German tanks, you have no AT guns, no tanks, then how to

do ? Ambush you do, gasoline bombs, damned brave men, soldiers, not with machines.

''America makes embargo: no weapons to Spanish Republic and Nazis and Fascists, they laugh and ship armies. Then how? You take them, by God, capture them, use whatever you can make together out of different.''

A hand gripped the Basque's sleeve and an angry voice followed out of the dark. Forget it, the voice said in the kind of pig German that all the slave workers spoke; it's like 1942 and Darlan. The Americans will now kiss the Fascists' ass. They like rich people.

The Basque pushed the hand away and looked at the colonel, shaking his head like a disappointed professor. ''You Americans — children! Children, and you don't know what the hell you're getting in here. You're brave, good equipment, idiots. Too bad; you could be a good man. Pity.''

In two commands he had his squad marching away, thumping even across the firelit cobbles.

When the slave worker talked about Darlan, he was talking about history the colonel barely knew and certainly didn't understand, but it was history that set a pattern America has repeated many times in the last thirty years, always to our disgrace, and always as a prelude to failure. It was the beginning of repeated performances that have earned us the contempt of the decent world and snatched from us the leadership of that world that we almost had in our fingers at the end of the Second World War. You should know about it. . . .

Come back two years from our Panzerspitz in Germany to the period of the First Great Disillusionment. It happened in French North Africa in 1942.

The French military in North Africa from 1940 to 1942 enacted and enforced anti-Semitic laws, maintained concentration camps, and collaborated with the Nazis with a great deal of flourish and saluting and tinkling of picturesque spahis. When America and Britain prepared for the invasion of French North Africa, our secret agents made contact with patriotic Frenchmen — many of them Jews — who provided invaluable intelligence, and on the day of the invasion actually rose in rebellion with smuggled American arms to help the Allied landings. They captured some of the worst French Fascists and held them prisoner during crucial periods of the attack. Jewish members of the Resistance had the marvelously rewarding experience of seeing the heads of the French secret police kneeling before them, revealing their true selves as they cried like children and begged for their lives in the face of Resistance machine guns. Because the landing and fighting took several days, the Resistance groups were overwhelmed by the regular French forces and put in prison while the fighting was still going on, but they had aided greatly ; among other things, they had held key Vichy French commanders incommunicado for some crucial hours, including Admiral Darlan, the commander in chief of all North Africa.

When our troops marched in, the world turned upside down. Our authorities chose to ignore the mass of the population and to deal with the thin scum of collaborators. We reinstated the dregs of the French armed forces in the seats of power, and stood by uncaring, while traitors who had served the Nazis locked up heroes who had fought for the Allies. For months after our victory, Vichy censors cut pro-Allied articles out of papers, Jews and anti-Nazi dissidents continued to starve in Vichy concentration camps with American MPs at the gates, and the Vichy secret police harassed citizens for the crimes of being Jewish and supporting the Allies.

French regular army regiments refused to accept Jews or anti-Nazi dissidents : troublesome *types* like these were graciously permitted to volunteer for the Corps-Franc, a madly underequipped, unpaid collection of *braves* who fought beside the Americans in the Tunisian mountains.

The overt anti-Semitism of the French regular army evoked some glittering American responses. George Patton believed French fairy tales about a " Jewish revolt " in Morocco and gravely transmitted this fantasy to our State Department.

American reporters, including the great A. J. Liebling, then with *Time* magazine and later *The New Yorker,* protested en masse to our State Department and to the French authorities: rebuffed, they went home to file their stories free of censorship, and so aroused public opinion that after five months the traitors and collaborators were removed from power, the anti-Semitic laws were repealed, and the stalwarts of the Resistance were out of jail and free to risk their lives for the Allies, but the world had had a sickening glimpse into the motivation and performance of our military caste and our State Department.

Resistance fighters from caves in Norway to forests in Poland breathed disenchantment and disillusionment and began to turn their backs on America. Here, at the very turn of the tide of the Second World War, the certifiable good guys had freed oppressed people, and then had handed them right back to the traitors who had been helping the oppressors oppress. The fall of America from possible greatness started right then and ended a long time later in Vietnam.

To be fair, the Second World War was awfully hard on the British and American military establishments: they found themselves in bed with unshaven Resistance fighters of assorted and sometimes alarming political persuasions, and at odds with impeccably groomed drill-stampers. They were asked to kill their twins, their doppelgängers, in behalf of various seedy individuals, and if they sometimes thought north was south, you couldn't blame them.

Back to our Panzerspitz: We attacked on to the east that night, following the tracers and explosions of our advance guard across Württemberg Province, forty miles before dawn, and nobody had time — for that matter, inclination — to stop to dismantle the Basque major's brave new world.

Our colonel kept a little obbligato going but nobody listened. "Getting in touch with military government," it ran. "Irregular forces. Got to have law and order, not a bunch of anarchists."

A couple of days later we were ordered to halt; the reason surprised us, and for that matter any part of the world that was paying attention. Georgie Patton's chorus of castrati had the whole world convinced that Third Army was leading the Allied assault on Festung Deutschland; the rest of us were supposed to be scrambling along in the wake. A BBC announcer came clearly over our radios one Sunday morning to tell us the truth when we were about two days' fighting past the Basque major's town. This very morning, said precise accents, the Twelfth Armored Division of the Seventh Army's Twenty-first Corps had the honor of standing farther east in Europe than any of the Allied forces, and we all looked over our shoulders and said, Jesus Christ, that's us! It felt more lonely than honorific, especially since we were the absolute needle point of the Twelfth Armored Division's advance, and it appeared we were really a long way out in the middle of a lot of Germans. The German counterattack on the night before became much more interesting.

At any rate, the laggards of Third Army, all weighted down with Georgie Patton and a thousand tons of press relations gear, were so far behind us on our left flank that Eisenhower got nervous and halted the hard-driving veterans of Seventh Army to let the lesser breeds catch up. I took the chance to drive back to look for some missing ambulances, and a few kilometers down the road the colonel passed us in his jeep going the same way. We beeped, but his response was not his usual chipper salute; he barely raised a finger and his head was sunk on his chest, causing me to wonder what the hell. He disappeared ahead.

In the Basque major's town I found the ambulances, but that was the least of my discoveries. The slave workers were still armed and were still in command of the situation. They were in evidence everywhere, standing guard posts with American MPs, parading in short, purposeful columns along streets, mounting guard at major buildings. An hour's gossip around town told me what had happened: the American press, by God, had done it again. Reporters from some wire services, two major newspapers, and elements of the liberal press had landed on the story of the slaves who had liberated themselves and run out the Germans and set up a free society, and they were trying to get it on all the wire services.

Soldiers were always delighted when the press lifted them into contact with the rest of the world; sentries beamed as they told me the fuckin' photographers were all over the place, taking miles of pictures of GIs and slave workers shaking hands and hugging each other and comparing guns, and asking soldiers a lot of crap about the free world and their brave allies.

I heard some of these interviews and I could only reflect that complete lack of political sophistication sometimes generated the truth. Yeah, said one soldier, it was nice having guys that were on our side in the town; it wasn't like them goddamn Krauts that would grin at you and stab you in the back.

Others made the profound observation that the liberated slaves felt like people who really liked us, and that felt pretty good.

Sentries commented to me that the slave workers certainly liked to parade and salute; they acted as if they really liked being soldiers again. When you talked to them you found out most of them were veterans of some army or other.

Then I found the colonel, and that was when God smiled, for the colonel was being composed into a tableau in the town square; the artists doing the composing were a platoon of photographers and reporters, and they had the division general and some high-ranking staff officers and our colonel in a kind of studied disarray, trying to look as if they had just run into each other, casual-like.

The rest of the tableau, as I hope for salvation, consisted of the Basque major and his squad, and as I walked up the major was extending his hand, by instruction, to grasp our colonel in a brother-in-arms handshake. The colonel's face was the ultimate tribute to upper-Hudson discipline; it was a mask with a grin pasted across it by order of higher authority. I've never seen such a dissociated baring of teeth.

The Basque major was way ahead of the situation; he had all the nuances firmly in hand and was exploiting the hell out of everything with a kind of subterranean, well-controlled glee that rumbled and flickered under a soldierly exterior.

For ten minutes while the reporters fired delighted questions he explained how inspiring it was to be allied with the Americans, who were, after all, the first revolutionaries. We heard selected comments about the new world of human freedom and dignity, without slaves, political or economic, everything like in the great

U.S. Constitution. He and his men had organized the town: the poor, the weak, children, German or not, they were being fed and sheltered. Humanity first, property second. Like the Americans.

He ended with an impressive wide British salute, returned perforce by the American brass, and led his men away thudding across the square to barked commands. With thanks from the press, the Americans dispersed, muttering, plucking fingers.

The colonel spotted me among the hushed spectators; he walked up, head on one side in his birdlike position of thought, the small smile moving to the left.

"Uh, propaganda stuff here. Press. Public relations."

I said I thought it had all been very well done, and the smile moved more eccentrically. We walked together, silent, across cobblestones. Just before we parted to our vehicles, the colonel said to something on the ground, "Well drilled; he had those people really well drilled, the way they march."

I said I thought they really looked military; encouraging, I thought.

He said yes, and we parted.

From then until the end of the war that Basque major was inside the colonel's head, ringing changes. I knew he was there because I kept hearing the colonel talk to him, and I'm sure I was the only one who understood those one-sided dialogues.

The colonel, speaking under field glasses while our P-47s blew a roadblock into flames: "Open country there, no cover. Don't know what I would do if I didn't have antiaircraft. How the hell would you ever hold men together? How *would* you keep them advancing?"

From a half-track, watching a hellish Fourth of July while the converging tracers and shells of 155s, 105s, tank guns, and planes turned a German army column into a lot of blazing junk:

"Well, velocity; gotta have muzzle velocity and heavy calibers; don't see how you can manage without them. Fire direction; gotta have fire direction; it all gets mathematical."

When we broke into our first concentration camp, the colonel, looking at the skin-covered skeletons:

"Right. He was right; the Germans are a bunch of damn criminals, savages, lunatics. You know, they don't deserve to wear uniforms: not soldiers. Is that how they were back then?''

After a lackadaisical attack by an infantry-tank task force, words mumbled into a fist propped over a map:

"By God, I wish we had that man in our infantry battalion; he at least has some enthusiasm for what he was doing. Gotta have the bare hands and the enthusiasm.''

One day our S-3 heard some of this and wondered aloud; I told him who was at the end of those murky sentences, and his explanation was that the colonel had been ordered, by God, to buddy up with the Basque major, and since the colonel was a man who lived by orders, he just had to rationalize his duties.

I didn't think it was that at all. I thought, and still think, the colonel was simply talking to another man whose outlines he was beginning to see through clearing mist, through a lifetime of foggy conceptions; the Dybbuk of Herrlisheim was deep in dialogue with the Basque major, and the two lonely soldierly ghosts liked each other.

A week later Bronc, the signal officer, and I were sitting in the command post watching the colonel look out a window through a couple of miles of twilight to a place where tracers were making arches and fans across darkening blue.

"The second sin is always easier," me to Bronc.

"Easier, crap, it's masterful. Practice makes masterful.''

"Christ," from the Old Man. "Small arms, nothing but small arms. Listen!''

We tuned obedient ears. All we could hear were faint pops, with no overtones of booming or slamming, no explosions of shells, no muzzle-blasts of big guns.

What we were looking at was the combat command on our right, CCR, in the midst of a German counterattack. Our division was attacking in three prongs and we, the left tine, were far ahead of the rest. CCR was in the midst of being attacked by some Germans in a forest, and their nervous commander thought they needed help and was saying so rather shrilly over the radio. Division had ordered us, CCB, to turn back southwest to attack toward CCR to take the Germans from the rear.

Problem was, it was twilight, and two friendly forces attacking toward each other in the dark would infallibly decimate each other; we'd hurt each other a lot worse than the Germans ever could. More important, anybody could see and hear there was nothing out there but small arms; CCR had a whole battalion of tanks, a battalion of armored infantry, and plenty of big guns; their commanding officer was lapsing into hysteria, spoiled by too many recent easy victories.

When the colonel tried to put this view across the radio to division, the receiver smoked with outraged authority: "No arguments. Attack. This is a direct order. Attack at once to relieve CCR."

The colonel said this usual yessir and took off the headphones. He turned to face the roomful of battalion commanders and staff.

"Meadows." He turned to the tank battalion CO, and then paused. "Ah," another pause. "Your situation is you have a lot of tanks out of gas. Take you some time to gas up, won't it?"

"Ah, well, not really, sir. I mean we can —"

"Some time, I said," with emphasis from the colonel, and he looked up from contemplation of his boots with a hard stare at Meadows.

"Oh, right, sir." Meadows was a young West Pointer but he did grasp things sometimes; he began to look relieved when he heard the code coming through the colonel's words.

"Yes, sir, have to gas up everything; need maintenance, too. Takes some time, you know."

"Right, get started."

"Davis." The colonel turned to the infantry commander. The infantry colonel, a savvy head from civilian life, fell into his role gracefully. Ammo was low, gas was out, he had to stock up everything, didn't know where the assault guns were, had to get weapons registered. Always took a while to assemble for an attack in the dark. The colonel nodded sympathy.

Artillery; same story under the colonel's hard gaze. They'd try, but it would take hours.

Now the colonel talked. They'd heard division; we'd attack as ordered, but *not* until we were absolutely ready. We were attacking toward a friendly force through enemy and dug-in positions. Very tricky. He expected thorough reconnaissance and thorough development of enemy positions, with absolute control of phase lines and limits of fire. Three enlightened and relieved commanders saluted and disappeared.

Per unspoken orders, the gassing and preparing took most of the night. The colonel kept division headquarters quiet; it was like watching a master of hounds tossing bones to still a yapping pack.

First there were a lot of communications about gassing, loading, and assembling; everyone knew this took a certain irreducible amount of time. Next came the magic word *deploying*. We were deploying. Deploying commands respect; it also takes time.

Reconnaissance elements were out; they were "feeling out" the enemy positions.

Strolling around the edge of town, I could see that our reconnaissance certainly was out, possibly half a mile out of town, leaning on their scout cars, looking at the fire ahead, wondering what the hell CCR was getting so nervous about.

Finally we were "developing the enemy positions." This cliché made division headquarters really happy; we heard enthusiasm over the radio. At last there were "conflicting reports from advanced elements; we have to assess who we are in contact with." This gentle hint that we might be fighting our own forces drew a respectful response from division and another period of blessed quiet.

Finally, just before dawn, our artillery battalion put on a large barrage and our tanks made a lot of racket, and the Germans were appropriately alarmed and got the hell out and nobody got killed stupidly.

Next morning as we packed for the attack on to the east toward Nuremberg, the colonel was stepping light, easy, and confident. The way he moved and everything he said defined a man who had come around another corner in his life; he kept dropping cryptograms to us all day, at halls or during map conferences, over shared brandy and K rations, and finally that night at our next command post twenty miles farther on.

"Three thousand men," heavy emphasis on each word. "People's brothers, fathers, and sons..."

Yessir, we agreed. Combat Command B consisted of three thousand men, and everybody was sure as hell connected with somebody back home.

"When you're doing it, when you're there, you know what's happening; it's the only way you can know. When you have to make decisions based on people's guesses, whole layers of guesses by layers of other people, then, by God, you just don't know. You can't...."

We all said, yessir, and tried not to look at each other.

Next night after destroying six roadblocks and routing a battalion of Germans, we were sitting in a *Gasthaus,* again waiting for the rest of the division. The colonel was talking again, quietly, half to himself. You do it right; only way you can do it is right. You can't do something wrong to please someone who doesn't even inhabit, I guess I mean inhabit, your world. Integrity; is that what they mean by integrity? It's when you *have* to do the thing you know you *ought* to do, regardless.

Our intelligence officer put it best when we gathered to talk and to wonder.

"Old Man's really out from under, by God, he's really out from under." We all knew what he meant. The Dybbuk of Herrlisheim was back to stay.

Final illumination: During the breakthrough fighting the safest place for us, the medics, was way up front where we were surrounded by thousands of infantry with tanks and machine guns and artillery, banging away in a perpetual uproar. It was all very spectacular and secure.

It was when we had to go back with the wounded through the suddenly empty countryside, through silent towns with the surrender flags and bedsheets all hauled back in, through forests that we knew still swarmed with German soldiers, that the nerves started to tingle. We lost ambulances and medical soldiers to German patrols. They were machine-gunned and they were captured; one was captured a couple of hundred yards from me down a different fork in the road. My heavy duty lay to the rear.

It was odd, though; I noticed that when I came back to combat command headquarters from one of those runs, feeling heroic and ready for some praise or at least a handshake, the colonel would almost sulk. He'd avoid talking to me for a whole day, and then he'd be frosty.

One day when we were both leaning on the railing of a balcony of a captured mansion, I started to explain the situation while he looked the other way, but then I decided that I'd be goddamned if I was going to have to spell out the hazardous duty I was going on; if the colonel couldn't figure it all out at this stage of the war without a diagram, he could pout forever for all I cared. I said the hell with it and went inside to get on the radio to find out about evacuation routes.

It wasn't until the war was over that I understood: in our mansion on the Danube the colonel came down with the flu, and after a few days of high fever and no response to medication, I decided to check him into an evacuation hospital where he could get X rays of his chest and some of the new miracle drug, penicillin.

The colonel had been quiet but fidgety, clearly uneasy, all the way over in the ambulance; at the admissions tent of the hospital there was the usual dull roar of rear-echelon indifference and incompetence, and I had to leave him for a time while I looked up the responsible medical officer. When I came back, the colonel looked small and white and worried, and suddenly I saw him as a man quite a bit older than I, sick and frightened.

"Doc," it was a child's voice. "You're not going to just leave me here," and I discovered I was holding his hand while I explained to him that I was going to stay with him until everything was taken care of and he was well bedded down with the top doctors in the hospital taking care of him. I saw him through the assorted layers of indifference that are usual in places like that and made sure that he met the head medical officer, but all the time I was doing this I kept thinking, Christ, he's scared, and it's the first time he could even begin to show that kind of emotion. He's been a commanding officer, and he couldn't even admit he was human most of the time.

That night Bronc and I talked our way into some kind of understanding of the man we'd spent the war with: he was a lonely man, a typical military bachelor; the army was his life and we, his staff, were his family, but he could never show that he was lonely or needed our companionship. We understood why the one bootlicker in our combat command had always been given a "superior" on his efficiency report. The colonel was vulnerable. As for me, when I wasn't around there wasn't any immediate medical support; if the colonel or others in the headquarters had been hit, they'd have to depend on the relatively distant aid men of the infantry and tank battalions, and the prospect must have been more alarming that I had ever realized, but it was not an alarm the colonel could admit, even to himself. As we talked images blinked with understanding: I saw the colonel sitting in his jeep with his odd rigid look, intermittently ruddy in the light of exploding shells, staring intensely straight ahead at nothing we could see: I remembered the time he walked into our aid station during the Colmar battle and simply sat still for a quarter of an hour while we wondered what the hell he was doing there until he stood up wordless and walked out again. I saw him always moving more slowly than the rest of us to get out of the way of shellfire, or standing in the middle of a road looking thoughtful while we all ran for ditches under the strafing of a jet plane before he gave in and walked to cover with artificial rigidity, and the attitudes and emotions and hesitations suddenly fell into place; they were the outline of a comprehensible man, a gentle, possibly even a timid man who would never admit gentleness or timidity. He had had to be fearless, professional, and aloof: he had had to order a lot of men to their death and mangling, and all the time, I was now sure, something inside him was shrinking, feeling pain, feeling terror, for himself and for them.

Governance; command; do they ever come effortlessly out of anyone's nature? Are there always masks? Is every commander an Ahab warped out of humanity by the exercise of his function, bending the direction and purpose of the voyage to his monomania?

When reason falters, try poetry: years after the war the colonel's face stared from certain lines.

"Government requires the exercise of the will and the human will is from the demon."

Scene by Auden; words spoken by the abbot of a Himalayan monastery staring into a spooky blue globe while he tries to enlighten the fatally flawed leader of a climbing expedition.

The abbot again: "Woe to the ruler, for to rule men one must appeal to their lusts and to their fears and he who does so is lost."

Well, maybe, Mr. Auden, but there are ways a man can be saved.

✳ 19

This Is the Way a War Ends

A FIREWORK BANGS AND FLASHES; it hisses in sparks to the top of the dark while children flinch and clutch their parents' hands, and then high, out of sight, the monster says "pop," and explodes in gentle rain of spangles and maidenhair, but while the children cry "ah" from faces turned up to floating red and blue, they still clutch in fright; they can't let go of safety, because it takes a certain time of beauty and ease to clear from any minds the roars, the flashing, the hissing, the loud terror...

Oh, the guns went bang, and the tracks went scream, and there we went, McNamara's Band, flat-assed out for the Danube in a cloud of fleeing Germans, all gunsmoke and dust, racing forty miles in a day to try to bounce an unblown bridge. There were three bridges, and we attacked them by combat commands. CCB's bridge, ours, on the left, went sailing toward heaven in five hundred feet of roiling smoke, blinking golden in afternoon light, and so did CCA's, over on the right flank, but in front of CCR, in the middle, there wasn't any smoke, and that was more interesting than all the fireworks on the flanks. The Danube was the last watery barrier left to the Germans, the last moat that might let them organize a defense in the Alps. Even the possibility of an

unblown bridge meant the chance of shortening the war by weeks
or months.

The gateway to the Alps spoke in that absent smoke. Our radios
screamed that we had a bridge, by God, we fuckin' well had a
bridge, and we did. Task Force I had raced into a town on the
riverbank, with half-tracks and tanks and scout cars laying a
storm of fire to front and flank, catching the local Germans deep
in dreams of wurst and beer and Rhinemaidens — or maybe Danube strumpets — and by the time the defenders got themselves
nerved up to peep out of cellars, some American soldiers were
cutting the airplane bombs out from under the bridge and a
stream of other American soldiers was cascading across the bridge,
erupting out on the south bank, fanning into a bridgehead. Re-
magen number two!

Hitler gave that bridge what was left of his personal attention;
he screamed a lot of gibberish about knocking it out within twenty-
four hours and rallied everything the OKW could find to try to
do it. The remnants of the Luftwaffe tried to bomb it, and assorted German river heroes tried to float mines downstream, but
the effort was fatally flawed. The planes were the sputtering old
Stukas, the terrors of 1940, now no more than pathetic bunches
of matchsticks when our flak and our fighters hit them (so swift
is senescence). The mines were deflected easily by our engineers,
who'd become very good at that sort of thing, and the bridge
stood and a whole armored division attacked over the last great
water barrier of Germany.

Sometimes battles become confused checkerboards: on our right
flank an infantry division known to us as the American Volksturm* attacked across the Danube, got itself counterattacked,
and screamed for help — about par for this division. Our combat
command swung right out of the bridgehead to take the attacking
enemy in the rear, and there was a day of hard fighting as our
men pressed the Germans against the bridgehead. The Germans
fought with terminal fanaticism: it was a day of especially mind-

*Volksturm: The German home guard, organized late in the war from the old, the infirm,
and the very young, a pathetic mob that shambled about trembling, a pathetic sacrifice
to modern firepower.

less violence. A young white aid man, a volunteer replacement from the medical company to the rear, had run out between the lines, waving a Red Cross flag and carrying a litter to help a wounded black soldier kicking and screaming on the ground. The Germans waited until he was actually opening the litter to make assurance doubly sure, and then cut him in two with machine-gun fire before riddling the wounded man. The attack had been a little sluggish, but then a war cry rolled along the black lines.

"Let's go get them mudderfuckers!" The words compressed and danced in a booming, frenzied, repetitive chant. The men fired bazookas and rifle grenades and squeezed the thumb-pieces of machine guns and drenched the town in explosions while they rushed in squads, firing and snarling until the Germans hung out white flags and sent a couple of soldiers out to ask for surrender. A black sergeant and a corporal were holding the bodies of the white aid man and the black soldier he had tried to rescue, rocking them and crying hard, saying, "Oh shit them bastards!" "Look what them bastards done. Look what they *done!*" The German emissaries asked only one condition for surrender : that we respect the Red Cross and care for their wounded. *Chutzpah* is a Yiddish word, but the Germans had taken it to heart.

We spent the night just outside the bridgehead wondering where the huge shells were coming from, whistling low over the inn ; we turned over in our sleeping bags on the hard floor and told each other that the Germans never shelled their own towns. They must be trying to hit the crossroads a couple of hundred yards away. Next morning we learned that the very infantry division we were rescuing had been shelling us with their 155 howitzers; they'd been trying their damnedest to hit us, and only some poor work at the fire direction center had saved our lives. It took frantic radio communications with one of their forward observers to keep our tank battalion from being wiped out by a ten-battalion artillery concentration. High-level incompetence galloped on, and we ran ahead of it to the south, to German territory where it was safer. We were told to hole up for the night in a little city that had been cleared by another task force of our division earlier that day ; as we drove into the main street some white-faced Polish slave girls ran up to gasp to us that the Germans were marching back into the other side of town.

Our small headquarters unit halted in the street and set up a roadblock with our one tank and three half-tracks while the colonel quietly ordered a massacre over the radio. The colonel and I sat swinging our legs on a half-track while the result of a dozen or so orders boomed and flashed at the end of the town; the engineers came in from one flank, a whole battalion of tanks swung in from the other, erupting over the crest of a hill with a hundred machine guns and fifty cannon firing, and the infantry played mortars and assault guns on the unfortunate Germans advancing in extended order over open fields. The threat fled southward, leaving an impressive number of its component parts sprawled and bleeding. Quiet night in the town.

Next morning the front had been torn away; we drove unopposed for miles past solid columns of trucks jammed with German prisoners stretching to the horizon; thirty thousand, forty thousand, fifty thousand, glum, frightened, appeasing, the faces stared out from under green peaked caps. Every rag and tag of vehicle left of the Wehrmacht went chugging and puffing past; sodden, pallid, mud-splashed German WACs* clutched their presumed paramours on motorcycles; the Wehrmacht went by ten feet away from us, stunned, masked, staring, beaten.

We were strung along a road somewhere in northern Bavaria when we heard that the President was dead. At first most of us didn't believe it. Days like that imprint themselves: I still remember how the sunlight looked on the half-tracks and tanks as I walked along the column, dazed, and the way the men's voices sounded, as they called the news to each other. Oh my God, they said, and Jesus, what happens now?

The enlisted men, after shock, were mourning: I saw veterans who had faced down every kind of violent death bending over gun barrels and steering wheels, crying. Something had vanished

*There was no designated Womens Army Corps in the Wehrmacht, but there were thousands of *Helferrinen*, women in uniform who carried out various clerical and other duties. Their chief function was indicated by their slang name among German soldiers: *"Lust-mädel."*

from the air over and around us, a face and a presence we had
leaned on more than any of us had realized, and his passing left
us with a kind of fear we didn't know existed.

Some officers, I was sure, would have liked to make cynical
comments, but in that atmosphere even the densest knew that
their rank wouldn't protect them from violence. The people had
lost someone who had always given them the sense of a friend at
the pinnacle of power, and their emotions were not restrained.

God, I thought, the world's a dark uncertain place, very suddenly.

Mountains have a way of jumping at you; when you come over
Togwotee Pass in Wyoming, you don't see the Tetons until you
round a particular bend, and then they fill the sky, in seconds,
all teeth and towers and drifting clouds and glaciers, so big you'd
think you could see them from any place in the United States.
Same thing with Mont Blanc; a ten-foot rise in the road, and
there you see it, filling the sky with ice and whiteness, and where
the hell was it all until that second? That's what the Bavarian
Alps did — they sulked behind some folds of earth and trees and
then suddenly they leaped out to fill the southern sky; after a
world that we knew was going to consist forever of little villages
and fir forests and roadblocks, there we were looking at the end
of the war. Down on the other side of those mountains was Italy,
with Fifth Army coming up our way through the passes; there
was no place left for the Germans to go.

Pretty mountains, not yet pleasant. Everybody pointed out that
we had to fight our way through those goddamn things, and we
looked at the dense contour lines defining thousand-foot walls
and steep V's of valleys where a squad of men with an antitank
gun could hold up an army. There were a thousand Cassinos in
there. More important than any real danger, those mountains
held a fairy tale; the Germans had duped Ike and American
intelligence again by creating a myth about the *Gebirgsfestung,*
a mountain redoubt stocked with arms and munitions to last for
years, manned by fanatics who were supposed to set off a *Göt-
terdämmerung* to end all twilights. That fairy tale was why we,

Seventh Army, were racing down south of Munich, into the passes
of the Bavarian Alps, to cut off the Germans' retreat into this
cloud-cuckoo-land. Actually there was no mountain redoubt and
there were no gallant fanatics, and we swept banging through
roadblocks and evergreen forests through the foothills and into
the passes south of Munich where we ended the war. This ridiculous maneuver cost us a significant part of Europe. If we'd kept
on going east, we could have reached Prague ahead of the Russians and brought half of Czechoslovakia into what we quaintly
call the free world. Churchill wanted us to; he kept begging
Eisenhower to ''let the armies race and meet where they would,''
but the power of fairy tales on American intelligence should never
be underestimated.

We stopped there, down under a world of snow peaks in the
last town that we would take, Benediktbeuren, near the rippling
blue and cold of the Kochel See, and we sat, still and surprised,
smelling the spring wind over snow and through firs, looking at
names on the map like Oberammergau and Garmisch-Parten-
kirchen right in the next valleys.

Suddenly three thousand veteran soldiers became a clutch of
old maids; nobody wanted to be the last casualty in the war. The
notion of death, until this time something always present, accepted, like a low humming in the air, was, this close to a horizon
and sunlight, intolerable, and we all thought sadly of the young
artillery observer killed a couple of days ago in the foothills, our
last casualty, as it proved. Safety first, safety everything; the
edge of that town was outposted as nothing in the history of
warfare; a weasel couldn't have wormed through the network of
machine guns and tanks and artillery pieces we ringed around
us. None of us thought this was foolish; we understood completely
and were comforted as we threaded the iron maze. The goddamn
stillness, you see, made everything different; the closeness of the
end.

Entertainment in our valley: We watched with keen delight
our Yugoslav Liberation Army, ten soldiers, prisoners of war,
formerly of the Yugoslavian Royal Guard, as they brushed up
their uniforms, shined the silver eagles on their lamb's wool hats,

helped themselves to German weapons, and went out in the mountains on patrol. They volunteered to round up SS troops, the gangs of tag-end fanatics hunkered in caves and thickets waiting for the second coming of Adolf Hitler. Our Yugoslavs were a revelation: they were tough soldiers, fierce with self-respect, with a savage readiness, rare among liberated prisoners, to go out and fight. Most other nationalities, including Americans, when freed, just wanted to get something to eat and go home, but our Yugoslavs stalked the Germans and kicked their asses down mountain roads and saluted with savage grins when we drove past the house they had liberated for a headquarters, and snapped to the commands of their top-kick with real pleasure. We kept them loaded with rations and ammunition. They were great allies, and there was much mutual liking.

From behind our old friends of Herrlisheim, the Texas National Guard, the Thirty-sixth Infantry Division came through to get in at the kill. These were the men who had been fighting ever since Salerno in 1943, and they had had a well-deserved rest for a couple of months, but now they wanted to be in at the crash of the crazy edifice, and we opened our lines to let them through. There weren't any walking infantrymen anymore; everybody in the Thirty-sixth Division rode in some kind of captured German vehicle, from Volkswagens to Mercedeses. Some of our tanks went with them as they attacked one valley over and picked up General von Rundsted, and another valley over, where they captured Göring. We waved and cheered when we saw them; if anyone deserved to be in on the glory and the loot, it was the Thirty-sixth Division.

I wrote in my diary that we had now tiptoed into the schizophrenia and old lace stage of the war, when a patrol came in with some German civilians dressed in tweedy suits and pullover sweaters. The men claimed that they were scientists and were babbling about some kind of a wind tunnel; our patrol had found them hiding in a cave. It turned out that they were one of Wernher Von Braun's teams of rocket scientists; he had hustled them all south as fast as he could to get them out of the way of the advancing Russian pincers, and most of them were picked up in the American, French, or British zones. A few teams, however, were captured by the Russians, and with typical German dedication to duty they went right to work building rockets for the Soviets.

> *"Once the rockets are up,*
> *Who cares where they come down?*
> *That's not my department,"*
> *Says Wernher Von Braun.**

A little crazier; an antique German training plane came flipping and tossing over the tops of the fir trees, forced down by a cone of fire our flak gunners put over until it crash-landed in a meadow. I ran out to the wreck with a platoon of soldiers from D Company. The pilot hadn't been hurt, and by the time we got to the wreckage he had stumbled out and was standing at attention, trying to look defiant. He held out a paper to me: it stated that the bearer, Unterleutnant So-and-so, was under orders to fly from the airport at Garmisch, carry out one combat mission, and then be officially discharged from the Luftwaffe. The last line stated that on completion of his mission he could not be considered a member of the German armed forces and it was therefore the duty of the Allied forces to consider him a civilian and send him home.

The tone was typically Germanic and imperious, and it was a real pleasure to wad it up, throw it away, and tell the big blond dolt that he was a prisoner no matter what it said on this piece of paper. One of the infantrymen seized his arm to march him off, but he shook the man's hand away and bellowed a stream of offensive German, ending with a loud, clear, unmistakable reference to "*verdammt Neger,*" several times repeated. None of those black infantrymen were German scholars, but they didn't need to be; I assumed the Aryan dunce would die right there, with all that black firepower around, but there was a sudden quiet behind me. I looked around to see some of the men with their weapons half raised, but the platoon sergeant was knocking their muzzles aside, waving them to follow him. They assembled a little

*Quotation from an inspired song by Tom Lehrer.

distance away, leaning together and talking in low, hard voices. "You," I heard someone say, "you're about his size." Then everybody nodded and they all walked back.

It took me a few minutes to figure out what they were up to as they put down their weapons very ostentatiously and formed themselves into a square about the size of a boxing ring. The man they had picked, a squarish, heavily built staff sergeant, walked up and tapped the German on the chest. The German tried to look brave.

"Tell that Kraut he's going to have to fight fair fist, Doc. He's going to have to fight me fair fist."

The soldiers waved hands to the German and pointed to him that their weapons were on the ground, then folded their arms formally to make it clear they weren't going to use them.

"Anyone calls any of us boys a nigger from here on is gonna have to fight, but it's gonna be fair. Ain't nobody gonna hurt him 'cept me."

I put it in the best German I could; it was an affair of honor, I explained. He had insulted these soldiers, and nobody was going to shoot him, but if he really thought he was an *Übermensch*, and these black men were *Untermenschen*, he'd better get ready to prove it now. These weren't "*verdammt Neger*," I told him, they were honorable black men, "*ehrliche Schwarze*."

It wasn't much of a fight. The German stood erect with his hands out in a military parody of a boxing stance, something like the old woodcuts of James J. Jeffries, and he swung so awkwardly the sergeant seemed surprised, as if he couldn't believe that anybody was that unwieldy. Then the sergeant hit the German so hard he flew a good six feet before he landed. The lieutenant staggered up and tried to stand at attention (Germans think military posturing is the solution to any crisis), but he got hit again about three times, fast, and this time one of the soldiers caught him as he fell.

The soldier walked up and talked down to the bloody face.

"Okay, white boy. I said, 'Boy,' hear? Call me nigger one more time, boy. Please."

I couldn't translate all those overtones to the lieutenant, but

I explained that if he wanted to get out of there with his facial bones intact, he'd better apologize. The German looked as if he might be mulish, but I could see him running his tongue along the inside of his cheek where his teeth had been, and he mumbled some words that I told everybody were an apology.

The black medics cleaned him up and a couple of soldiers marched him off with surprising gentleness.

I asked the sergeant where his home was.

He came from Mississippi, he told me, and he gentled his knuckles as he talked. "Jackson, Mississippi." These last words came out very slowly and thoughtfully while he blew over his fists.

Jackson, Mississippi, I thought, get ready for some interesting subsurface forces.

Southeast Army Group surrendered a few days ahead of the rest of the Germans; on May fourth our war was over. We couldn't stand the stillness and we all got sick.

Across France and Germany our men had been as healthy as so many wild stallions; except for gunshot wounds and freezing, they were invulnerable. When I used to tell soldiers it was dangerous to drink out of dirty streams, I heard condescending chuckles about how it would certainly be the shits if they got sick and had to go back and lie on a nice clean hospital bed for a couple of weeks, and they went on and they stayed healthy. Their cellules snorted at diesase; they said among the bacilli, "Ha ha!" but the quiet did them in. In a couple of days over half that combat command walked or crept to the aid stations, with disploding gastrointestinal tracts, with lungs spewing infection, with heads banging and backs bent in aches. From frontal sinuses to excretary orifices and below, the combat command throbbed and declined.

The words *let down* conveyed some kind of meaning; we used them to produce that sense of the expected that sick people need, but we didn't know their real significance until Hans Selye in Montreal years later published his classic work on the physiology of stress. The human animal — or any animal — perceives stress with its sensory receptors and transmits alarms through the brain to the neural pituitary, thence to the glandular pituitary, thence to the whole endocrine system of the body, and finally to the several masses of cells. The adrenal glands charge the body with adrenaline and cortisone, the exchange of energy in the muscles and liver cells alters, and the lymphocyte system, the source of resistance to disease and invasion, is stimulated to its highest level of activity. The human under chronic stress actually becomes a changed animal in composition and function, and up to a point this is useful, for the animal is at peak efficiency for survival, but there are two dangers. Overwhelming stress, far beyond the capacity to respond, can exhaust all physical resources and lead to rapid death; more commonly, the sudden withdrawal of stress brings a swift drop in the levels of the circulating hormones and chemicals and a decline in cellular function so that the whole organism enters a period of terrible vulnerability to any destructive force. There you have CCB in early May, throwing up, and there you also have the man who abruptly retires from active, productive life, dying a year later of coronary disease, or there, look around you, and you have a society gone hedonistic and totally gratified and disintegrating into anarchy. Strenuous imperative: Life for humans can consist only of climbing endless topless mountains, or eviscerating perpetually renewed dragons; there's no safety in ease.

The evening before we left the valley I went with Bronc to investigate a report of a German signal installation up the road. We drove in a jeep carrying rifles because things were still unsettled, and we found the station, a few miles into the mountains, deserted. We walked through a litter of telegraph wire and discarded helmets, ornamental swastika daggers, and a whole packrat's fantasy of military junk, pathetic tinware of a despicable crusade. Nothing was left now but the litter. I walked on to the edge of a meadow where a stream made swift, chuckling noises, and I leaned against a pine tree, looking across grass to evergreens, rocks, and snow. Through time and space, through sights and sounds; I was on the instant standing in Ontario, the M-1 resting on my elbow was my old 30-40 Krag, and I was waiting for a moose's antlers to part the edge of the forest. There was the sane world, back there for the reaching, waiting. Out of the whispering of the late afternoon wind I heard the sound from a little way above me:

"Cuckoo," the bird was saying over and over again. "Cuckoo." It was the first "cuckoo" I had ever heard, and what was surprising was that the sound was precise and beautiful in a startling way. I used to wonder why anyone bothered writing music about anything as silly as the sound of a cuckoo, but this sound wasn't silly; it had musical shadings and a dying fall that I hadn't anticipated, coming from a bird too typical to be real, ten feet above me in a fir tree over a Bavarian mountain meadow, pronouncing a finale, and who or what could pronounce it better?

We marched back out of the mountains on a sunlit day to some Bavarian towns in our occupation zone. Enough time was passing to loose a feeling of carnival, an atmosphere we reached into timidly as we crossed columns with the great fighting units of the American army, identifying vehicles from the 101st Airborne, and the Third Infantry Division, and even some liaison vehicles up from Italy with Eighth Army markings and bereted Britishers. Everyone seemed cheerful but dazed; the realization that the war was won took time to sink from cerebral to emotional.

In the lovely towns of mid-Bavaria where we sprawled with some thought of patrolling and security, we still moved in a haze of altered consciousness; waking dreams and sleeping ones were hard to separate, and all of us saw and heard things we never admitted to each other until much later. Our dead came talking to us; their ghosts marched through the Bavarian sunlight; we heard them out of rustlings on warm nights, the words very clear, precise, repetitive.

Pico: I saw Pico a lot. "I had to go out there, Major." Pico used to say this half apologetically, half defiant. "That wounded guy was crying, not just screaming, you know, he was crying like a little kid, and I knew that Kraut machine gun was there, I had to go or I couldn't have looked at myself. It wasn't dumb, what I did...."

Or Salvo Gagliardo: "Damnedest thing, I didn't know the guys in my company really liked me all that much, you know, Doc, till I got shot off that tank and they went crazy and blew every Kraut soldier in the town right off the map. The way they went screaming and crying and kicking doors open and blasting in them with guns and grenades, all because they liked me and I was dead. Well, hell, I tried to be an okay officer, Doc, you know that, but it's too bad you don't find out about things like this until after you're dead. Hell, maybe I would have been embarrassed. . . .''

Or Chuck. I used to see Chuck Willis more than anyone else, mostly at night but sometimes in the daytime reveries, always with those great round holes across his body where the twenty-millimeter flak gun had torn him in two, and he always said the same things. ''Where else was there for me to go, Doc? What could I do now, be a mercenary? Can you picture me parking my ass in the Onwentsia Club playing who-do-you-know-and-what-school-did-you-go-to with drunks and profiteers? Can you see me trying to keep a straight face while the Longmeadow Hunt went bouncing around, all merchants and stock certificates, trying to act like English gentry? Where could I go after all this? Maybe I'm the lucky one, Doc; I got off at the top. . . .''

May 6, 1945, VE Day, the end of the European war. Where we were we couldn't hear a thing, not the massed artillery racket booming in Red Square, or the fireworks and bands in Paris, or the fireworks and fornication in Brussels, or the hundred and ninety-six thousand loyal British voiceboxes packed before Buckingham Palace reverberating to Churchill's V-signs and to limp, smiling royalty, or even the steady roaring columns of sound reaching for the clouds above Times Square. Where we were, in Wasseralfingen, Bavaria, there were, for celebration, sunshine and water running in a brook behind the street below the balcony where I sat when I heard the Armed Forces Network announce that Admiral Doenitz had surrendered all German forces, land, sea, or air. No guerrilla resistance, no Werewolves, complete co-operation. *Punkt.*

In the next room the colonel and the battalion commanders

were bent over maps, talking about occupation areas and patrols. When I walked in I found it awkward to tell them the news; it seemed almost frivolous compared with the serious business on the table.

I excused myself for interrupting, and I explained that Germany had just surrendered completely, with no possibility of resistance. Official. Signed by Doenitz.

The battalion commanders looked at our colonel, wondering how to react, but the colonel, as clearly, didn't know, and he let his eyes wander from me to the three commanders to the pane of gold on the tall window behind them. Then he decided to be pleased.

"Well," it came out with a pause and nod; and, "well," again. He nodded at each of the three colonels individually to emphasize the meaning of his monosyllables.

They smiled cautiously.

"Well, thanks, Doc." The three battalion commanders smiled thanks silently and waved hands, and they all bent back to the map, to work that had at that instant been rendered pointless, because they couldn't really stop thinking and being what they were and what they thought they ought to do, any more than a top that was still spinning. If they lost their centrifugal force, I thought, they might fall right over.

Bronc and Davis and a half-dozen more of us sat in my room that night on the second floor of the mansion that was our headquarters, drinking; with every drink, we said we were toasting victory, but at first it didn't feel reasonable. Finally somebody commented that we didn't need to be blacked out anymore. Being blacked out had been such a way of life since we reached Europe that there was some argument about it: we couldn't believe that people didn't need to be blacked out to be safe, but finally somebody tore the blackout coverings off our windows and we ran all over the house tearing down blackout hangings and flinging windows wide. It was the sensation one could feel only once in a lifetime; it was like first lovemaking, the daring and the free happiness of pouring all that light into a dark that no longer held fear. Some of us ran outside and stood by the brook, looking

up at others leaning out the windows and shouting down to us.
The house became a wall of squares of light in a street of dark,
frightened boxes, a painting by Edward Hopper, all gold rec-
tangles, and glowing near-parts, and glints on gutters. People
took turns running into the house and standing in windows and
shouting toasts to the others down in the street by the brook;
after we toasted the United States of America and all our Allies
severally, and the memory of Roosevelt, and the commanding
general of our division, and our combat command, and each of
us individually, we ended up shouting toasts for Secretary Beneš
of the Czechoslovakian government in exile because someone had
read his name in the armed forces issue of *Time* magazine a few
days before. Men laughed down from windows at others, who
shouted laughter back up from the brook and the street and from
under the trees.

That night we all saw what we had never seen before, back
when our lives were ordinary and accepted and unfrightened;
we saw the miracle of humans shining in light, the way God meant
them to, and what was out there now for them to call to was the
gentleness of a May night, rustling, gurgling in stones, kind, not
to be walled away.

That felt like victory.

✳ 20

The Concentration Camps

THE FIRST CONCENTRATION CAMP we saw was near Landsberg on the Lech River, near the fortress where Hitler was imprisoned after his putsch. We were last in the column of combat commands after the Burgau fight; as we rolled in, rumors flew down the battalions about a death camp ahead. Our only Jewish officer in the headquarters drove on ahead to see if he could lend a hand; that was a mistake. When he came back a couple of hours later, his face was the glassy white one reads about but rarely sees, and his eyes had the look of glazed marbles. In my aid station he sat down, mumbling, ''Those poor people; oh, God, those poor people.'' Then he vomited. After I calmed him down with brandy and barbiturates, Bronc and I filled the jeep with loaves of bread from the mess truck and started out for the camp.

A mile before we found it we saw the first bodies lying in the freezing mud along the roadside. Blue-striped pajama suits were soaked around what looked like skeletons. I walked over to the first body, lying on its face, and turned it over with some idea of hauling it out of the way of vehicles; the face came up toward me, dribbling mud, and I flinched from the shape of a scream. The eyes were wide beyond any human anatomy, great, blank rounds of staring glass, the skin of the face was shriveled down to taut, thin leather, the nose was a knife edge, the facial bones were thrust out rather than hidden by the incredibly thin covering, the soft tissues of the face were collapsed right onto the bone, and the only structures still full-sized, the teeth and the eyes, were bared in frozen agony, a terminal sustained scream.

I dragged the body to the roadside; incredibly light, it was a child's body, a bird's body. In the next half-mile we must have passed twenty more, and I noticed that many were lying face down in the mud, arms flung ahead as if reaching for something. Later we heard that they had indeed been reaching; they had crawled out through the mud trying to kiss the gas-cans on our scout cars before falling dead.

Shots; shots again, single shots, slamming blasphemous sounds in that open-air sepulchre, where the *whush* of our tires and the wind in the fir trees had been the decent sounds around the dead. Snipers? As we came around a bend, the camp came into view, barbed-wire wings flung wide around rows of low huts stretching off into mist. The gate hung open; near it we saw a mass moving in a way I'd never associated with human activity, moving crazily, jerkily, like a many-limbed sea creature flinging about in agony. As we came closer it resolved into separate forms, prisoners in the same thin pajamas, seeming to fall and rise in erratic motion like a bizarre *Totentanz*. Closer still, and I realized I was looking at the last extremity of human weakness; the poor creatures were clinging to each other, leaning, falling, pulling themselves up while they wobbled insanely, many of them crouching on all fours in the mud, using all their remaining strength in a desperate attempt simply to lift their heads. Following their fixed gaze, I saw a downy-lipped lieutenant from the military government holding a clipboard in one hand; in his other he held a forty-five that he fired in the air, apparently to fix everyone's attention. The prisoners weren't frightened by the gun, since they obviously understood it was a device to help them organize or register or something, all of which seemed wildly inappropriate, but when they saw us driving up, our jeep filled with loaves of bread, they turned for us in a mass, crying, whining, crawling, reaching, utterly out of control of the lieutenant or his clipboard or his gun.

I have never before or since seen completely involuntary, uncontrollable mass human behavior, but as the mob closed around us I realized they could no more restrain themselves than they could have kept from falling if they'd been thrown off a cliff. The sky disappeared behind a wall of staring, irrational eyes and wildly upthrust claw-hands. Christ, I thought, we'll be torn to pieces, these people simply can't stop themselves; but the final horror was the touch of that frenzied boil of humanity. The people were so weak that the most agonized clutch felt like the gentlest brushing of feathers; the hands that clawed across my face reaching for the bread felt like the fronds of ferns; they were thistledown remnants of humans.

After a couple of trips to the jeep I had the help of one of the prisoners, a young Russian not as starved as the rest, and we managed to tear loaves in two and stuff them into hands. The mass fell back, tearing and gulping, and I had a chance to look at individuals. The monstrous eyes, great round bird's eyes, owl eyes, unlike anything I'd ever seen or imagined in a human face, were, I now realized, the result of the starvation that had drained all the orbital fat away — there were no supporting tissues around the eyes, and the eyeballs lolled, huge, in the tight-skinned sockets.

The faces were skulls, bones painted brown, and the fingers clutching the bread were thick wires that crooked with enormous effort, moved by muscles that must have been mere wisps.

A young Jew talked to us between mouthfuls of bread; first he kept repeating the words *"Freunde, Freunde,"* stroking us and the bread, in a strange, inhuman voice. Starvation, I learned, produced this high, rasping, seabird voice through wasting of the pharyngeal tissues; sounds resonated on the nasal bones, high shrill, avian.

"Mutti, Vati, Bruder, Schwester," he went on, *"alle verbrennt, verbrennt, verbrennt,"* and as he repeated "burned, burned, burned," he tried to cry; the taut-parchment face tried to wrinkle and the great eyes screwed up, but there didn't seem to be any

functioning tear ducts in those painfully bared eyeballs, and the skin was too taut to pull itself into the folds of grief; his whole body instead shook with the wracking, tearing effort to sob as he whined the words ''burned, burned,'' over and over.

The lieutenant thanked us reluctantly; he admitted he was slightly obliged for the bread, but he really couldn't wait to get back to whatever he was doing with his clipboard. We wandered off through the camp.

The huts were A-frames, with roofs that came down to the ground, and the roofs, we noticed, were a peculiar combination of green and a glowing black. As we came closer we saw that the black was char; the huts had been partially burned, and looking though the holes in the roofs we could see dirt floors. Under the walls of some of the huts were peculiar scooped-out gouges in the earth, with what seemed to be claw marks around them. Some men of Graves Registration Units we met carrying bodies on litters told us they had found many of the bodies half out of the huts, twisted in the earth in the gouged-out holes, wildly contorted, with bloody slits in their chests and abdomens. Later we heard that the claw marks in the ground were indeed clawings; some men of the Todt, the German engineer organization, had been detailed to kill as many of the prisoners as possible before our reconnaissance troops broke in. They had locked the prisoners in the huts, thrown gasoline on them, and set fire to them. When the half-crazed inmates had clawed their way out from under the walls — it was raining, the mud was soft — the Germans had bayoneted them.

All through the camp, through the lifting mist, we could see soldiers carrying bodies, lugging containers; the rear elements had for a wonder sorted themselves out swiftly and efficiently. Our loaves of bread wouldn't be needed now. We left.

That night, sleeping on the floor of the *Gasthaus* that was our command post, I stared into the dark while the images of the day raged through my head. I had seen hundreds of people die of wasting diseases, of cancer, of terminal kidney or heart disease, of infections (in those dark pre-antibiotic days), but not in the wildest ravaging of a virus or a malignancy had I seen the human body reduced to the stage of those prisoners. Nothing in all the lexicon of medical horrors could have so shriveled the flesh from around the bones and from under the skin, leaving those varnished skeletons, those incredible painful bird's eyes, those unearthly nasal screams.

That's what it was all for, I thought, that's what they finally did, Rommel dashing about being knightly and brilliant, Krupp and Bohlen and the best scientists in Europe sifting logarithms, statesmen and clergy and every prop of governance looking sober and quoting wisdom, that's what the hell it was all for, that's what they accomplished.

Counterpoint: We meet the enemy and they are pigs.

Our first command post after we left the Alps was a mansion on the Danube, formerly the property of a lieutenant general in the Luftwaffe. It was lovely, three-storied, blown about by willows, glowing at night through gold-laced windows. Inside, someone had gone to a lot of trouble to make sure that not one square foot was free of adornment; bulging Rhinemaidens fled the attentions of cretinous dwarfs across tapestries and through lampstands; passions of frills and loops and overblown furbelows writhed through the rooms and along the corridors.

Floating on the waters of this Nazi swamp, *fleurs du mal;* the wall of the master bedroom was hung with whips, many tastefully decked with human hairs tied into their short lashes, while another wall was lined with books about perverted sex, the interlineations, marginalia, and exclamation marks through them all making it clear that Lieutenant General and Madame had done a lot of slavering.

Sadomasochism, homosexuality, bestiality, necrophilia, nothing had been slighted. For light reading there were rows of pseudo-anthropological studies about the vileness of the Jewish race, with anatomic reproductions of Jewish bone structure, lip folds, and other stigmata; there were whole chapters given over to sniggering caricatures of Jewish old people and children and endless anectodal evidence to prove that the Jews were a malignant, freakish mutation to be totally, savagely extirpated.

Across the hall from the master bedroom was the light of the household, the family shrine. In a small room, a table was arranged as an altar, with a white linen cloth draped over it. A massive copy of *Mein Kampf* a couple of feet square was propped open on it; it was bound in white leather and flanked by bulging brass candlesticks with tall white candles. *Introibo ad altare Dei.*

The local newly liberated Russian and Polish slave workers were very happy to work for our headquarters. They cooked, cleaned, and maintained the grounds with great enthusiasm, and when they weren't busy often reminisced about Madame Lieutenant General, their recent employer. She had been a rare and vicious bitch, they told us; when she had worked them all to exhaustion on short rations, she delighted with threatening them with a trip ''to the camps'' to keep them working until they dropped. There had been sexual abuse of younger slave workers and frequent little cultural illuminations to make clear to all of them their perpetual role as subhumans, lucky to be able to serve the descendants of Siegfried.

We weren't as sympathetic as we might have been, understandably, when Madame herself turned up at the gate one night scowling, demanding to be let into the garden where lettuces and other greenery were beginning their spring riot. The guards explained, courteously at first, that this was a military headquarters; *Eintritt verboten.* When she shrugged this off, I pointed out that the slave workers who had actually created the garden were going to have first crack at anything that grew there. Madame and cohorts, I couldn't help commenting, looked remarkably well fed, as well they might, having lived off the loot of a continent.

After a few evenings of surly persistence, I told her with some emphasis that her husband had been a damned Nazi villain, an accomplice in mass murder, and further, that if she had pestered a German military headquarters as she did ours, she'd have been shot or led off to a military brothel. I might as well have been singing to a stone. The prototypic Teutonic face set in abused stubbornness, and the ears were stopped with that peculiar Germanic clay impervious to guilt. She was a handsome woman, certainly, and her projection of outraged nobility was convincing; I remember thinking that she might have been a Trojan mother wailing her slain sons or weeping over Hecuba rather than a German pervert sniveling because she couldn't get into her back garden.

A few nights later she produced a gaggle of demoiselles obviously whistled up to witness her martyrdom and our barbarity. With an audience, Madame outdid herself; I noticed even our sentries were beginning to look sheepish, when I heard behind me the pleasantly nasal Midwestern, small-town tones of the motor officer growing nearer down the garden path, penetrating the guttural dirge. Madame's lamentations stopped, chopped with a knife edge; silence. She stared over my shoulder with the first emotion other than indignation I'd seen her register, a compendium of dismay, shock, helpless horror. When I turned around I understood, for under one arm Al was carrying a large bundle of the whips that had hung on the bedroom wall, and in the other he was juggling a collection of the sex books.

"Lady wants her property, she ought to have her property, Doc. Hers is hers, right? Tell her." I told her, polite, solicitous. I assured her we weren't going to confiscate her personal property, not us law-abiding Americans, no sir. Weren't these whips hers? Al snapped a couple, making their character plain to the enthralled audience, while I wondered aloud if the hair we had found tied into them had been hers or her husband's. Madame could hardly move. Her face was an interesting shade of boiled crimson. I stood beside her, opening one of the books, flipping it open to some fat female bottoms being whipped, Amazons bestriding helpless males, bestiality. I commented in a conversational tone we had noticed lots of them in the bedroom. Did they read this stuff every night? I shook my head tolerantly; no accounting for tastes, as Frederick the Great once commented. Behind me I felt the demoiselles breathing hard, peering, nudging; the fascination of morbid sex drew all thoughts of race, war, nation, or self-pity clean away.

By this time Madame had turned from crimson to a kind of stock white. Poor bitch. Imagine having your wildest sexual fantasy detailed for the garbage man and the cleaning lady, as well as some adolescent cousins. The demoiselles whispered and giggled off down the riverbank while Madame backed away, shaking her head, looking genuinely pathetic. If she had been human, I suppose I might have felt sorry for her. At least the crepuscular visitations stopped.

Captain Levy, a medical officer traveling back to Dachau, stopped at our mess for lunch; he and I naturally sat together and he told me where he worked — in a typhus hospital in the concentration camp. There had been a number of British and American hospitals organized in the camp, he told me, chiefly to deal with the typhus then raging among the human wreckage with appalling results.

I asked him how they were treating them (this was in the days before antibiotics; there was no definitive treatment for typhus).

Well, he hesitated, they had started out just feeding everybody. They had dumped all the army rations they could find into a big stew and ladled out as much as everybody could eat. The patients did fine, he commented; even with their TB and their beriberi and their typhus they started gaining weight and healing infections — and then some flaming ass in the quartermaster corps discovered a regulation forbidding the feeding of GI rations to foreign civilians and cut off their supply. The medics were told to get food from a German warehouse in Munich, but the general of the X Infantry Division for some arcane reason had the key and wouldn't give it up and there was, for practical purposes, no food in the American field hospital.

The whole table stared. "What the hell are you doing?" I asked.

"Scrimping out leavings of rations," he mumbled, acutely embarrassed. "Sometimes we have to use our plasma for food. I mean it," he assured my disbelief. "We make up the damned plasma units and feed the stuff to them with a spoon."

The mess was silent, genuinely shocked. I dropped the subject until we were standing near his jeep as he left, when I pressed him further with incredulous questions. Could we help? Wasn't somebody doing something? Couldn't they just go out and scrounge food for these people ? Finally I asked if he thought I could help if I came down. I had nothing special to do where I was. He assured me they'd be glad of any help, and next day, with permission from division surgeon and my commanding officer, I drove my ambulance down the autobahn past Augsburg to Dachau and the Seventy-seventh field hospital. My motives weren't entirely altruistic; not a dozen physicians in the United States had ever seen typhus, and the chance to work with a rare and almost legendary disease was irresistible, particularly after four years of mindless army surgery. More practically, I had some vague idea of showing the helpless rear-echelon medics how to forage for food as we'd done all across Germany. As I drove along I mused that in May of 1945 Germany still bulged with the looted food of all Europe and it was hard to imagine in that cornucopia why concentration camp inmates should go hungry. I made sure my carbine with the usual sixty rounds was in the rack in the ambulance, and I noted the cows and pigs thronging the fields all around Dachau. There didn't seem to be any real shortage of animal protein.

After I'd been thoroughly dusted with DDT powder, I introduced myself to the commanding officer, a squatty major named Karff: from what Levy had told me I gathered he was trembling toward promotion.

"Always glad of extra hands, Major," he assured me and sent me off to dump my gear in a barracks.

I began daily rounds and patient care in the typhus ward in one of the giant green barracks with the mocking "*Arbeit macht Frei*" still lettered in white across its front.

The room seemed bigger than a gymnasium; it was filled with long rows of cots a few inches apart, each holding a shriveled remnant of a human fighting with pathetic resources against diseases that could tear the life out of vigorous, well-nourished people in their prime.

Starvation was the diagnosis that met the eye; the faces and the voices were those of the cold, muddy nightmare near Landsberg with the same naked, painful eyeballs, the same fleshless lips, the same bird-rasping voices, and, under the blankets, remnants of bodies of unbelievable fragility, every tissue wasted right down tautly around the skeleton, deep concavities between ribs, plunging hollows where the skin fell from the rib cage down to the almost empty abdomens, arms and legs where there was no muscle one could feel. I marveled at their ability to move.

After an initial tour of the ward, I sat down with the physicians of the unit to look at X rays. I hadn't actually looked at an X ray since we left the States; from the vantage point of a battalion aid station, the ability to look at something as medical as an X ray was a luxury. In addition to the four American physicians, there were two foreigners. One was a young Yugoslavian who had been surgeon of a "Divisie" in the partisan army and, until recently, a prioner in Dachau. The other was an elderly Dutch physician who had been in Dachau for a long time; he had been, he informed me proudly, a member of the Dutch Communist party. The Yugoslavian hadn't been in long and was almost back to normal health; dressed in an American army uniform, he functioned as a ward officer. The Dutchman was a collection of bones barely mobile; he had been starved almost to death. He was still in his blue-striped pajamas, which fluttered loosely around his feeble frame as he walked, but he sat among us with great professional pride, squinting at the X rays, manifesting a dignity that could come only from a man so near death asserting the achievement of his life.

We began by looking at X rays of chests. Most of the lungs showed evidence of tuberculosis, many in stages so advanced it was obvious there could be no cure. A great number of the hearts were enlarged, some grotesquely, suggesting severe heart failure. The physicians of the ward explained that I was looking at the terminal stages of beriberi, when the heart, having been pathologically overactive, declines to a swollen, feebly pulsing organ. (Studies of American survivors of Japanese prison camps five and ten years after the war showed that at this stage the disease is irreversible and that even though feeding and vitamins appeared to restore health for a time, the heart muscle was so scarred that the victims died slowly of progressive heart failure over a period of years.)

Typhus is a savage disease; added to starvation, tuberculosis, and beriberi, it ravaged the wards like a machine gun. The steady flow of new cases into the unit, I was told, was balanced — sometimes more than balanced — by the dead who left. The louse, the transmitter of the disease, was being attacked throughout the main camp, but the infestation was so profound, the population so large, and the preexisting infection so widespread that new cases kept turning up every day.

I didn't realize it at the time, but I was in the middle of what was probably the last major typhus epidemic in the history of the human race. In 1945 there was no treatment for the disease once it had started, but it could be largely prevented by DDT delousing and by a typhus vaccine that was at least fairly effective. When the first broad-spectrum antibiotic appeared in the late forties, the rickettsial diseases, including typhus, suddenly became minor nuisances instead of lethal, large-scale scourges.

Typhus is caused by an organism of a peculiar class named the *Rickettsiae,* smaller than ordinary bacteria, larger than viruses. The *Rickettsiae,* named for their discoverer, Ricketts, are remarkably widespread, since they have penetrated almost every part of the globe, surviving in insect reservoirs until they attack the definitive human victim. Each region has its characteristic and slightly different disease; all have some features in common. Rocky Mountain spotted fever is transmitted by ticks, tsugsugamuchi fever by the Japanese river mite, rickettsialpox by the mouse flea. All the rickettsial infections are acute, febrile illnesses characterized by a rash and a varying degree of mortality. The mortality of typhus tends to be very high.

"Classic" louse-borne typhus was endemic to, and often epidemic in, Eastern Europe, the Near East, and Russia. The disease figured in European literature as a daemon ex machina; typhus often destroyed besieging armies, saving cities, or conversely, left cities full of dead ready to contaminate conquerors. Napoleon's armies were ravaged by it as they dragged their lice from the English Channel to Moscow; the protagonist in Turgenev's *Fathers and Sons* died of typhus acquired while performing a postmortem examination, thereby figuring forth the helplessness of the enlightened ''nihilistic'' generation in the face of an antique horror. Pathologically, typhus is characterized by an acute inflammatory and necrotizing process in the cells of the capillaries throughout the body, a kind of swift inflammatory degeneration of the lining cells in the smallest blood vessels, often with catastrophic results for the area or organ where this takes place. The disease begins with fever, followed soon by a rash. After a time the characteristic degeneration of blood vessels in the skin transforms the rash into a dark, red-purply process that mottles most of the body, hence the term ''Fleck Typhus'' or spotted typhus.

Since there was no definitive treatment for typhus in 1945, all that could be done was to treat the specific manifestations of the disease and hope for survival. The basic problem of recognizing typhus in the first place before coming to grips with its complications and permutations was very difficult for American physicians, who had never seen a case. Our chief resource was the young Yugoslavian, who, in his army career, had lived with typhus in the primitive, lousy encampments of the partisans. Like everyone else close to the disease, he had learned to dread it and to look minutely for its presence and its manifestations. He was a recent graduate of the University of Belgrade just before the war and had had no sophisticated postgraduate training, but he knew typhus, I suppose, better than anyone else in the world. As we walked down the wards, he demonstrated the characteristic rash, the early stage with a deep pink eruption that blanched under light pressure, the second, a mass of dark red hemorrhagic eruptions, dark massy speckles all over the body.

Even in the short time the hospital had been functioning, the American physicians had started to learn the danger signs. Invasion of the central nervous system produced a peculiar agitation, followed within hours by delirium. On the first day I began to see patients who would suddenly begin babbling wildly, trying to lift themselves from the cot, so weak they needed only a hand or a finger to restrain them. Most of the time, I learned, death followed within twenty-four hours, with convulsions and agonal screaming. After a couple of days of going around with Tito Minor, as our young Yugoslavian was delighted to be called, I had also learned to look for a rapid heartbeat and a falling blood pressure indicating invasion of the circulatory system. Tito Minor would take a pulse, note a blood pressure reading, and put a blanket back with a headshake. *"Bald todt,"* he would mutter, and he was almost always right. Within a day or two a shocklike state would produce deadly cold, a weak, rapid, thready pulse, a blue color to lips and earlobes, and gasping, wheezing death.

We treated the central nervous system complications with sedatives and anticonvulsants; circulatory collapse was treated with digitalis and adrenaline — the latter to sustain blood pressure (it was the only pressor agent then available). Nobody was sure the treatment helped very much, and the death rate was appalling once the more virulent stages of the disease took over. I remember standing with Tito Minor one evening watching a man die of terminal inflammation of the brain and spinal cord. He suddenly drew up in the terrifying position called opisthotonus, commonly seen in the last stages of tetanus, when the body is arched like a drawn bow, only the heels and the back of the head touching the bed, muscles drawn to an unbelievable rigidity. The man's groans turned to screams; the screams seemed to cycle with the convulsive arching of his body, growing louder and higher in pitch while his body pulled into more intense contortions until one feared the spinal cord would shatter. In midscream he collapsed, the sounds cut off, the muscles loosed in a series of jerking releases, and the man was dead, a pathetic, shriveled testament to the virulence of the *Rickettsiae* and the savage degeneracy of humans.

To which add the final mocking element: The only real treatment we could offer was food, and my friend had been right. The medical bureaucrats had pulled off the final, staggering stupidity of the Second World War. It was the absolute top of an impressive list, starting with the clods in Italy who threw combat men from Cassino in jail for coming on leave without neckties, proceeding through the record of the criminal incompetents in army ordnance who sent our men into battle with obsolescent death-trap tanks, reaching flood tide with the rear-echelon satraps who kept regiments of able-bodied men busy with janitor work far behind the lines while we sent sick and wounded infantrymen back out to fight, and finally, small but dazzling, incomparable, this paradigm, this illumination of a kind of mindlessness that percolates through our corporations, our governments, our institutions, our armed forces, corrupting, castrating, infuriating, wasting, and finally destroying — here it was, focused to a brilliant point of light. We couldn't feed the patients. Army regulations said we couldn't feed them army rations at a time when those rations were the specie of Western Europe, traded for sexual favors, for war souvenirs, for black-market profit, moldering in mountains in every depot, generating towering profits for manufacturers and traders and pilferers, wasted and dumped in garbage cans by the ton, but denied to our poor patients whose only hope for life they were.

As I walked along the rows, patients called to me, beckoned me. By now the word was out that I spoke German, the lingua franca of prisoners and victims, and they tried with varying degrees of desperation to convey to me that surely some monstrous mistake was being made, something that I or any rational man could correct with a word.

"Hunger, hunger," this often with clutching of sleeve to hold my attention. "Herr Major, we are starving. I don't believe this. We were finally rescued, we never thought we could be rescued, we never thought it was possible, but we were rescued by the Americans; after everything we were rescued, and now we're starving."

A meal might consist of a cup of milk and two crackers from a K ration. One inmate looked at this repast and commented bitterly to another, "*Guten Appetit!*"

"Please," one mumbled, "I'm dreaming. This is a nightmare."

Translations were incredibly involved; a Hungarian might speak to a Czech who knew enough German to speak to me. An enormous effort went on to convey to me as a sympathetic ear the mass conviction among the prisoners that nobody understood that they weren't getting enough to eat. They were sure that if somebody simply understood . . .

I kept asking the administrative officers. They were trying, they answered, with memos and phone calls to Third Army, largely ignored. Military government officials were manifesting their true colors early in the game. Nothing was their fault or their responsibility. See the people at the captured food warehouse in Munich. See the general who had the key to the warehouse; he wasn't around? Then see his aide. Not around either? Well, what could you do?

The medical officers themselves had gone around to the local Germans for food, meeting, of course, a blank wall. Didn't the Americans have all the food in the world? How could the poor, starving Germans possibly part with anything, pressed as they were by four years of war? The rear-echelon medics lived with the pretense of law, and it hadn't occurred to any of them simply to take food from the well-stocked larders around.

After a week, desperate myself, I went to see Major Karff, the commanding officer. I explained that there was a critical shortage of food.

Yes. His nod was solemn. Agreement. "Some administrative problems. Administrative."

I waited. Silence. Apparently the word *administrative* had been hauled in from the wings to explain and excuse everything.

"They're starving." I blurted it. "These people are really starving to death. Right in this United States hospital."

"Starving is a strong word, Major." (Calming, conciliatory, minimizing, smiling, tolerant.) "Supply problems...."

I described that day's menu on the wards. I asked the major if he thought he or anybody else could live on it.

"A couple of cups of milk a day," I finished. "The only treatment we have for these people is food. It could save a lot of their lives, but we aren't feeding them."

The major spread his hands. I thought of a French general in 1940, bathing in happy, relieved hopelessness, in cleansing disavowal.

"We can do something," I put the point strongly. "I can do something, but I'll need help." Raised eyebrows, genuine surprise, unspoken question. I went on. "I have a carbine and sixty rounds of ammunition in my ambulance. Give me some men from the mess crew and I'll bring in all the fresh meat we can use.''

"Fresh meat?" The major started to beam. Apparently he thought the fresh meat was going to be for him.

"There," I pointed out the window. The major's gaze followed my finger, focusing on some cows and pigs in nearby fields. Then he swung back to me. The dawn of comprehension was followed swiftly by a high noon of genuine alarm.

"You mean those cows, that livestock?"

"Just shoot the goddamned things. Make stew. Feed these people. The military government can pay them or something later, and what if they don't?"

"Just take them? Take people's property?" The idea was still battering at the outworks of the major's mind. Tough sledding.

"Major, the Germans did this to these people. They can damn well feed them.''

"*Take* people's private property?"

"Hell, the Germans took their lives, if you want to think of it that way. Food, medicine, it's life-saving. It's an emergency." The words were tumbling out. I had to penetrate that glassy incomprehension. Inhalation, retreat to back of desk, official pose, steely gaze.

"Major, the United States Army doesn't steal. We are not criminals.''

I forbore to point out that the army killed and burned as a matter of duty, because a category was knocking.

"Foraging," I said, "it's just foraging. Foraging is okay, it's official. Armies forage; they have foraging parties. Officers are in charge of foraging parties. If an army didn't forage when it ought to, people would get court-martialed.''

The major hung fire. I had him by the throat. The official resonance of the word *forage* was something he couldn't get around. It was standard military jargon, and he knew it. It suggested something he ought to do that he wasn't doing.

I pressed on. "Sherman, Stuart, Grant — all the great American generals did it. Had to. Armies are supposed to forage when they don't have food. Rules of war.''

The major looked trapped; I began to relax, thinking I had

snared him in officialese and that the mess truck would soon be forthcoming, but I reckoned without the major. He was, after all, a career survivor; he had survived too many half-witted encounters, too many *imbecilia bureaucratica* to be hoist by any engine of mine. In a way it was wonderful to watch him recover. With the deepest, most studious, kindly explanatory air he began a lecture, not really much sillier, now that I think of it, than many I have since heard from learned podia or corporate board-tables.

"Armies forage, of course; they always have, but armies forage *to feed their own soldiers.* That's their duty; that's legal. Rules of war. On the other hand, if armies took people's private property and gave it to other civilians..." (long pause, tapping of fingers on desk with each word) "that, Major, would [pause] be [pause] stealing!"

Silence. I waited for a silly giggle or some other more obvious sign of lunacy, but the studious lecture continued. The major looked steely-eyed. He pointed at me.

"You'd get in..." (again a pause) "trouble."

Apparently I continued to look untroubled, or at least unimpressed, for the major fused and fired his ultimate weapon.

"You'd get..." (very long pause) "a REPRIMAND!!!"

Studied silence. Hand that had pounded on desk now pointed a finger to the floor, indicating nethermost hell reserved for damned souls who have gotten themselves reprimanded.

I tried to talk, but nothing came out. Discuss mercy and reason with Caligula? Shout a message to Antares? My head was spinning with a feast of pure unreason. I left.

Across the muddy yard I slammed into the mess and began talking agitatedly, angrily, with some of the other medical officers. They all knew about the problem; they were all distressed; why not ignore the major and order the mess crew out on our own? Nobody could argue with success, and anyway, none of us was going to stay in the army after the war. We were all going home to residencies or to practices, and what the hell did we care what our army 201 files looked like? Certainly no one was going to get into very serious trouble for feeding concentration camp prisoners — not in May of 1945. I didn't convince anyone and, in fact, the more I talked the more I sensed embarrassment, a growing hostility, a concentration of a lot of frustration and guilt on me as an outsider daring to make them more uncomfortable than they were already. After all, they had tried within their own lights.

Two officers came in and sat down while we were talking; fragments of the conversation reached them.

"Oh, shit." The speaker was a red-faced, food-stuffed officer punctuating his words with forkfuls of food. "Hunger, hunger" — he gave the words the German pronunciation as the inmates did — "that's all I hear. I'm sick of it. We're doing our best; I'm in that fuckin' ward all day on my feet for hours and do you think they appreciate it? Hunger — all I hear is this goddamn complaining."

His neighbor gave a relieved giggle and began to chant, "Hunger, hunger," in the singsong whining tones of the prisoners, shaking his head to convey wonder at their effrontery.

The two made a jeering chant of the phrase, repeating it to each other. I felt Levy's hand on my shoulder, restraining me, and I realized I had been about ready to plant a plateful of food on the fat officer's mocking mouth. I walked out.

Across the yard in the ward I made rounds with the Dutch physician, stopping while he rested, sitting down every third or fourth bed. We had offered him rations like ours, because after all he was a working physician and insisted on staying on his feet as long as he could, but he refused. To have accepted extra food, he explained, would have been a betrayal of his friends, his patients, as he thought of them. I kept thinking that I should ignore him and simply carry him off someplace and feed him, but he probably would have refused even then. I thought then, and I have thought many times in the years since, that nobody who hasn't been desperately hungry or close to real starvation could begin to grasp the sacrifice of that splendid old Hollander. It was a triumph of idealism and dedication over the atavistic lifesaving reflexes of the human organism beyond anything in my experience. We wanted to bring him food and put it in front of him to try to make him eat, but that would have tormented the old man beyond endurance, so we let him sit there on the cot with his friends and patients, munching a couple of K ration crackers, quietly accepting with them the agonies of slow starvation.

Next day Tito Minor asked me to drive him to a bookstore in the village of Dachau to find a German-English dictionary. I was delighted; a few hours out of the camp was welcome, and somehow, even in Nazi Germany, the idea of a bookstore conveyed an aura of learning and decency. I half-expected to find some scholarly old gentleman who had been hiding volumes of Heine and Brecht from the Nazis, but when I confided all this to Levy, he snorted.

"We looked that place over when we moved in. It's wall to ceiling Nazi propaganda, race books, stuff about *Übermenschen* and *Lebensraum*. Scholarly old bookseller my Jewish ass!"

When Tito and I walked in the door, any shred of illusion vanished; the proprietor was a rodent-faced version of Joseph Goebbels, deep in hunched conversation with two Germans. Since I took pains to look uncomprehending and talked loudly in English to Tito Minor, I was soon hearing phrases about the goddamned Jews in the camp, and all this ridiculous fuss the Amis were making, and why didn't people get them all killed in time?

I waited until the conversation, subdued on our entrance, had hit its stride before introducing myself in my most fluent German, explaining what I wanted. The effect was marvelous: the two customers backed against a shelf, staring at me as if I'd pointed a gun, while the proprietor pasted the sickliest smile I've ever seen across his receding chin and froze. At that stage of the war most Germans supposed we had some equivalent of the Gestapo, since they couldn't imagine running a war or a country without one. Obviously they felt they had been blabbering unguardedly in the presence of an *Obersturmbannführer*.

A dictionary, I reminded the bookseller forcefully. He ran to get one.

"We work at the camp there." I pointed out the window. "In the typhus hospital."

Rodent-face began to talk. Wasn't it awful; my God, they were appalled; they never suspected.

The words *nie gemütet* — never suspected — uncorked all the bad tamper I'd been holding back for days. Ever since we'd crossed the German border all we had heard was how nobody suspected, nobody was a *Naziparteigenosse*, nobody ever dreamed, if they had only known, and besides, what could they do? We really didn't give a damn, and reactions had varied from uh-huh to bullshit, but to hear this same whine right in the village of Dachau, in the lee of the horror of horrors, blew all restraint to the winds.

"Didn't suspect, you goddamn pimp." I found myself dragging Rodent-face to the window, holding his head out, pointing him toward the camp a mile away. "What the hell was there not to suspect when you saw all those furnaces and barbed wire and railroad sidings and trucks loaded with human beings coming in to get burned? Christ, the stink must have knocked you over. Couldn't you see? Couldn't you smell?"

I picked up the dictionary. Rodent-face started to say something, but before he did I seized a piece of paper from the counter, wrote "requisitioned for the inhabitants of Dachau" across it, and started for the door. Before I went out I turned back, trying to say something more impressive, more chilling. The Germans hadn't moved; their expressions had hardly changed.

"*Leb' 'wohl, Naziparteigenosse*," I told them, "Live well, Nazi party members, soon comes the American Gestapo," and with that completely empty but satisfying threat I slammed out to the jeep.

At the end of three weeks, the food shortage improved; somebody got the word somewhere, and I had the pleasure of hearing a prisoner tell me he had "*mehr als genug*" to eat one day. It was time to go back to my unit, and I packed up and left.

How many had died of the stupidity? Hard to say — there was so much else to die of. On the way through the village of Dachau I stopped at military government headquarters with some idea of tracking down the responsible dunce, or at least finding out if the machinery could possibly admit to having broken down.

Military government headquarters was very well bestowed in a mansion, and the officer in charge, typically, was a quartermaster corps captain who stood behind a large desk wearing riding breeches and highly polished boots, twiddling a riding crop.

I tried in reasoned tones to explain what had happened, but the captain kept shaking his head all the time I talked and ended up by telling me that it really hadn't. I next told him what I'd actually seen the prisoners eat, and he implied strongly that I was making it all up. We both started shouting; the captain retreated behind his desk and struck what he obviously thought was a military pose, hand on hip, riding crop tapping the desk. In the first place, he explained, I was all wrong; there had been lots of food in the camp all the time, and anyway, it wasn't his responsibility.

Whose was it?

Not clear, certainly not his.

Well, how would he have known there was enough food if it wasn't his responsibility? It must have been in his department?

Lines of administrative responsibility, problems I wouldn't understand.

I exploded. I told him he was either a fool or a liar; I pointed out the incongruity of his Georgie Patton get-up in the light of his real role in the army, i.e., that of a glorified grocery clerk. I commented further that he was an incompetent grocery clerk. (Military joke: Only two members of the quartermaster corps died in the whole war: a case of toilet paper fell on one and the other died laughing.)

Again I slammed out of doors and I realized I was being bad tempered, emotionally exhausted, floundering, and ineffectual. I should have gone to the inspector general of the Third Army and nailed the culprits; someone should have burned, but by now I was sick of the camp, sick of my own footling efforts, sick of the mindless bureaucracy I saw closing around us, and I simply turned my ambulance north and headed toward the mansion on the Danube.

Even as I drove along the autobahn, somewhere in the large centers of Germany businessmen in uniform were finding it easier to deal with former Nazis than with the heroes of the concentration camps. One Demaree Bess, a writer for the *Saturday Evening Post,* was to comment with stupid loftiness that one couldn't turn the government of postwar Germany over to men who were still capable of hiding fish sandwiches under their beds, thereby betraying his bottomless ignorance of the real greatness of mind and soul that had been penned in the concentration camps and of the grinding compulsions of starvation. In offices in New York and Boston men whose moral imperatives began and ended with greed were limning the corporate structures of the next incarnation of Krupp and I. G. Farben; all through Germany the military govenment units, staffed by the incompetent rejects of the combat army, the men with no war to forget, the compromisers trapped in immediacy and the need for personal advancement, were creeping through everything we had conquered, leaving trails of expediency and compromise across the footsteps of heroes, while back in our mansion in the willows, we, the innocent warriors, still in the glow of victory, propped our boots on the marble tables, drank our captured beer, and talked of battles won and the battles still ahead of us in Asia. What a relative pleasure it would be to match our long-barreled seventy-six-millimeter guns against the cracker-barrel tanks of the Japanese!

✳ 21

Long after Clausewitz

OBSERVATIONS OF WAR BY NONWARRIORS:
"Wars do not produce changes; they simply underline those changes that have already taken place." — Gertrude Stein. A partial truth, but not bad for someone who never smelled terror.

"Man is meant for war and woman for the delectation of the warrior; all else is folly." — Nietzsche. All the silly little bastard knew about war he learned by watching Prussian guardsmen parade behind a band; he spent his life shivering at the very thought of a female.

"War is a sexual phenomenon, with a prolonged uproarious tumescence, a shattering climax, and a particularly awful post-coital triste."

"War states the condition of the society that produces it. Definitions and values glare in bright relief. The rifleman shivering his way to mutilation is a drudge in a military sweatshop; his only reward is survival. If he lives with some functions intact, he faces a struggle against poverty, a race already lost to the clever faces that stayed tidy, coining security during his time in Hell. The employers and exploiters of the rifleman generate careers, income, and reputation by spending the poor devil's life; they have the advantages, unique among employers, of the cloak of national and godly virtue, and of the power to enforce their exploitation at pain of death.'' — My own personal, hitherto unpublished, observations.

A statement about war by a warrior:

''The most frequently extinct thing in the world is civilization; it's so helpless. All it is, finally, is marks on pieces of paper and stones cut into certain shapes. That's all they can leave behind, Sophocles, Socrates, Shakespeare, Taine and Shelley, Praxiteles and Michelangelo. Burn that paper, smash those stones, and they never existed. Gone. Off into outer cold space. They never happened. The burners and the smashers are always just outside, riding around, waiting. How do they break in? Simple goddamn things. Mongol recurved bow, Spanish armor, Arab cavalry tactics; the stupid things anyone could do, but it's the criminals and lunatics that do them, and there goes the architecture and music and poetry of Eastern Europe and the archives of the Mayas and the library at Alexandria. All waste motion; the guys who wrote and created and built might just as well have stayed home, eating chocolate and screwing their girlfriends.

''If you let dunces control your weapons, the way we do, you're selling the human race to oblivion. You better have some fucking brains concentrating on your calibers and blades or away you go, off into the dark out there, and you might as well have saved yourself a lot of trouble.'' — Rambling statement by Colonel O'Flaherty, intellectual West Pointer just back from Africa to tell us about the lessons to be learned from the debacle of Kasserine-Faïd in 1943. He was standing in the moonlight in a tank battalion motor park, reeling from two deep hours at the Officers' Club, in the middle of a philippic about the War Department, which was sending us to cremation in junk like the Sherman tank.

Sometime after the war, W. H. Auden caught the colonel's thought in four lines:

> *Guard, civility, with guns,*
> *Your modes and your declensions.*
> *Any lout can spear with ease*
> *Singular Archimedes.*

International understanding, lack of, Russian-American, 1945.

Mother Russia and kindly Comrad Stalin were ugly, scary fairy tales for the Russians who worked in our headquarters. By the end of the war we had adopted at least a platoon of them; the Ukrainian boys stayed with us, and we liberated the others from a German camp in Colmar.

They acquired American uniforms and weapons from the piles that were always around, and they worked so hard that the mess crew and the motor-park gang never had to scrub a pot or tighten a bolt. The four Ukrainians were with us so long we thought of them as American soldiers; they even stood sentry outside the command post — usually a nominal duty. The day of the German attack at Herrlisheim, the duty wasn't so nominal; as I ran through the courtyard, I saw Leonid at his post, unslinging his carbine, grinning. "Goddamn Germanski, Doc, huh? Goddamn Germanski," and with this reasonable comment our sixteen-year-old soldier ran with the others to stop a panzer division.

When we told them they were going back to Russia, Leonid cried. The others severally brooded, swore, and kicked things. They tried logic: they had worked out a superb postwar program if we would just listen. They all wanted to go to Detroit and work on jeeps. Wasn't that sensible?

We asked ourselves why the hell not; these men had endured shelling and strafing and night-fighting and assorted terrors right at our sides. They were brave, loyal, and competent, and they had proved it, which was a great deal more than could be said for the war profiteers and rich cowards who flitted to America without let in the dangerous years.

We asked about immigration or special dispensations, but bureaucracy slammed shut. We were still officially cooperating with Uncle Joe and it would have made him even more murderously paranoid than he already was to discover how many of his countrymen saw America as a fiery blessed beacon, a land beyond happy clouds, where a man could grow cabbages in his own dirt, and where you could call a president or a senator a son of a bitch without getting shot (our Russians loved to hear that; they repeated it to each other, muttering "Son of a beetch!").

We shipped them back to persecution and imprisonment for the mythical crime of letting themselves be captured, and for the even darker crime of having to do with the Americans. Stalin and the Russian rear-echelon cowards were more vicious than the American type. They really hated men who had faced the danger they hadn't, and it became party line after the war to sneer at veterans as tedious windbags.

We lost some fanatically dedicated prospective citizens because the State Department and the military government had their eyes crossed.

Home, the dreamed-of.

On an elevated train in Chicago, suddenly and shamefully in civilian clothes among crowds of returning soldiers, I was floundering in a sense of loss, as painful as if a friend and guide had just died. The wings and flanks were loose, untethered. The great impelling force, the goal, had faded; the gray Illinois sky was dead. What do I do? Why?

Make a living. Make money. Provide for my family. Take advantage. The world was diminished and life had lost power and direction.

The furious, the propelling, need for dedication! We need a clan or a god or a flag to expend ourselves for; we need purpose at the end of all the cynicism and shuffling. Louis-Phillipe; *enrichessez-vouz!* That's a swamp, the muck is suffocating.

Today we hear an eyrie of little eyasses who cry up greed; we're to believe that the only good is self-seeking and -serving, and that paper and gold are legitimate worship, but how do we fit into that shriveled universe the man who throws himself on a grenade to save his squad? Darwin again; we're still speckled about the planet only because the impulse to die fighting the cave bear so that the tribe might live somehow erupted in our genetic spirals. Jenner refusing money for his conquest of smallpox, Hopkins writing his poems for the pure secret creation of beauty, Socrates with the peripatoi, Mozart inflaming sound, Pico running across the snow; it's the same blessed mutation, as powerfully inscribed as the urge to beget.

And, last, time and departure.

There must be somewhere a plane where everything exists, shining with its own merit, eternally. If there isn't, what's the point of decency? The Iroquois or the Nazis could eradicate a people who spoke and worked kindness and beauty; extinction descends, but is everything lost? We can't believe that it is, or creation stops.

Someplace in the eye of some God there must be eternal being and value, but for us, we're trapped in time. It's a passage, of people, loves, events, spaces, happy approaching, terribly sad leaving.

Leaving: One afternoon, I stood at the foot of the glacier on the highest peak of the Wind River Range and watched my two sons disappearing up over tumbles and monsters of talus: my sons now at the edge of manhood, of movement out into life, were specks appearing and sliding on tongues of ice below staggering snow-towers and the boiling clouds of the Continental Divide.

I knew they'd be back at camp in a few hours, but I also knew they were leaving forever the places in life where the three of us had been, and I turned in my emptiness to my oldest friends, my friends since childhood, the foaming green water and the pines, and clung to them, really clutching with my hands.

I felt the same departure one fall afternoon in Fort Lowell Park here in Tucson watching the volunteers dressed up in their old Indian-fighting army uniforms go through a happily sloppy drill and fire a cannon and march off behind their fifes and drums. They were almost in step and "The Girl I Left Behind Me" shrilled splendidly over the rattling drums, and as I watched the gangling little band dwindle through cottonwood and mesquite, I was in the grip of that same rending sense of departure and loss. Why? Was I watching our own youth and dedication carried off on the dark torrent? Was it a mourning for what we were and what we hoped in our marching brightness? Was it possibly only an unexpected farewell to some very old friends glimpsed in the gathering dark and the mountains and the clouds beyond that bravely stepping little band?

Time and departure . . .